ALEXANDER

A portrait statue from Magnesia of the 3rd–2nd century B.C.

JUDAISM IN
THE GREEK PERIOD

FROM THE RISE OF
ALEXANDER THE GREAT TO
THE INTERVENTION OF ROME
(333 *to* 63 B.C.)

BY

G. H. BOX, M.A., D.D.

GREENWOOD PRESS, PUBLISHERS
WESTPORT, CONNECTICUT

Originally published in 1932
by The Clarendon Press, Oxford

Reprinted from an original copy in the collections
of the Princeton University Library

First Greenwood Reprinting 1971

Library of Congress Catalogue Card Number 73-109712

SBN 8371-4288-1

Printed in the United States of America

EDITORS' PREFACE

THE problem of the teaching of Holy Scripture at the present time presents many difficulties. There is a large and growing class of persons who feel bound to recognize that the progress of archaeological and critical studies has made it impossible for them to read, and still more to teach, it precisely in the old way. However strongly they may believe in inspiration, they cannot any longer set before their pupils, or take as the basis of their interpretation, the doctrine of the verbal inspiration of Holy Scripture. It is with the object of meeting the requirements not only of the elder pupils in public schools, their teachers, students in training colleges, and others engaged in education, but also of the clergy and the growing class of the general public which, we believe, takes an interest in Biblical studies, that the present series has been projected.

The writers will be responsible each for his own contribution only, and their interpretation is based upon the belief that the books of the Bible require to be placed in their historical context, so that, as far as possible, we may recover the sense which they bore when written. Any application of them must rest upon this ground. It is not the writer's intention to set out the latest notions of radical scholars—English or foreign—or even to describe the exact position at which the discussion of the various problems has arrived. The aim of the series is rather to put forward a constructive view of the books and their teaching, taking into consideration and welcoming results as to which there is a large measure of agreement among scholars.

In regard to form, subjects requiring comprehensive treatment are dealt with in Essays, whether forming part of the introduction or interspersed among the notes. The notes themselves are mainly concerned with the subject-matter of the books and the points of interest (historical, doctrinal, &c.) therein presented; they deal with the elucidation of words, allusions, and the like only so far as seems necessary to a proper comprehension of the author's meaning.

THOMAS STRONG⎫ *General*
HERBERT WILD ⎬ *Editors.*
GEORGE H. BOX ⎭

AUTHOR'S PREFACE

THE present volume, forming Vol. V of the Clarendon Bible (Old Testament), embraces a period in the history of Israel of many-sided importance. It coincides to a large extent, with the Hellenistic age, which was so fruitful and significant for the world at large, and not least for the little province of Judaean Palestine. The contact of Jew and Greek, indeed, marked one of the turning-points in the history of the world. It profoundly modified, without destroying, the essential character of Judaism itself, liberating religious energies which overflowed with momentous consequences into the world outside.

The expansion of Judaism is one of the most striking consequences of the Jewish reaction against the Hellenic onslaught on the Jewish religion in the second century B.C. which manifested itself in the recrudescence of an intense nationalist spirit and the foundation of a native dynasty.

How small and isolated Judaea was till late in the Greek period appears from a remark by Polybius writing in reference to the beginning of the second century B.C. He refers to the Jews of that time as 'those who lie round about the sanctuary called Jerusalem'. All this, however, was changed at the latter end of the century and later by the Maccabean princes till Rome intervened.

Sufficient attention has not hitherto, perhaps, been given to the influence of Alexander the Great on Judaism and the Jewish people. *A priori* it would have been expected that the career of Alexander would have made a deep impression on the Jews, which would have been reflected in their literature. That, in fact, this really happened to a larger extent than has hitherto been commonly supposed is made clear, the author hopes, in the selection of passages from the Hebrew Bible which follow, and also in the additional note on Alexander the Great in Jewish Legend.

But perhaps the most momentous consequence that flowed from the conquests of Alexander was the pervasion and subtle influence of Greek thought and culture which affected everything with which they came into contact. It is the presence of this diffused and disintegrating influence which gradually affected Judaism and led to changes in its texture. This, in turn, led to a crisis in the inner development of the religion till all the instincts of the Jew were aroused in protest and revolt. It is this inner conflict which marks the most significant phase in the development of the old religion during the Greek period, with consequences which can be seen in such a book as Ecclesiastes or even Ecclesiasticus.

Another important phase in the development of Judaism during this age is the growth of the Greek-speaking Jewish diaspora. This appears in its most obvious and concentrated form in the position of Jews and Judaism in the city founded by Alexander and named after him—Alexandria. What may be called a special type of Judaism was here produced. Though fundamentally Jewish, this type of Judaism expressed itself in Greek forms— it produced the Greek-Jewish Bible, LXX, and even used Greek for purposes of worship in the synagogue. It also produced a literature more or less outside the scope of the Palestinian Jewish scriptures. Its spirit is seen in striking form in such a book as the *Wisdom of Solomon*, as well as, later on, in the work of Philo and the Sibylline oracles. This type of Judaism, moreover, exercised a profound influence on the Christian Church, which for some centuries used the Greek form of the sacred books as its Old Testament.

On the other hand, the Judaism of Palestine, though deeply influenced by that of the diaspora, tended more and more to differentiate itself by clothing its literature in Hebrew form, and by conserving and popularizing the Hebrew Canon of the Old Testament.

The rise of Rabbinical Judaism is somewhat difficult to trace with precision. In the opening words of the Mishnaic tractate, commonly called *The Sayings of the Jewish Fathers*, the chain of tradition traces back to 'the men of the great synagogue', that vague body which bridges the gulf between the last of the prophets and the later bearers of the tradition, beginning with Simon the Just. What follows is also vague, except for such a name as Simeon ben Shetach, till we reach the names of Hillel and Shammai. Simeon figures as a prominent Pharisee at the court of Alexander Jannaeus (102–76 B.C.), and his successor, Queen Alexandra Salome (76–67 B.C.). Simeon was, in fact, the brother of Queen Alexandra and was mainly responsible for the change of policy which she inaugurated towards the Pharisees. Simeon figures in the tradition as the leader of the Pharisaic party and is said to have been influential in modifying the old Sadducean interpretation of the Law in favour of the Pharisaic.

We may regard Simeon as in some respects a forerunner of the later Rabbinical teachers of the Law; but Rabbinical Judaism had hardly emerged yet in its characteristic form—that was to come later.

Enough has been said to show the many-sided importance of the period embraced in the present volume. To have attempted a survey of all the relevant literature that falls within this period would have required a much larger amount of space than was available. All I have attempted to do is to select and group the typical passages from the available literature; but I venture to hope that these selections are sufficiently characteristic to stimulate the interest of the students who may have occasion to use this volume and to encourage them in some cases to pursue the study of a fascinating period in larger works, some of which have been indicated.

My warm thanks are due first of all to my wife and my younger son, Mr. Herbert Box, for assistance in the preparation of the manuscript, and secondly to the officials of the Clarendon Press for facilitating the task of getting the book into printed form and for the collection and arrangement of the illustrations; thirdly, to my fellow editors the Bishop of Oxford and Bishop Wild, who read through the proofs and corrected numerous errors; and finally to my elder son, Dr. P. H. Box, who kindly undertook the preparation of the index.

My large indebtedness to previous writers has, I hope, been sufficiently acknowledged in the book itself.

G. H. B.

KING'S COLLEGE, LONDON, *August* 1931.

CONTENTS

Contents

LIST OF ILLUSTRATIONS

List of Illustrations xiii

LIST OF PRINCIPAL DATES

B.C.

336. Assassination of Philip of Macedon and Accession of Alexander.
335. Alexander in Thrace and Illyria.
334. Alexander starts on his Persian Campaign.
334–333. Conquest of Lycia, Pamphylia, and Western Pisidia.
333. Conquest of Cilicia: Battle of Issus.
332. Siege and capture of Tyre: Alexander conquers Egypt.
331. Foundation of Alexandria: Settlement of Syria: Alexander occupies
    Babylon, Susa, and Persepolis. Battle of Arbela (Gaugamela).
330. Alexander at Ecbatana: Death of Darius.
329–328. Alexander winters at Bactria.
328. Alexander conquers Bactria.
327. Alexander invades India.
326. Crosses the Indus.
324. Reaches Susa.
323. Alexander at Babylon: June, Death of Alexander.
319. Syria annexed by Ptolemy.
313. Ptolemy crushes revolt in Cyprus.

B.C.

312. Seleucus establishes himself at Babylon.
310. Ptolemy makes Cyprus an Egyptian possession.
308. Ptolemy makes peace with Cassander and secures Cyrene.
301. Battle of Ipsus: Death of Antigonus.
300–250. Date of the Chronicler.
285–247. Ptolemy II, Philadelphus.
247–222. Ptolemy III, Euergetes.
223–187. Antiochus III the Great, King of Syria.
203. Capture of Jerusalem by Antiochus (Jerusalem under domination of Syria for about a century from this date).
198. Battle of Magnesia.
187–175. Seleucus IV, Philopator.
180. Composition of Ecclesiasticus (?) (Ben Sira).
175. Accession of Antiochus Epiphanes.
168. *Abomination of Desolation* set up in the Temple of Jerusalem.
166–165. Revolt of Jews begins. Victories of Judas Maccabaeus, and re-dedication of the Temple.
161. Defeat and death of Judas at Eleasa.
158–142. Jonathan, brother of Judas, at head of Jewish insurrection.
146. Carthage destroyed by the Romans.
142. Assassination of Jonathan.
142–135. Simon, brother of Jonathan, succeeds.
132. Translation of Ben Sira into Greek.
135–105. John Hyrcanus, Head of Jewish State.
108. Hyrcanus destroys Shechem and the Samaritan Temple of Gerizim.
105. Aristobulus I, King of Judaea.
104–78. Alexander Jannaeus, King of Judaea.
78–69. Salome Alexandra, Queen of Judaea.
68–63. Hyrcanus II and Aristobulus II (Civil War).
63. Intervention of the Romans: Jerusalem surrenders to Pompey.
Hyrcanus II appointed Ethnarch and High Priest to act in conjunction with Antipater. (In Egypt about this time The Wisdom of Solomon and 3 Maccabees may have been produced.)

SHORT TITLES AND ABBREVIATIONS

Cant.   = Canticles.

Chanukka = Dedication. The Jewish feast commemorating the re-dedication of the Temple of Jerusalem.

H.N.   = *Historia Naturalis* (of Pliny).

I.C.C.   = International Critical Commentary.

Kiddush   = Sanctification. A Jewish ceremony at the weekly inauguration of the Sabbath.

Midrashim = Jewish Commentaries of a popular and homiletic kind, usually based on the text of the Bible.

Pesh.   = Peshitto. The Syriac version of the Bible.

T.B.   = Talmud of Babylon.

Targums   = Aramaic translations of the O.T. books.

LIST OF SELECTED PASSAGES

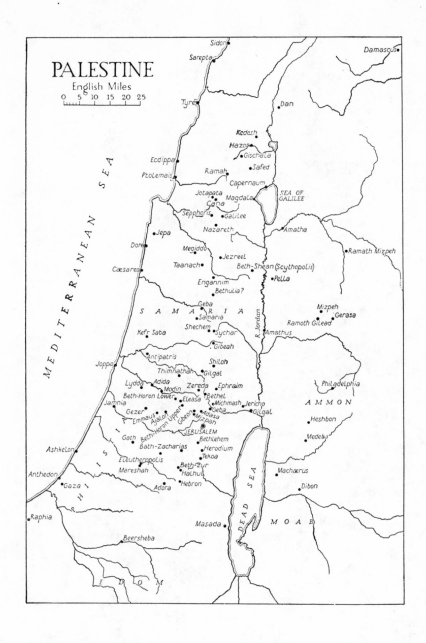

PALESTINE

English Miles

0 5 10 15 20 25

MEDITERRANEAN SEA

Sidon

Sarepta

Damascus

Tyre

Dan

Kedesh

Hazor

Gischala

Ecdippa

Ramah

Safed

Ptolemais

Capernaum

Jotapata

Magdala

SEA OF GALILEE

Cana

Sepphoris

Galilee

Jepa

Nazareth

Amatha

Dora

Megiddo

Jezreel

Ramath Mizpeh

Caesarea

Taanach

Beth-Shean (Scythopolis)

Engannim

Pella

Bethulia?

Geba

Mizpeh

S A M A R I A

Samaria

Gerasa

Kefr Saba

Shechem

Sychar

Ramoth Gilead

Amathus

R. Jordan

Antipatris

Gibeah

Joppa

Thimnathah

Shiloh

Lydda

Gilgal

Adida

Zereda

Ephraim

Philadelphia

Beth-Horon Lower

Modin

Bethel

Jamnia

Eleasa

Michmash

Jericho

A M M O N

Gezer

Emmaus

Geba

Gilgal

Gath

Ajalon

Beth-Horon Upper

Gibeon

Adasa

Heshbon

Mizpah

JERUSALEM

Medeba

Bath-Zacharias

Bethlehem

Eleutheropolis

Herodium

Ashkelon

Beth-Zur

Tekoa

Anthedon

Mareshah

Halhul

Machaerus

Gaza

Adora

Hebron

Dibon

Raphia

Masada

DEAD SEA

M O A B

Beersheba

E D O M

P H I L I S T I A

INTRODUCTION

HISTORICAL BACKGROUND OF THE NEARER EAST FROM THE FOURTH TO THE FIRST CENTURY B.C.

THE period with which we are concerned embraces the Hellenistic Age and falls naturally into two main divisions: (I) the pre-Maccabean Greek Age, and (II) the early-Maccabean and late-Maccabean Ages.

The first of these divisions (I) embraces the period from Alexander the Great to Antiochus Epiphanes (*circa* 330–168 B.C.); the second (II) ranges from 168 to 63 B.C.

We are thus concerned with the Greek period from the rise of Alexander the Great down to the intervention of Rome under Pompey in 63 B.C. Strictly speaking, the Hellenistic Age extends considerably beyond the time of Pompey, in fact, down to the last great Jewish rising against Rome, which culminated in the defeat of Bar-Kokba in A.D. 135, when Jewish political independence was finally annihilated. But it will be convenient for the purpose of this volume to carry the story down to the first Roman intervention only; to do otherwise would carry us well beyond the boundaries of the Old Testament proper. The two great crises which profoundly influenced the development of Judaism during this epoch were the Maccabean rising and the Roman wars.

I. THE PRE-MACCABEAN GREEK PERIOD (333–168 B.C.)

(a) *The foundation of Alexander's Empire*

Alexander, surnamed the Great, son of Philip II of Macedon, was born in the year 356 B.C. and ascended the throne of Macedonia at the age of 20 in the year 336. He was of Greek descent, though, possibly, there was some mixture of foreign blood. In early youth he had as his tutor Aristotle, from whom he learned many useful lessons which profoundly affected his character and career. From his father, Philip, he inherited a capacity for affairs and genius for military things. His emotional nature he inherited, to a large extent, from his passionate mother. 'Aristotle taught him ethics and metaphysics with some politics. Later, he wrote for him a treatise on the art of ruling and another on colonization. He also gave him a general interest in philosophy, scientific investigation and medicine.'[1] The results of Aristotle's teaching were seen later in Alexander's zeal for the health of his army and his scientific interest in extending the bounds of knowledge. Between the ages of 16 and 18 Alexander had some military ex-

The city of Thebes to-day

perience, but at the age of 19, owing to family disputes, he went into exile. Next year Philip was assassinated, 336 B.C. Alexander asserted his claim to the throne and acted with energy. The political situation outside Macedonia was difficult. The various Greek States appear to have regarded their former treaties with Philip as at an end when Philip died. Alexander dealt with the situation energetically. He first turned to Greece and in 336 secured control of Thessaly without a blow. Thessaly was especially important because she could supply cavalry. Thebes,

[1] See *Cambridge Ancient History*, vol. vi, p. 353.

Ambracia and Athens were overawed, and Alexander was elected general of the reconstituted League for the invasion of Asia. He began operations in the spring of 335 and conducted a successful campaign in the region of the Danube.

A report having spread to Greece that Alexander was dead created a serious situation. Alexander had reason to fear a combination of military states against him—Thebes, Athens, Aetolia and Sparta. He acted with characteristic energy and speed and

Greek soldiers in the time of Alexander. Infantrymen of the fourth century charging and receiving a charge

rapidly marched to Thebes. The Thebans were defeated and the city taken. Thebes suffered much. The city itself was razed, and many of its inhabitants sold into exile. The effect was immediate. Every Greek State hastened to submit.

In 335 B.C. Alexander returned to Macedonia and began his preparations for the invasion of Persia.

The reasons why Alexander invaded Persia were, doubtless, complex; he represented Pan-Hellenism and inherited the task; doubtless, too, he was attracted by the adventurous side. But deeper reasons may be sought in the insatiable need for Hellenic civilization to expand. It was compelled to break the narrow bonds that confined it.

We have said that Alexander inherited a task; his father, Philip, had long been preparing and had accumulated resources which facilitated the task of his son. It must be remembered also that Hellenic culture and civilization appealed irresistibly to all who were Greek. He enlisted this enthusiasm and almost fanatical zeal to spread Hellenic culture, ideals and institutions over the rest of the world.

In the spring of 334 Alexander at the head of the Army of Macedonia and the League crossed the Dardanelles.

His forces consisted of rather more than 30,000 infantry and 5,000 cavalry. Of the infantry 12,000 were Macedonians and 12,000 were Greeks, the remainder being light-armed troops. The cavalry included the famous corps of Companions, drawn from the upper classes of Macedonia and numbering some 2,000 men. This army, by its combination of different forms of equipment, constituted itself into a machine of overwhelming power. It also possessed a siege-train and a corps of engineers which constructed pontoons and siege-machines. A daily official record of the expedition was kept by a secretarial department. We are told that several philosophers and literary men accompanied the expedition as well as geographers, botanists and other scientific experts. Ptolemy, the son of Lagos, wrote a history of the expedition based on the official journal, and much of our knowledge of Alexander's campaign is derived from this official source.

The first clash took place at the Granicus, where the Persians had collected a considerable army, including a substantial number of mercenary Greeks.

They concentrated their cavalry on the bank of the river, put the Greeks behind them and waited. Here Alexander nearly lost his life, but after a desperate struggle he won a decisive victory. Eight Persian nobles of high rank were killed. One of the formidable possessions of the Persians was a fleet, 400 strong, greatly outnumbering that of the League, on which Alexander had to rely. He determined to ignore the fleet and carry on the war on land. The decisive battle was fought at Issus in the north-east of the Mediterranean in 333. The numbers of the Persian Army engaged are uncertain, but certainly did not reach 600,000 as was currently believed. Darius' army was, no doubt, somewhat larger than Alexander's. Alexander at this battle probably had from 20,000 to 24,000 infantry and 5,000 horses. Darius fled at the critical moment of the battle, and his chariot and bow were captured, as well as his tent.

The victory at Issus put Alexander in possession of the western

Alexander and the Persians. Part of the front of a sarcophagus at Sidon showing Alexander killing a Persian noble in battle

part of the Persian Empire, but Asia Minor was only half conquered. Alexander proceeded to complete his arrangements for
the government of the country. He proclaimed a régime of
democracy and won over the Greek cities to his side.

It has been suggested that Alexander first conceived the project
of conquering the Persian Empire after the battle of Issus. In any
case, it was sound policy to take the offensive. His first objective
was Phoenicia—it was essential to destroy the Persian fleet.
Byblus and Sidon welcomed him with open arms. Tyre was not so
ready, and Alexander made preparations for a siege. The Tyrians
really believed that their city was impregnable. Here Alexander
erected his famous mole, to which there is possibly an allusion in
Habakkuk 1¹⁰ (*He heapeth up dust, and taketh it*). After a desperate
struggle and with the aid of a hastily gathered fleet Tyre was
captured, after holding out for seven months, July 332, and became a Macedonian fortress. Alexander was now master of Palestine and proceeded to march against Egypt, which he reached
in November, 332. The Persian satrap submitted at once, and
wisely, for the Egyptian population hailed the advent of Alexander as the avenger. One of his first acts was to plan the great
city of Alexandria, designed to be a great trade centre and to
take the place of Tyre in the Mediterranean. After settling the
government of Egypt, which he placed under two native governors
of Upper and Lower Egypt, he returned in the spring of 331
to Tyre and settled the Government of Syria. Meanwhile the
Persians had been reorganizing their forces. In July, 331,
Alexander crossed the Euphrates and later the Tigris. He now
marched towards the village of Gaugamela,¹ eighteen miles north-
east of Mosul, where the Persians had established themselves under
Darius. After a hard fight, at the crisis of which Darius fled,
Alexander gained a signal victory. He now advanced on Babylon,
where he was warmly welcomed. Next he advanced to Persepolis,
where he stayed till the spring of 330.

The further progress of Alexander marks a stage in which he
now becomes the Great King, the Lord of Asia. It is interesting to
note that the title of King, which he now began to use, he never

¹ This is sometimes called the Battle of Arbela, though Arbela is about
fifty miles east of Gaugamela.

The ancient city of Erbil (Arbela) from the air
Royal Air Force Official—Crown copyright reserved

Alexander in legend. A scene in a Persian MS. representing Alexander holding a council with his Seven Sages (*see* p. 10)

used on his Macedonian coinage. An incipient plot among the generals against Alexander's life was ruthlessly suppressed. Parmenion was put to death, although there was no evidence against him.

During the winter 330–329 B.C. he was still in the far east. In the spring of 329 he crossed the Kabul valley. Bactria was occupied. Later the Oxus was crossed. Later still, the Jaxartes. In the spring of 328 Alexander again crossed the Oxus. Spitamenes was defeated, and Sogdia finally conquered. The daughter of Spitamenes, Apana, was subsequently married to Seleucus, and she became the mother of Antiochus I. Alexander continued his Persian policy on a still more grandiose plan. Since the death of Darius he had adopted on state occasions Persian dress and Persian court ceremonial. He proceeded to add to these the Persian custom of prostration for all who approached the King. To the Greeks prostration implied worship offered to a divine being. Officially he became the god of his Greek allies. 'Alexander never thought that he was a god; he was ironical on the subject in private, and in public he regularly alluded to his father, Philip. The thing to him was simply a matter of policy, a pretence which might form a useful instrument of state-craft.'[1] This provoked protest on the part of some of the Macedonians, who asked that the custom should be confined to Asia.

The next stage in Alexander's progress was the invasion of India, with an army which may have consisted of some 35,000 fighting men. It must be remembered that the India at this time known to Alexander was much smaller than the real India. The India which he invaded was the country of the Indus. He never knew the Ganges or Eastern Hindustan. He started from Bactria in the early summer of 327. In September, 325, he dropped down the eastern arm of the Indus to its mouth. He proceeded to Susa, which he reached in the spring of 324. The conquest of the Persian Empire was now complete. The close of Alexander's career took place in Babylon. In the midst of preparations for an Arabian expedition the autocrat was attacked by a fever, which he was unable to throw off. The final scene, in which his veterans filed through the room where the dying monarch lay, was tragic

[1] *Cambridge Ancient History*, vol. vi, p. 399.

and grand. He was just able to raise his head as they passed, in token of recognition and farewell. He died June 13th, 323, not yet 33 years old, having reigned 12 years and 8 months.

(b) The division of Alexander's Empire

Alexander died at the height of his fame and achievement. His personality and character and marvellous career made a profound impression on the ancient world. That he consciously aimed at World Dominion is a legend, though he doubtless believed in the spread of Greek culture and Greek ideals.

He soon became the hero of legend, and the Alexander romance flourishes in some twenty-four languages. In Graeco-Egyptian romance he is the subduer of Rome and Carthage, and in Jewish legend he plays a very prominent part.[1]

Among the forces that make for the evolution of world-civilization Alexander plays a supreme part. 'He lifted the civilized world out of one groove and put it in another; he started a new epoch; nothing could again be as it had been. He greatly enlarged the bounds of knowledge and of human endeavour, and gave to Greek science and to Greek civilization a scope and an opportunity such as they had never yet possessed. Particularism was replaced by the idea of "the inhabited world", the common possession of civilized men; trade and commerce were internationalized, and "the inhabited world" bound together by a network of new routes and cities, and by a common interest. Greek culture, heretofore practically confined to Greeks, spread throughout that world; and for the use of its inhabitants, in place of the many dialects of Greece, there grew up the form of Greek known as the *Koine*, the "common speech". The Greece that taught Rome was the Hellenistic world that Alexander made.'[2] The great Macedonian certainly helped in no small degree to plant in the world the ideal of a universal brotherhood.

Alexander left no heir to the empire; but a posthumous child was expected of Roxane. In these circumstances, Perdiccas, perhaps the most distinguished of Alexander's generals, summoned

---

[1] See further Additional Note III, p. 225 (Alexander in Jewish Legend).
[2] *Cambridge Ancient History*, vol. vi, p. 436.

a council and proposed that they should await the issue of
Roxane's confinement, and if the child were a boy, make him king.
The infantry, however, objected to this arrangement, preferring
another candidate, Arrhidaeus. He assumed the title of Philip III.
The men who figure as the Diadochoi, the successors, were the
most prominent among Alexander's generals, and among these the
struggle for supremacy soon became fierce. It went on in warlike
fashion from 321 to 301 B.C. The principal generals at Babylon
were Perdiccas, Ptolemy and Leonatus.

Perdiccas tried to keep the empire together by concentrating all
power in his own hands. Ptolemy, however, did not believe in
centralization and thought the empire must be broken up. Perdiccas came to his end in Egypt, where he was put to death by his
own troops in 321. Ptolemy had taken possession of Egypt in 323
and had attracted to his cause, by his popularity, a considerable
number of Macedonians. In 322 Ptolemy conquered Cyrene. The
inevitable rupture between him and Perdiccas soon materialized.
Perdiccas spent the winter of 322 in preparation. The clash came
in 321. In the spring of 319 Antipater, the regent, died, and with
him all legitimately constituted authority ceased. Nominally, two
kings reigned in Alexander's stead, one an infant and the other
an idiot.

With the death of Antipater the forces of disruption asserted
themselves. Ptolemy, now master of Egypt, invaded Syria, which
he annexed (319). The war was continued in 318, the protagonists
being Eumenes in Asia and Polyperchon in Europe, who stood
for the kings; while Antigonus in Asia and Cassander in Europe,
supported by Ptolemy, were warring against the central power.
Ultimately, the opposition came to a head between the policy of
Antigonus and that of Cassander. Antigonus, who was master of
Asia by 316, aimed at securing possession of the whole empire for
himself, without reference to the royal house. He entered Babylonia and demanded of Seleucus an account of his revenues.
Seleucus escaped to Egypt, and persuaded Ptolemy, Lysimachus
and Cassander that the ambition of Antigonus threatened their
very existence, and the three rulers formed an alliance. Cassander,
already master of Macedonia, Epirus, Thessaly, Athens and much
of Greece, wielded a formidable power. Ptolemy was securely

established in Egypt. Lysimachus had but a small army, but he held the Dardanelles. The following years, 315–312, are marked by the war between Antigonus and the Coalition. Hostilities began in the spring of 315. With his main army he himself invaded Syria. Ptolemy retired before him into Egypt after garrisoning Tyre and taking all the Phoenician warships. Another Siege of Tyre now took place, Antigonus being before the city for thirteen months before he succeeded in capturing it. In 313 Ptolemy succeeded in capturing Gaza and recovered all Syria and Phoenicia. About this time he settled some Jews in Alexandria. Seleucus seized this favourable opportunity to return to Babylon, and the Seleucid era, beginning in Syria in October 312, according to which the Seleucid kings reckoned, dates from Seleucus' return to Babylon.[1]

In 312 Antigonus recovered Syria and Phoenicia. He continued his efforts to weaken Ptolemy in Egypt, but without any great success. By 311 the position between the two rival combinations was more or less that of stalemate, and peace was made between Cassander, Lysimachus and Antigonus, and later Ptolemy also made peace. Seleucus was not included in the peace-treaty. Ptolemy was secured in Egypt, and Antigonus controlled Asia. Cassander retained Epirus and continued to hold Macedonia. Ptolemy had lost Syria and Cyrene. He secured Cyprus and continued to hold a very strong position in Egypt. The realm which made up Antigonus' kingdom included Asia Minor to Armenia (except Bithynia and part of western Pisidia), the whole of Syria and, apparently, Mesopotamia. Following the example of Alexander he retained various subordinate kings (in Phoenicia) and Mithradates. In 302 Mithradates was executed for treason, but a son escaped and became the ancestor of the kings of Pontus.

The Treaty of Peace of 311 really marked the progress of the empire's dissolution, which was completed ten years later. Antigonus desired to subdue Seleucus and capture Babylon. In 310 and 309 he ravaged Babylonia but failed to effect his primary purpose. Meanwhile (310) Ptolemy declared war again on Antigonus. Ptolemy in 309 was in Cos, and a year later (308) a son was born to him there, the future Ptolemy II. At this time Ptolemy was working to secure control of Greece. In the spring of

[1] Sometimes called the era of Contracts.

308 he crossed the Aegean and announced himself as the liberator
of the Greeks, but without effect. This move of Ptolemy's roused
Antigonus, and for the next six years he was engaged in a second
struggle to master the empire. The actual conduct of the war was
in the hands of Demetrius, his son, who was loyal to his father and

Gaza to-day

a brilliant commander. The war was carried on against Ptolemy.
In the spring of 306 Demetrius sailed to Cyprus with a large fleet
and an army.

Ptolemy was bound to intervene and put to sea with his whole
remaining fleet to relieve Salamis. In a battle between the fleets
Ptolemy lost 120 warships and transports carrying 8,000 mercenaries. Salamis surrendered, and Antigonus was triumphant.
Antigonus thought that Ptolemy might now be finally demolished
and invaded Egypt with 88,000 men and 83 elephants. But again

the attack failed, and Antigonus had to lead his army back to Syria. Ptolemy assumed the title of King in 305.

Meanwhile, the war had been carried on throughout Greece, and in the spring of 303 Demetrius, having liberated Central Greece, started to reconquer the Peloponnese. He reconstructed the League of Corinth on Pan-Hellenic lines and was elected by the League as a general in Alexander's place.

(c) The Jews in Egypt and Alexandria

The four kings now renewed the coalition of 315, this time to destroy Antigonus. The end came in 301 in the famous battle of the Kings, fought at Ipsus. Antigonus was defeated and killed, and with his death the division of Alexander's empire became inevitable. In the final division, Seleucus, as we have seen, established his dominion over Babylon. He himself dated his reign from 312 (the victory at Gaza). After the battle of Ipsus, in addition to Babylon and a large section of Asia Minor he added Syria and Armenia to his kingdom. Ptolemy, the son of Lagos and Arsinoe, born perhaps in 367, was some years older than Alexander. He became, first, satrap (322–307 B.C.), then king (305–285 B.C.) of Egypt. The founder of the Ptolemaic dynasty, he was surnamed Soter and is also usually styled Lagi. It was Ptolemy I who incorporated Palestine in his dominions. At the death of Alexander Coele-Syria and Judaea were assigned to Laomedon but were seized by Ptolemy.

According to Josephus, Ptolemy seized Jerusalem on a Sabbath day, when the Jews did not fight, in 320 B.C. In connexion with these events Ptolemy is said to have taken many prisoners from Judaea as well as from Samaria and to have settled them in Egypt. During the century that followed the battle of Ipsus Palestine became a bone of contention between the Ptolemies and the Seleucids. Seleucus regarded Coele-Syria and Judaea as part of his rightful dominion and only acquiesced in Ptolemy's domination because he was obliged to do so. Ptolemy himself was engaged in Palestine in military operations several times—in 320, as we have seen, and again in 312. At the latter date, although he was successful at the battle of Gaza, he found it expedient to evacuate Palestine temporarily and on his departure razed to the ground several important strongholds (Acco, Joppa, Gaza, Samaria and Jerusalem). A large number of Jews apparently migrated to Egypt at this time.

Warfare of the Diodochoi. A clay statuette of a war elephant of the third century B.C. found in Asia Minor. It probably reproduces a statue commemorating one of the victories of the Hellenistic kings over the Galatians

The founding of Alexandria by Alexander himself, to which we have already referred, was a master stroke of policy. The site of the city was carefully chosen and was calculated to divert the rich trade of the Red Sea and the Nile. It contained two splendid harbours, well able to accommodate large fleets. The city itself was divided into various quarters, native Egyptian on the west, Greek and official quarters in the centre and the Jewish quarter in the north-east. There the Jews lived together under their own law and were represented on the municipal council by their own leaders.

Ptolemy not only brought captive Jews to settle in Alexandria but also encouraged others to come voluntarily. In course of time the Jewish community became very powerful, and from the beginning of the Greek period the numbers of the Jews in Egypt at least equalled, if they did not surpass, the numbers in Palestine itself. A peculiar type of Judaism flourished in Alexandria, to which we shall have to refer in detail later. It was remarkable for its combination of Greek and Jewish ideas and produced a characteristic and peculiar type of literature. For the greater part of the century which follows the battle of Ipsus Palestine was under the rule of the Ptolemies, though the house of Seleucus never abandoned its claim.

In 295 B.C. and again in 219 the Seleucidae were temporarily in control of Palestine. It was not until the reign of Antiochus III, surnamed the Great, 223–187 B.C., that they felt themselves strong enough to press their claim, and from 218 to 198 Judaea was the scene of violent warfare. By his great victory at Paneas on the Jordan in 198 B.C. Antiochus won Judaea and Phoenicia, and from that time until it regained its independence in the time of Simon Maccabaeus, 142 B.C., Judaea was under the control of the Seleucidae.

On the whole, the Jews in Palestine came to regard the rule of the Ptolemies with favourable eyes. The sentiment of the Jews in Egypt, especially in Alexandria, where they enjoyed many privileges, was favourable to the Ptolemaic dynasty, and doubtless helped to create a similar sentiment among the Jews of Palestine. Josephus, *Contra Apionem*, ii. 4 and 5, highly praises the kindness of the Ptolemies towards the Jews, and it seems to have been a cardinal principle of the leading circles of Jews in Jerusalem to depend on the Ptolemies in opposition to the Seleucidae.

(d) The Ptolemies

The establishment of the Ptolemaic dynasty in Egypt and its long-continued rule there constitute a remarkable phenomenon. Although beset with difficult political problems which often re-

The Ptolemies in Egypt.   Restoration of the great banquet-tent of Ptolemy Philadelphus, based on a contemporary description

sulted in crisis, and though constantly engaged in war with other Greeks, and though vastly outnumbered by the native population, the Ptolemies and the Greek communities in Egypt maintained their authority till the intervention of the Romans. Egypt's natural position was one of great strategical advantage. It was practically invulnerable to outside attack.

Alexandria and its fleet commanded the only entrance. The domination of Palestine on the eastern side was, and still is, a vital Egyptian interest. The only possible rivals of Alexandria are the ancient seats of commerce in Tyre and Sidon, and these were part of Palestine. Further, the supply of wood from the Lebanon district was essential for the building of ships.

It may be useful at this point to set forth in tabular form a list of the more important members of the Ptolemaic dynasty:

Ptolemy I, son of Lagus, surnamed Soter. King of Egypt 305–285.

Ptolemy II, Philadelphus, 285–247.

Ptolemy III, Euergetes I, 247–222.

Ptolemy IV, Philopator, 222–205.

Ptolemy V, Epiphanes, 205–182.

Ptolemy VII, surnamed Philometor, known also as Ptolemy VI, 182–146.

Ptolemy IX, Euergetes II, known also as Ptolemy VII and more commonly as Physcon, 146–117.

Cleopatra III, reigned with her sons, Philometor (Soter II) or Lathyrus and Ptolemy Alexander, from 117 B.C. onward.

An allusion to Ptolemy I occurs in Daniel 11^5 (King of the South). The second Ptolemy, surnamed Philadelphus, who succeeded to the throne of Egypt in 285, made his position strong in Coele-Syria and Palestine about 274. Like all the Greek kings, he delighted in building cities, among such in Palestine being Philadelphia, Philoteria, and Ptolemais. He married his sister Berenice to the Syrian King Antiochus II for political reasons, and this union is referred to in Daniel 11^6.

According to the famous story embodied in Aristeas, the LXX came into existence during this monarch's reign. The nucleus of truth in this legend is that the Pentateuch was translated into Greek at the time and possibly under this monarch's auspices. The rest came into existence later, but probably was substantially complete by the time of Ben-Sira's grandson (*circa* 132 B.C.).

The Rosetta Stone, which contains a decree of Ptolemy V, Epiphanes, in hieroglyphics, demotic and Greek

The third Ptolemy, Euergetes I, came to the throne in 247. He is referred to in Daniel 11[7-9]. According to this passage the Egyptian monarch was remarkably successful in military operations in Syria and brought back to Egypt much booty, including the idols of the conquered. This Ptolemy favoured the Jews, and, according to Josephus, actually visited Jerusalem and offered sacrifice in the Temple. A long story is told in Josephus, *Antiquities*, XII. 4, sc. i. According to this, the High Priest, Onias II, an avaricious prelate, held back twenty talents of silver, which were contributed yearly as a voluntary offering together with the taxes, from the king, who threatened reprisals. The danger was averted by Joseph, the nephew of Onias, who was appointed tax-collector not only for Judaea but for all Coele-Syria. Some interesting synagogue inscriptions refer to this monarch.[1]

The fourth Ptolemy, surnamed Philopator, who came to the throne in 222, is referred to in Daniel 11[11-12]. This passage reflects the desperate state of war which went on in Palestine between Antiochus the Great and Ptolemy IV. In 217 B.C. Ptolemy won a brilliant victory at Raphia. The apocryphal book of 3 Maccabees refers to events in connexion with this Ptolemy. Though the details are invested with a certain amount of legend, the story given narrates of this Ptolemy that he visited Jerusalem after the battle of Raphia and announced his intention of entering the Temple, but was prevented from so doing by a divine interposition. After his return to Alexandria, he planned a massacre of all the Jews in revenge, but the elephants, which were to be the agents of the destruction, attacked the royal troops instead, and the Jews celebrated their escape by an annual feast. The story given in 3 Maccabees has been much discussed. It has been referred to another Ptolemy, Physcon, and even to events under Caligula.

Ptolemy V, surnamed Epiphanes, came to the throne in 205 as a child of 5. During his reign the struggle for the possession of Coele-Syria raged at its fiercest. Antiochus the Great finally annexed Palestine to his empire (202), and the Egyptians, who tried

---

[1] A synagogue inscription discovered in Lower Egypt refers to this king. It reads 'In Honour of King Ptolemy and of Queen Berenice his sister and wife, and of their children. This synagogue the Jews (dedicate).' The inscription is in Greek.

to retake it, were defeated and wholly destroyed at Sidon. This Ptolemy died in 182 B.C. The eldest son, Ptolemy VII or VI, surnamed Philometor, came to the throne in 182, while still a child. The conflict with Syria was later renewed and in 170 B.C. Antiochus IV, Epiphanes (175–164), attacked and defeated the Egyptians as described in 1 Maccabees 1[18-20]. As the result Philometor was dethroned by the Alexandrians, his younger brother being set up in his stead, known as Euergetes II. Antiochus now intervened in favour of Philometor. He apparently intended to assume supreme control in Egypt but had to withdraw under Roman pressure.

The Ptolemies as a rule treated the Jews very favourably. Thus Jonathan Maccabaeus enjoyed considerable honour (1 Maccabees 10[57-60]). It is interesting to note that the Onias Temple was built under Ptolemy Philometor at Leontopolis. Ptolemy died from a wound received in battle in Syria in 146 (cf. 1 Maccabees 11[14-19]). The next Ptolemy had to fight his brother's widow, Cleopatra. The grandson of the author of Ecclesiasticus went to Egypt in the 38th year of Euergetes II. (See his preface to the Greek translation of Ecclesiasticus.) As this Ptolemy reckoned his reign as beginning in 170 the 38th year would be 132, an important date in the history of the Canon of the Old Testament.

(e) Palestine under Egyptian Rule

We have already noted that for nearly a century after the battle of Ipsus, 301, Palestine was mainly dominated by the Egyptians. On the whole, the Egyptian rule was mild, and, so long as the tribute was paid, little interference came from the dominant power. The head of the Jewish Community was the High Priest, and for the most part the Jews were allowed to control their internal affairs. During this period Greek influence and Greek institutions penetrated Palestine in all directions. These influences, as we shall see, came to a head in the first half of the second century B.C.

(f) Conquest of Palestine by the Seleucids

The empire which Seleucus Nicator consolidated was based at first on Babylon. The western part of his dominion came to be known as Syria, a shortened form of the ancient Assyria; and

Seleucus made the capital of this western portion the city of Antioch on the Orontes, near the north-east end of the Mediterranean. This famous city had its site at the point where the Orontes breaks through the Lebanon, and where the roads from Euphrates and Coelê-Syria converge. Its seaport was Seleucia. The city itself was built partly on an island in the river and partly on the northern bank. It was strongly fortified and soon became one of the most prominent seats of Hellenic civilization. Its natural line of expansion was north and south. It was not, however, until 198 B.C. that Antiochus the Great secured permanent control of Palestine. The Hellenization of the East, begun by Alexander the Great, was zealously developed by the Seleucidae. They were great city builders. Greek cities sprang up in Palestine, both during Egyptian rule and even later. Among these were Abila, Gadara and Seleucia. The last-mentioned was situated on the shore of Lake Merom. In all the cities founded by the Seleucids both in Asia Minor and Syria they carefully pursued the policy of granting the Jews full civil rights. This was the case in the capital, Antioch, where the Jews retained their privileges until the time of Josephus (*Ant.* XII. 3, sc. 1).

It will be convenient at this point to give a table of the Seleucid Monarchs with dates, similar to the one we have already given of the Ptolemies:

Seleucus I, Nicator, 312-281.
Antiochus I, Soter, 281-261.
Antiochus II, Theos, 261-246.
Seleucus II, Callinicos, 246-226.
Seleucus III, Soter, 226-223.
Antiochus III, The Great, 223-187.
Seleucus IV, 187-176.
Antiochus IV, Epiphanes, 175-164.
Antiochus V, Eupator, son of Antiochus IV, 164-162.
Demetrius I, 162-150.
Alexander Balas, 150-145.
Antiochus VI, son of Alexander Balas, proclaimed king by Tryphon, 146, died 142.
Antiochus VII, Sidetes, son of

Demetrius I, declared war against Tryphon, who had taken the place of his brother, Demetrius II, then a prisoner of the Parthians; 138, died 129,
Antiochus VIII, Gryphus, 125-113, and from 111-96.
Antiochus IX, Cyzicenus, half-brother of Antiochus VIII, died 95. He rose against Antiochus VIII in 113 and controlled Syria for three years.
Antiochus XII, Dionysus, youngest son of Gryphus, the last of the Seleucids to come into contact with the Jews.

Marble statuette of the Tyche (Fortune) of Antioch, the capital of the
Seleucids. The figure under her foot represents the river Orontes. (3rd
century B.C.)

(g) *Palestine under the Seleucids*

Our information regarding the condition of the Jews of Palestine, both under the Ptolemies and under the Seleucids, is very defective. What was the inner history of the Jews during this period? That they were profoundly influenced by the spread of Greek culture and Greek institutions is certain. In his *Jerusalem under the High Priests* Dr. Edwyn Bevan has brilliantly described the seductive and irresistible attraction of the new culture that followed in the wake of Alexander's advance. New institutions, like the gymnasium and the theatre, sprang up; new political forms and organizations; a new taste in literature and art—in short, a whole range of new ideas and interests filled the life of Hellenized cities, beside which the old pre-Hellenic life seemed dull and empty. Greek became the language of the educated, and largely the language generally understood in such cities as Damascus, Tyre, Ascalon, after they had reorganized themselves on the Greek model. Dr. Bevan goes on to remark: 'If we had looked about us there would have been a great deal in the Syrian cities of those days to show us the predominance of the new power. . . . As a building, the gymnasium would have shown us the familiar forms of classical architecture. The new political organization would require new buildings—a hall for the senate, and such like; and the new social life would create the indispensable *stoas* cool, pillared galleries for lounging, and all these would be Greek in form. Dress, too, would be then, as now, inseparable as an outward symbol from the particular form of civilization. . . . We should have seen the *epheboi* of Tyre or Ascalon with their broad-brimmed Greek hat and fluttering chlamys, and the richer men and women not easy to distinguish by their appearance from their contemporaries in Ephesus or Athens.'

Nowhere except in Egypt was Hellenic influence more powerful than on the eastern shore of the Mediterranean. Greek cities abounded in this region during the Hellenic period—Raphia, Gaza, Ascalon, Azotus, Jaffa, Caesarea, Dor and Ptolemais; while, further east, Greek influence was powerfully consolidated by the confederation of cities known as the Decapolis, which apparently included Damascus. In fact, during the later Hellenic period the

Hellenization in Palestine. The Forum at Gerasa (Jerash), one of the Decapolis cities in Transjordania; a view taken from a tower of a Greek theatre

whole district east of the Jordan, including Trachonitis, Batanea and Auranitis, appears to have been Hellenized. Even such important centres as Samaria and Panias were subjected to the same process, having been planted with settlements of Macedonian colonists at an early date. The little Jewish community was thus immersed in Hellenic influences. They made great inroads even in Jerusalem itself, and seemed to be carrying everything before them. A vivid picture is given of the effects of this in the opening chapters of the book of Maccabees.

With the accession of Antiochus Epiphanes (175–164 B.C.) things came to a crisis. The first act of Antiochus was to deprive the legitimate High Priest, Onias III, of his office.

At the beginning of the second century B.C., when the Seleucids seemed permanent possessors of Palestine, it must be remembered that Judaea was the only Jewish land and Jerusalem its only city. The Jewish community occupied a very circumscribed area. Polybius, speaking of the Jewish community of this time, refers to those Jews that lived around that temple which was called Jerusalem (cited by Josephus, *Ant.* XII. 3. 3, sc. 136). This description is accurate. Palestinian Judaism was bound up essentially with the existence of its Holy City, and what gave its significance to Jerusalem was that it was the city of the Temple. For the maintenance of a Holy City it was indeed essential that a certain amount of the surrounding country should lie within its sphere of influence, but the boundaries of this territory had, since the days of Cyrus, not exceeded a day's march from Jerusalem on any of its sides.

In the time of the Maccabees, Hebron was a hostile town in possession of the Idumaeans. These, under pressure from the Nabataeans, had forsaken their proper home domain and settled on lands which had once belonged to the Jews. On the western side of the mountain country, Gezer during the Syrian wars was the nearest point to the mountain country to which Greeks could resort for protection when fleeing from the central highlands. Everything westward of that point—the whole maritime plain with its towns—was Greek. On the eastern side, the Jordan formed the boundary, Jericho being a Jewish possession. On the northern side Jewish territory had been slightly enlarged, so as to

.

Funeral stele of a Phoenician priest of the fourth century
B.C., found in Phoenicia. The sculpture shows strong Greek
influence, and illustrates the spread of Hellenic culture on
the eastern shore of the Mediterranean

include three small districts, which had originally belonged to Samaria, namely the district north-east of Bethel, that from Lydda on the eastern edge of the maritime plain, and that from Ramathaim, which lay in the hills north-east of Lydda.

According to another account derived from Hecataeus, Alexander's army in Babylon contained a Jewish contingent. It seems clear that the Jews submitted at once to Alexander, abandoning their allegiance to their Persian governors. The Jews of Babylonia also submitted to Alexander peacefully.

The policy of Hellenization, to which we have already referred, was initiated by Alexander himself. The first Palestinian city which was so treated was Samaria, which had risen in rebellion against the Greek domination. In consequence, the native population was decimated and a military colony was set up. Another town that was Hellenized was Bethshean, which now became known as Scythopolis. Opposite Scythopolis on the east bank of the Jordan, stood Pella. All over Palestine and the neighbouring lands this process went on. On the sea, north of Joppa, there grew up Apollonia; north of this, Straton's Tower. On the edge of the wilderness the capital of Ammon, namely Rabbath-Ammon, in honour of Ptolemy Philadelphus was named Philadelphia.[1]

The towns inhabited by the Greeks maintained Greek municipal law. Proud of their autonomy they announced the fact by their coinage. Many of these cities controlled a substantial amount of land immediately around them. Many of them with the assumption of Greek names adopted also Greek myths. Greek legends grew up which falsified history. Thus in the second century B.C. it was seriously believed in Jerusalem that the Jews had entered into relations with the Spartans and were bound to them by agreement. The author of the first book of Maccabees has inserted in his narrative a spurious letter of a Spartan king. The danger of all this was that if this luxurious crop of legends was allowed to grow, all recollection of the earlier history would disappear. This danger threatened even Jerusalem itself. It was, however, warded off. The

---

[1] Professor Macalister, in his book *A Century of Excavation in Palestine*, notes how much the work of excavation reveals the widespread character of the Greek remains. To a large extent Greek buildings obliterated the earlier structures, on the sites of ancient settlements. See further Additional Note IV on Greek and Latin names among the Jews, p. 226.

traditional belief in Abraham was too strong to allow it to be displaced by Dionysus.

It is necessary to emphasize the fact that both the Ptolemies and the Seleucids were ardent Hellenizers. By the time that Antiochus the Great secured control of Syria and Palestine the process of Hellenization had been going on for more than a century. The two forces which had met under these conditions and were heading for inevitable conflict were Greek culture and the Jewish religion. The crisis came to a head in the reign of Antiochus Epiphanes, and to the elucidation of this we must now turn our attention.

(h) Antiochus Epiphanes

The monarch who figures in Daniel as the 'little horn' and appears there as the final and supreme embodiment of the evil power is known to history as Antiochus IV, Epiphanes. He was a younger son of Antiochus the Great, who, it will be remembered, after a successful career of conquest was compelled by the Romans to give up all the results of his aggressions except Coele-Syria, and, further, was forced to pay a large tribute. The young Antiochus was sent by his father to Rome as a hostage in the year 190/189, and there he passed his earlier years until he was a young man. On the death of his father his elder brother, Seleucus IV, succeeded, 188–176 B.C. In the latter part of his reign Seleucus was compelled to send his own son and heir to the throne, Demetrius, as a hostage to Rome. By this arrangement Antiochus was released and allowed to leave Rome. Though he carried away with him an intense hatred of all things Roman, he loved Hellenism, and was an ardent Hellenizer in all respects. He visited Athens, and became chief magistrate of the city. Soon after this Seleucus was murdered, whereupon Antiochus left Athens, returned to Syria and secured the throne for himself. Demetrius the legitimate heir was still kept as a hostage at Rome.[1]

In the book of Daniel 11$^{21\text{-}2}$, the proceedings of Antiochus are referred to, and he is described as a contemptible person who gained the throne by fraud. Shortly after this his sister Cleopatra, Queen of Egypt, died 173 B.C., and the regent proposed to claim

---

[1] He ultimately escaped and secured his throne, 162–150 B.C.

on behalf of her young son, Ptolemy Philometor, the possession of Coele-Syria.

The assertion of this claim led to hostilities between Antiochus and Egypt. His success led him to intervene in the internal affairs of that kingdom; he backed one of his nephews as king and took hostile action against the other by laying siege to Alexandria. For some reason he did not press the siege but retired, leaving a garrison of Syrian troops in Pelusium. This first Egyptian campaign took place in 170 or 169 B.C. It is referred to in 1 Maccabees 1[16-19] and in Daniel 11[25-7]. According to 1 Maccabees 1[20ff.], it was on his return from this expedition that for some reason he manifested a strong feeling of hostility against Judaism and entered the Temple, plundering its sacred vessels and treasures.[1] Antiochus was obliged to return to Egypt without delay to secure his gains; the two brothers, young Ptolemy Philometor and the other, were now united against him. This second expedition may have taken place in the spring of 168 B.C. It looked as if the independence of Egypt would be brought to an end, and the Ptolemaic kingdom annexed to Syria. But just at this critical moment the battle of Pydna took place (June 22nd, 168 B.C.) and decided the fate of the Greek Macedonian empire under King Perseus, ending in a decisive victory for the Romans. This led to Roman intervention in Egypt —it was not at all consonant with Roman policy to allow a victorious Syria to absorb Egypt. An embassy was immediately sent to Egypt, and confronted Antiochus on his victorious march. The head of the embassy, Popillius, produced a decree of the Senate demanding his immediate and complete withdrawal from Egypt; an answer was required before Antiochus left the circle drawn around him by the legate. Antiochus yielded. He returned to Syria 'in high dudgeon indeed and groaning in spirit, but yielding to the necessities of the time' (Polybius). It was apparently on his return in this mood that he made his assault on the Jewish religion which was to prove so momentous in its consequences for the world.

---

[1] 2 Maccabees 5[11-20] refers to violent measures against the Temple taken by Antiochus on his return from the second Egyptian campaign. Possibly, this spoliation of the Temple is identical with that referred to in 1 Maccabees. According to 2 Maccabees it was provoked by an insurrection of the Jews, acting on a rumour that Antiochus was dead.

Antiochus was an able monarch, devoted to Hellenic culture
and bent upon strengthening his somewhat heterogeneous realm.
Though he had been obliged to yield to Rome just when the prize
was within his grasp, he seems to have been successful in other
directions in strengthening his kingdom. To celebrate his victories
he determined to hold a great festival at Daphne, near Antioch
(? spring 166 B.C.). Perhaps it was in the summer of the same year
that he marched on his great campaign towards the East in an
attempt to subdue the Parthians. This expedition was organized
on a large scale, and Antiochus attached so much importance to it
that he left behind a regent during his absence, who was to control
the country in the name of his young son, who received the
title of king. The detailed history of this campaign is unknown.
Antiochus apparently won a good many successes, but died in
the midst of it from disease (164).

The character of Antiochus exhibited many of the faults and
weaknesses associated with Hellenic culture. He was boastful,
vainglorious, fond of display to the verge of eccentricity, extrava-
gant, ready to go to any extreme in captivating the multitude.
With the appearance of geniality he was at heart a reckless tyrant.
Profoundly believing in Greek institutions he desired ardently to
bind together and consolidate his empire by Hellenizing his subjects. He is depicted in Jewish documents as the incarnation of
wickedness, a type of Antichrist, the embodiment of the spirit
of the world in opposition to God. The writer of Daniel, who was,
of course, a contemporary, though a highly prejudiced witness,
refers to him as a 'contemptible person', and represents him as
a deceitful schemer, concealing his purpose and feelings under
a plausible exterior and working to gain his end by cunning;
according to the same authority, his character was marked by
overwhelming conceit and arrogance, shown by his assumption of
divine rank and his sacrilegious attack on the Jewish religion.
Polybius describes him as a clever intriguer, a master of dissimula-
tion, but also impulsive and capricious. Professor Porter says
(*Messages of the Apocalyptical Writers*, pp. 87 ff.): 'He was a man
of energy and ambition, attempting magnificent things in war and
in art, and accomplishing much. His ruling passion was Hellenic
life and Hellenic culture in its external aspects, and he aimed, as

Alexander had done, to make Hellenism the dominant and unifying element throughout his realm. He made gifts of splendid buildings, temples, altars, colonnades, to Athens and to many other cities. His whims and extravagances more than offset his good qualities. He seemed to observers at times a high-souled king with cultivated manners, and then again so eccentric as to be almost crazy.' His conduct was characterized by a strange waywardness, and he was capable of doing the most incongruous things.

The title he assumed, Epiphanes, is explained by the inscription on his coins, where the word for 'God' appears—$\theta\epsilon\grave{o}s$ $\grave{\epsilon}\pi\iota\phi\alpha\nu\acute{\eta}s$. The worship of the ruler was no new thing, having been in vogue from the time of Alexander onward. It was regarded as a useful means of welding the population into a certain amount of unity. A non-Jewish population had no objection to this cult, but it ran hopelessly counter to Jewish feeling, and Antiochus, by pushing it further than his predecessors, helped to precipitate an inevitable conflict.

Why did Antiochus vent his indignation upon the Jews? It was on his return from Egypt, 'in high dudgeon,' that he spent his wrath in an attempt to crush the Jewish religion. Coele-Syria was the scene of his operations, preliminary to his expedition against Egypt, and it has been suggested that it was probably the Jews who made his tenure of that region insecure. In any case, his action was somewhat precipitate, for it must be remembered that Hellenism at this time was making rapid strides in Jerusalem itself (cf. 1 Maccabees 1[11ff.]; 2 Maccabees 5[7ff.]). 'The malady which had long been incubating now reached its acute phase. Just in proportion as Hellenism showed itself friendly, did it present elements of danger to Judaism. From the periphery it slowly advanced towards the centre, from the *diaspora* to Jerusalem, from mere matters of external fashion, to matters of the most profound conviction.' [1]

The Jews themselves by their intrigues and divisions had given Antiochus an opportunity for interfering in their internal affairs. The struggle of the Tobiads in violent opposition to the High Priest, Onias III, soon grew from a mere personal quarrel into a serious division within the community. The conservative element

[1] Wellhausen.

sided with the High Priest, and depended on the support of the
Egyptian King, rather than on that of Antiochus. Through the
intrigue of the Tobiads Antiochus was induced to depose Onias,
173 B.C. Jason, a brother of Onias, largely by bribery, got himself
appointed to the office, and at once took the lead in promoting

Coins of Antiochus Epiphanes, having on the reverse the
inscription *ΒΑΣΙΛΕΩΣ ΑΝΤΙΟΧΟΥ ΘΕΟΥ ΕΠΙΦΑΝΟΥΣ*. The
upper coin shows the young Antiochus with curls and diadem,
while the lower shows a bearded head representing Antiochus
assimilated to Zeus. The figure on the reverse in each case
represents Zeus seated on a throne

Hellenism in Jerusalem. The upper classes, led by Jason, especially
the priesthood and nobility, now displayed a perfect frenzy for the
adoption of everything Greek. Greek names were assumed, e.g.
Jason for Joshua, Menelaus for Menahem. An arena for public
games was set up in the neighbourhood of the Temple, and Greek
customs and Greek dress were largely adopted. Jason, however,
was not able to maintain himself in his office very long, being
succeeded in 171 by a certain Menelaus, who managed to buy the

office for a large sum. In order to raise the necessary money, Menelaus was obliged to resort to unpopular measures, and it may have been in connexion with some disturbances resulting from these proceedings that Antiochus came into collision for the first time with the Jews.

The angry king on his return from Egypt took measures to punish the refractory populace, and carried off the Temple treasures. Menelaus, who had been obliged to flee, was restored to office. These violent measures, especially the desecration of the Temple, produced a reaction. The Hellenizing movement, which had been making such marked progress, received a check. A more violent reaction, as we shall see, was destined to follow.

It should be noted that the deposition of the High Priest, Onias III, marked a definite break in the line of legitimate High Priests. Menelaus, who held the office later, was not even of a priestly family. According to 2 Maccabees 4[32ff.], Onias was treacherously murdered near Antioch (cf. Daniel 9[26] and 11[22]). Others think that he survived and fled to Egypt, and there set up a rival Temple at Leontopolis. It is more probable, however, that this Temple was built by Onias IV, a son of the murdered Onias III.[1] In any case, the erection of such a Temple upon foreign soil is evidence of the deep cleavage that existed at this time in the ranks of Judaism.

Rather than sanction the usurpation of a non-priestly line the orthodox, or a considerable section of them, were prepared to support the representatives of the legitimate high-priestly line in organizing a rival Temple outside Palestine and in defiance of the Biblical law about the one central sanctuary (cf. Deut. 12[5ff.]).

---

[1] This Temple, erected about 170 B.C., existed until A.D. 73. It is a remarkable fact that such a sanctuary should have been built outside the Holy Land and received recognition from orthodox Jews.

II. THE MACCABEAN EPOCH

(a) *The causes of the Maccabean revolt*

The deeper causes of the Maccabean revolt are to be sought in the fundamental differences that divided Judaism and Hellenism. To both Jews and Greeks the contrasts between Judaism and Hellenism at this time were most glaringly obvious. Nothing is more characteristic of Judaism than its intense hatred of idolatry, which led the Jews to despise and reject all forms of Art.[1] They were naturally averse to the associations of Greek games—the gymnasium—with their attendant licentiousness. The Jews on the other hand loved the simple domestic joys of home life, and their devotion to the services of the Temple and the faith of their fathers was intense. All this doubtless appeared barbarous and contemptible beside the voluptuous life of the Hellenic cities. 'Hellenism protested against the narrowness, barrenness and intolerance of Judaism; Judaism protested against the godlessness and immorality of Hellenism. Both were right in their protests, and yet each in a sense needed the other.'[2]

(b) *Persecution and the reaction*

It was inevitable that Antiochus should regard the existence of Judaism with its obstinacy and its deep prejudices and party strifes as a nuisance. In fact, it must have appeared to him a source of insecurity to his tenure of Coele-Syria. He therefore determined to get rid of this obstacle by drastic means. He accordingly issued an edict imposing certain pagan rites on all suspected persons. He wished to abolish Judaism at one stroke. He accordingly set up the Abomination of Desolation in the Temple —this was an image of the Olympian Zeus set up on the great altar of burnt-offering in the Temple court; the sacred scriptures were burned; the practice of circumcision was forbidden on pain

[1] This generalization needs perhaps some qualification. As a matter of fact, in process of time many features of Greek art were adopted by Jews, even in their synagogues; but fundamentally the spirit and tendency of Judaism were as described above.

[2] C. F. Kent, *The Makers and Teachers of Judaism*, p. 191.

of death and all the horrors of a religious persecution descended on the land (168 B.C.).

Doubtless, many among the Hellenizing party conformed and duly worshipped Olympian Zeus in the desecrated Temple. But there were many who refused to identify themselves with the Apostates, and more especially the party of the 'Pious', as they were called (Hebrew *chasidim*), who are referred to in the books of Maccabees as the 'Assidaeans'. This party refused to conform with the requirements of Antiochus' decree. At first they contented themselves with passive resistance and allowed themselves to be butchered rather than fight on the Sabbath. But soon more active measures of resistance were organized, first by Mattathias at Modin, where the officers of Antiochus appeared and demanded from the Jews participation in the heathen offering. When a Jew proceeded to make the incense offering required, Mattathias, seized with indignation, slew him and raised the banner of revolt. He was succeeded by his heroic son, Judas Maccabeus (166–161), who was a master of guerrilla warfare and inflicted more than one defeat on the Syrian commanders. A brief summary of these events is given in the book of Daniel (cf. Daniel 11³¹ff.). Lysias, who had been left as regent by Antiochus, was instructed to crush this movement, but the generals he sent against Judas, namely, Ptolemaeus, Nicanor, and Gorgias, were defeated one after another (165). Lysias himself was compelled to flee to Antioch. Antiochus, as we have seen, died in 164.

Judas made himself master of Judaea in 165 and so remained till the summer of 163. His first act was to restore the polluted Temple of Jehovah to its sacred uses. The temple was re-dedicated in the December of 165, according to tradition exactly three years after it had been desecrated. The feast of dedication has remained one of the most popular of Jewish commemorations ever since. It is referred to in John 10²².

We have seen that Antiochus died in 164, during his expedition against the Parthians. Again there were troubles about the succession. Meanwhile, the Hellenists in Jerusalem were in a difficult position. They still had one point of vantage, the citadel, which was garrisoned by Syrian troops. Once more they appealed to the central authority at Antioch for protection against their enemies.

In response to this call Lysias in 163 invaded Judaea with an imposing army. He was accompanied by the boy-king. Judas in vain tried to stem the advance at Beth Zachariah, but was defeated and forced back. But the situation at Antioch made it expedient for Lysias to get back home as quickly as possible. In consequence, he made terms with the Jews, very favourable to the latter.

Soon, however, a very important factor entered on the scene. It will be remembered that the son of the murdered Seleucus, by name Demetrius, had been sent to Rome as a hostage while a boy. In 162 he escaped from Rome and landed on the coast of Syria and was at once hailed with enthusiasm. He became king. The regent Lysias was put to death. Demetrius was energetic and strong and soon found it expedient to intervene in the affairs of Judaea. At this time a person comes into the story whose Hebrew name Jakin was Grecized into Alcimus. He belonged to the priestly class. This man pressed his claims at Antioch, where he assumed the role of opponent of the Hasmoneans[1] and intrigued to get himself nominated as High Priest. The intrigue was successful, and Alcimus was sent to Jerusalem under the escort of a considerable force of Syrian troops commanded by Bacchides. At first Alcimus was received in a friendly way by the *Chasidim*, the party of the Pious.

The Hasmoneans[1] were thus isolated. The party of the Pious no longer worked in co-operation with them. Bacchides expelled the Hasmoneans[1] and their followers from Jerusalem; but Judas and his brothers were still the centre of the forces of resistance, and Demetrius within a short time found it expedient to send another expedition, this time under Nicanor. Nicanor tried to enter into friendly relations with Judas and was apparently ready to come to an arrangement with him; but orders came from Antioch to arrest Judas, who, however, promptly disappeared. Nicanor failed in his immediate object, and meanwhile Judas, having collected his guerrilla bands, challenged the Syrian force to battle. This resulted in a great victory for the Jews. Nicanor perished on the field. The battle of Adasa was Judas's last and greatest victory. The Syrian monarch promptly dispatched another large force, this time under Bacchides. Judas felt constrained to fight and perished on the field of battle (Eleasa, 161 B.C.).

[1] i.e. the Maccabean family.

Bacchides cleared the country of rebels and installed the Hellenizing party under Alcimus in power. The surviving Hasmonean brothers, Jonathan, Simon and John, took refuge with their followers in the wilderness. Alcimus, however, died shortly before Bacchides left Judaea.

It is significant that the party of the Pious withdrew their support of the Hasmoneans during the later part of Judas's life. His brother and successor Jonathan (161–143) was thoroughly worldly in his outlook and achievements. He was astute and cunning, a wily diplomatist who used all the arts of intrigue to gain his ends. And in the later history of the house the same cleavage, as we shall see, reveals itself from time to time between the ruling house and the party of the Pious. The book of Daniel, as has often been noticed, adopts a somewhat cool attitude towards the Hasmonean cause. In this apocalyptic work we have revealed to us the innermost feelings and struggles of the *Chasidim*, and the religious importance of the book is of the highest. It aimed at inspiring the truly religious with the spirit of martyrdom. The book gives only a brief summary of the great tribulation—the pollution of the Temple, the apostasy of many, the persecution of the faithful (cf. $11^{31\text{ff.}}$; 7^{25}; $8^{11\text{-}14}$; 9^{27}). It is noteworthy that the beginning of resistance by Judas is referred to not altogether with warm approval (11^{34}: 'Now when they shall fall, they shall be holpen with a little help: but many shall join themselves unto them with flatteries'). The *Chasidim* at first followed the policy of non-resistance, but the exploits of Judas go beyond the limits of the book.

It seems clear that the Pious section of the nation was content with the attainment of religious freedom. For that end it was willing to struggle, but not for purely national ends. The Maccabean princes were essentially secular rulers, necessarily involved in the tortuous web of statecraft and diplomatic intrigue. It was impossible to unite the two interests—the spiritual and the secular headship of the State—in one person without damage to the spiritual side. As Dr. Edwyn Bevan remarks: 'What was the issue of the battling of Judas and his brethren? The establishment of a dynasty by whose dominion the national life was poisoned, and whose presence at the altar the religious denounced as a pollution.

Perhaps this explains why the general conscience of Judaism so soon allowed the memory of Judas and his brethren to fade, why it ultimately abstained from putting any book of *Maccabees* in its sacred canon.' [1]

(c) *The struggle for political independence*

The ill-timed attack of Antiochus Epiphanes aroused both the religious and the political consciousness of the Jews. Judaism consolidated itself, became tougher and more self-conscious. The devotion of the people to the Law was intensified, and the effects on the religion are marked in this period and onwards.

Political independence was not so easy to attain. Nevertheless, it was attained, and the story of how this was accomplished remains to be told.

On the death of Judas three of the five brothers were left, Jonathan, Simon and John. John soon after died. For the most part the Hasmoneans at this time had to content themselves with wandering in the wilderness, where they carried on guerrilla warfare. Judas, as we have seen, perished in 161. Jonathan and Simon were able to return to Judaea in 158 while Demetrius was still on the throne. Apparently this took place with the acquiescence of the Syrian government. Jerusalem, however, was still held by the Syrians. Jonathan was allowed to establish himself at Michmash. Jonathan, who was a clever politician, bided his time and soon had an opportunity to profit by the turn of events. About the year 152 a pretender, who claimed to be the son of Antiochus Epiphanes and called himself Alexander, assumed royal power and established himself at Ptolemais. Though he was undoubtedly an impostor, he received a good deal of support from outside. This diversion had marked effects on Judaea. Syrian garrisons were withdrawn by Demetrius, who found it expedient to conciliate Jonathan in the hope of winning him over to his own side. The Hasmonean Jonathan was allowed to re-enter Jerusalem and authorized to maintain a military force. The next step of Jonathan was to obtain the high-priestly office, and Alexander was ready to buy Jonathan's support by conferring this dignity upon him.

[1] *Jerusalem under the High Priests*, p. 99.

In the autumn of 152 he appeared before the people at the Feast of Tabernacles in the·vestments of the High Priest. Two years later, 150, Alexander defeated Demetrius. During the reign of this usurper Jonathan kept on good terms with the Syrian court; Alexander was consistently favourable to Jonathan, in spite of the desperate attempts of the Hellenizing party to turn him in the opposite direction. But soon further complications with regard to the dynasty arose.

Another candidate for the Syrian throne now appeared—this time a younger Demetrius, the son of the king of that name. In 148–147 this Demetrius (II) appeared in Syria. He was quite a boy at this time, not more than 14 years old. War at once broke out between the parties of Alexander and Demetrius II. Apollonius, the governor of Coele-Syria, sided with the new pretender. Jonathan, however, was true to his allegiance to Alexander. A battle took place near Azotus (Ashdod). Jonathan and his forces were completely victorious. He had rendered Alexander a signal service. But the reigning Egyptian king intervened in favour of Demetrius, and Alexander lost his authority. An attempt in 145 to recover the kingdom led to his rout and subsequent murder. During these troubles Jonathan tried to eject the Syrian garrison from the citadel of Jerusalem (the Akra), but without success, though he made favourable terms with Demetrius II. The Syrian garrison, however, was allowed to retain its possession of the Akra.

But troubles soon broke out again. A widespread revolt reflected the general dissatisfaction. Disorders culminated at Antioch, where the crowd attacked the royal palace; the king's mercenaries, in retaliation, set the city on fire. A panic ensued, and the mercenaries took advantage of this to start a general massacre. The Jewish contingent took part in this. The dynastic troubles, however, were not at an end. The same year (145) a movement was started to set up as king an infant son of Alexander, known as Antiochus Dionysus. The movement was led by a general named Tryphon and was joined by the Jews. Jonathan and Simon were treated with favour by Tryphon, Simon being made governor of Palestine. The Hasmonean brothers were now at the head of considerable national forces and proceeded to initiate a number of operations, acting as officers of king Antiochus against the party of Demetrius. These extended far afield; Gaza was besieged and taken, and we hear of operations in Galilee and Damascus.

Of the rich opportunities thus afforded them of consolidating the Jewish power they made full use, and places won from Demetrius were garrisoned by Jewish levies.

In this way Joppa, Beth-sur, and Adida became Jewish strongholds. Whether Jonathan engaged in diplomatic relations with Rome is doubtful. Some scholars, however, including Schürer, believe that the account given in Maccabees is authentic. Jonathan's proceedings, however, did not escape the observation of Tryphon, who understood perfectly well what the wily Jewish leader was doing. Having, as he thought, exhausted the usefulness of Jonathan, he took advantage of Jonathan's presence on a friendly visit to him at Ptolemais to have him arrested.

When the news reached Jerusalem, consternation reigned. Simon rose to the occasion and prepared for a struggle with Tryphon. The military defences of the capital were strengthened; Joppa was made safe for the Jews by the ejection of the Gentile population. A new policy of expansion was adopted, and Jewish settlements were pushed out beyond the boundaries of Judaea.

Tryphon threatened Judaea with invasion, but without result. He, however, put Jonathan to death. Simon buried his brother at Modin and as the last survivor took up the inheritance. Tryphon, having murdered the boy-king Antiochus Dionysus, attempted to assume royal honours himself. This action led to a final breach with the Jews. Simon seized the opportunity to negotiate with Demetrius. He secured the removal of all dues which had been enacted by the Seleucids, and the following year, 142–141, the Syrian garrison in the Akra surrendered, and political independence was now practically attained.

(d) The reign of Simon (142–135)

Simon, who now assumed the leadership, had won a reputation for moderation and wise counsel. He was prudent and statesmanlike. In war he had shown himself a skilful commander. The years of his rule are pictured in the books of Maccabees as a sort of golden age. In the glowing words of the author of 1 Maccabees 14⁹:

'The ancient men sat in the streets, they communed all of them together of good things, and the young men put on glorious and warlike apparel.' In a great assembly of the nation Simon was proclaimed High Priest and military and civil governor of the Jews, and this office was declared to be hereditary ('for ever' till a trustworthy prophet should arise. I Maccabees 14[41]). Simon was a wise ruler and intent upon building up the state on a firm

Simon's annexation of Gezer. A graffito found at Gezer, probably reading Παμπρας Σιμωνος κατοπαζῃ πυρ βασιλειον, 'Pampras (says): may fire overtake Simon's palace'. It is an imprecation scratched on one of Simon's building-stones, probably by one of the dispossessed Syrians

foundation. He was devoted to the service and interests of his people. The Syrian kingdom was still recognized as Suzerain; but the political independence of the Jewish State was practically attained, and Simon's position was that of an independent prince. To strengthen his position he entered into relations with Rome. It should be noted that at this time the process of expansion which had already begun was continued. The area of the Jewish State was extended by conquest. Simon's chief gain in this direction was the annexation of the city of Gazara (Gezer). The strategical position of this city, guarding as it did the approaches to Judaea from the west and also commanding the great maritime highway from Joppa along the coast, was of great importance. The town was taken after a desperate resistance. The heathen population were deported and Jewish colonists installed in their place. The important town of Joppa was also controlled by Simon, and the Temple area was fortified. Thus Simon laid the foundations of a prosperous Jewish State. The expansion which took place in this way at the expense of Greek cities and Greek populations aroused the energies of the Syrian king, Antiochus VII, Sidetes. This monarch, one of the most energetic of the later Seleucids, was the

The first Maccabean coinage. Half-shekel (above) and quarter-shekel (below) of Simon, issued in 139 B.C. by permission of Antiochus Sidetes. The inscriptions are, 'of the year 4 of the redemption of Zion'

son of Demetrius I and died in 129 B.C. In 138 he took the field against Tryphon, Demetrius II, his brother, being a prisoner of the Parthians.

At first, Antiochus was friendly to Simon; later, he changed his demeanour and demanded from him the surrender of the conquered cities Joppa and Gazara and the citadel of Jerusalem, or in default a heavy payment. Simon refused these demands. A clash took place, and Antiochus' general, Cendebaeus, was defeated by the sons of Simon, Judah and John (137). This victory enabled Simon to enjoy peace for the rest of his reign. He was left undisturbed, though Antiochus Sidetes, who was an energetic monarch, intervened again in the affairs of Judaea, as we shall see later on, with decisive effect.

Simon was king in all but name; he wisely refrained from claiming the royal dignity and was rewarded by the spontaneous act of the people in proclaiming him High Priest and Ethnarch of the Jews. Unhappily Simon was assassinated by his son-in-law, Ptolemy, who was governor of the Jordan valley. The murderer intended to assume Simon's office but was frustrated by John Hyrcanus, Simon's son (135 B.C.). The reign of Simon was marked by other developments. In particular, it is probable that the Psalter was thoroughly revised, and possibly some Psalms of Maccabean date added to the collection. The services in the Temple were probably beautified, and the Temple Choirs extended. These points will be discussed more fully in connexion with the literature.

The tone of joy which pervades the later Psalms is noteworthy. It may reflect the feeling of deep thankfulness on the part of the community after the terrible trials and dangers of the earlier Maccabean days. The people were profoundly sensible of the magnitude of their deliverance and showed this in a deepened devotion to the divine law, which henceforth became the hall-mark of Judaism.

(e) John Hyrcanus and his Sons

On the death of his father John Hyrcanus (135–105 B.C.) proceeded to Jerusalem, where he was at once appointed High Priest and civil ruler of the Jews. With his accession to power Hyrcanus was confronted with a new danger. Antiochus Sidetes was by no means disposed to acquiesce in this independence of the Jewish State and again intervened to re-establish his authority in Palestine. The Syrian king invaded Judaea and laid siege to Jerusalem. After holding out for some time the city was taken (134).

John was compelled to make terms of peace and to pay a heavy indemnity of 500 talents; the population was disarmed, the fortifications dismantled, and the Jewish prince had to pay rent for the cities captured outside Judaea (Joppa and Gazara). Antiochus thus used his victory with moderation. John was left in full possession of Judaea, and we find him leading a Jewish contingent in Antiochus' army, which marched against the Parthians in a campaign in which the Syrian monarch lost his life (129 B.C.).

Henceforth Judaea was left alone and enjoyed its independence for the next sixty-five years until the intervention of the Romans.

John returned safely from the East and at once with character-istic energy began to carry out a policy of expansion. His aim was to consolidate the Judaean State by crushing unfriendly elements on its borders. His first campaign was in the region east of the

The ruins of the gate of the Maccabean castle at Gezer

Jordan. The towns Medeba and Samaga were captured and the surrounding territory annexed. On the north he captured Shechem, the principal town of the Samaritans, and demolished the hated rival Temple on Mount Gerizim. The Idumaeans on the south—the ancient Edomites—were also invaded and were compelled to accept Judaism by force. By a strange irony of fate, it was from an Idumaean family thus Judaized—the family of Antipater, who was appointed Governor of the conquered people—that Herod, the 'half Jew', who was destined to prove such a scourge to pious Jews, sprang.

Finally, John attacked the Greek city of Samaria, which under-went a long siege and was only finally reduced by famine. It is important to notice that Samaria was a *Greek* city, the seat of a Macedonian colony; the chief city of the Samaritans was Shechem, which had already been conquered by John.

The actual conduct of the siege was left by Hyrcanus to his two sons, Antigonus and Aristobulus, who were able to beat off repeated attempts to relieve the city made by Antiochus Cyzicenus, who was at that time ruling over part of Syria. The siege went on (?110-107 B.C.), and when the city was finally taken, the Jews did all they could to remove every trace of its former existence. About the same time they also secured possession of another important city, Scythopolis (the ancient Bethshan) on the edge of the plain of Esdraelon.

It is clear that the Hasmonean House was assuming the pomp and power of secular rule. Thus John employed mercenary troops and to a large extent lived the life of a military leader. He also functioned as High Priest, and this was naturally a cause of offence to the Pious, as we shall see. John died in 105 B.C. and was succeeded by his son Aristobulus, who was the first Maccabean prince to assume the title of king. Aristobulus exhibited the ruthless character so often associated with Oriental monarchy. He starved his mother to death, and imprisoned all his brothers except Antigonus; and even the latter fell under suspicion and was put to death.

His reign lasted but a single year; but it was long enough to enable him to conquer and forcibly Judaize the territory of the Itureans, which corresponded to a part of Galilee. This marks an important event in the history of Judaism. Galilee at this time was inhabited by a mixed population of Syrians and Greeks. There appear to have been very few Jewish families in the district. Galilee thus became what we find it in the Gospels—a province where the population is largely non-Jewish by race but Jewish in religion.

Aristobulus, who died in 104 B.C., was succeeded by one of his brothers whom he had imprisoned, by name Jonathan. This name, shortened into Jannai, was Grecized into Jannaeus. He also bore the Greek name of Alexander and is known to history as Alexander Jannaeus.

During his long reign (104-78 B.C.) he was engaged in perpetual

Ploughing on the site of Sebaste (Samaria). The columns are of the Hall of Justice built by Herod

wars and led the life of a rough soldier. He was indeed a sort of
Jewish Pope John XXIII. It is not difficult to understand that
such a leader came into violent collision with the party of the
Pharisees, who had acquired immense influence over the people
generally. A vivid illustration of this is given in the story extant
both in Josephus (*Ant.* XIII. 13. 5) and in the Talmud (T. B. *Sukka*,
48b), according to which on one occasion, while officiating as High
Priest at the Feast of Tabernacles, Alexander deliberately poured
out the libation of water on to the ground instead of on the altar
in accordance with the Pharisaic view. By this contemptuous
action—which followed Sadducean custom—Alexander greatly
incensed the assembled worshippers. Loud shouts of protest arose,
and they began to pelt the unworthy High Priest with the citrons
which they held in their hands. The tumult increased and was only
quelled by the intervention of the Greek mercenaries. It is related
that no less than 6,000 people perished on this occasion within the
precincts of the Temple.

After this event the Pharisees were irreconcilable and awaited
an opportunity for vengeance. Their chance came when Alexander
returned to Jerusalem after an unsuccessful campaign against the
Nabateans, having lost his army (94 B.C.). The Pharisees at once
fomented a revolt, and civil war raged in Judaea for six years.
When the king sought to end the carnage by coming to terms with
his adversaries, the Pharisees refused to be satisfied with anything
short of his death, and with this end in view made the mistake of
inviting the aid of their old foes, the Syrians. A large army under
Demetrius III invaded Palestine and defeated the Jewish king,
who was forced to flee for refuge to the mountain country of
Ephraim. The plight of Alexander, a fugitive from a foreign foe,
produced a strong reaction in his favour among the Jewish population, a large body of whom went over to the king's side. Demetrius was compelled to withdraw, and Alexander was dominant.
He exacted a barbarous and bloody revenge from his implac-
able foes, the Pharisees, who were driven into exile, while those
who did not succeed in escaping were crucified. It is said that
800 suffered punishment in this way. After this the king remained in undisputed possession of his realm. Towards the end
of his reign the Syrian monarchy was overthrown by Tigranes,

King of Armenia, 83 B.C., and Alexander profited by this to extend the boundaries of his dominion. He died in 78 B.C., while engaged in military operations east of the Jordan.

As we have seen, Alexander was essentially a soldier, intent on aggrandizing the Jewish state. Though by no means always successful in his military operations, at the end of his long reign of 27 years he had substantially increased the area of his kingdom, which extended on the north as far as Lake Merom, on the west embraced the maritime plain from Mount Carmel, and included on the east of the Jordan the ancient territory of Gilead and Bashan.

Unlike his brother Aristobulus, he was no friend of Greek culture. His conquests meant the devastation and destruction of Greek civilization in Palestine.

Alexander left two sons, John Hyrcanus, commonly known as Hyrcanus II, and Aristobulus. He was succeeded immediately, however, by his widow, Alexandra (78–69 B.C.), Hyrcanus taking the office of High Priest. Queen Alexandra was a wise and prudent woman; she reversed the policy of her late husband and recalled the Pharisees from exile, restoring them once again to power. They used their opportunity to revive the practice of the law, which was interpreted according to their own traditions; a system of elementary schools was also organized. Unfortunately they did not content themselves with constructive work of this kind but took occasion to persecute their opponents, the Sadducees. The latter found a champion in Aristobulus, who induced his mother to hand over the fortresses of the kingdom to him. He took care to garrison them with partisans of the Sadducees. The seed was thus sown for future troubles. Alexandra died in 69 B.C.

(f) The Rise of the Pharisees; their relation to the Sadducees

As we have seen, the Pharisees took a prominent part in public affairs during the reign of Alexander Jannaeus. The first mention of them as a party occurs in Josephus in his account of the reign of John Hyrcanus. They appear already as a powerful party during this prince's reign (135–105 B.C.).[1]

No doubt they were in existence at an earlier date. Their general

---

[1] See Josephus, *Ant.* XIII. xiii. 5–7.

aim was to make effective the work of the earlier teachers with regard to the Mosaic law, which was regarded as a system to be applied to every department of life and to be worked out in detail accordingly.

In the passage of Josephus already referred to an account is given of the rupture between the Pharisaic party and the ruling house. According to the story, the breach grew out of an incident at a banquet given by John Hyrcanus I, when one of the Pharisees indiscreetly suggested that the ruler should lay aside the high-priestly functions which he had assumed and content himself with the role of secular prince. When asked to give a reason for this demand the Pharisee is said to have mentioned a rumour (which in fact was entirely baseless) to the effect that the mother of Hyrcanus had been a captive.[1] This was the cause of the rupture. Hyrcanus is said to have withdrawn from the Pharisaic party, of which hitherto he had been a zealous member. In the Talmud, however (T. B. *Qiddushin*, 66 A), the story is referred to Alexander Jannaeus (104–78 B.C.), and this is probably the correct historical setting. Whereas the reign of Hyrcanus was, according to Josephus, peaceful and happy, we know there were violent conflicts between Alexander Jannaeus and the Pharisees, resulting in devastating civil war. Probably Hyrcanus continued to favour the party all through his reign and was under their influence. A violent quarrel between the ruler and the party took place under Alexander Jannaeus. In the reign of Queen Alexandra, and subsequently down to the time of Pompey, the Pharisees continued to exercise great political influence, not always wisely.

The explanation of the name Pharisee is uncertain. It may mean 'Separatist', perhaps originally given as a nickname by opponents who may have intended to brand the party as disloyal —those that separated themselves from loyal obedience to their king. Or it may have meant, originally, the expelled or 'dismissed', i.e. from the Sanhedrin.[2] A division certainly took place within the ranks of members of that body, so that it was grouped finally into two great parties, namely, the Sadducees (i.e. the

---

[1] This would be a legal disqualification for the High-priesthood.

[2] Other explanations of the name have also been suggested. See Hastings, *E.R.E.* ix, p. 832.

The Rise of the Pharisees 51

priestly group) and the Pharisees (i.e. the lay members of that body, representing the popular party).

In order to understand the development of this great party it is necessary to consider how their work grew out of earlier antecedents. As we have already remarked, this work was bound up with the teaching of the Law. The earlier teachers of the Law went by the name of 'Soferim', so called because they taught the people out of the 'Book of the Law'. The word 'Soferim', usually rendered 'scribes', really means 'bookmen'. They taught the plain and simple text of the Mosaic Law. Of course, a certain amount of interpretation went on, but without the elaborate exegesis of the later Pharisees. The period of the Soferim ended with Simon the Just (the first of that name), about 300–270 B.C. It therefore ceased just about the time when Greek influence began to permeate powerfully Jewish life in Palestine.

During this period the circumstances of the Jewish community in Palestine underwent no great change. The revised book of the Law, accepted from Ezra, was thus adequate to meet the needs of the Jewish community. Simon the Just, the last of the Soferim, was himself High Priest, and, no doubt, the teachers of whom he was the head were mainly recruited from the Priests. Under this system Priests and teachers of the Law were combined. After the death of Simon, however, the activity of these teachers as an authoritative body seems to have broken down. Owing to changing conditions the old control exercised by the High Priest and the priestly Soferim was no longer possible. New customs and practices gradually arose, for which there was no authority either in the text of the Law or in priestly tradition, and established themselves among the people. Still, the need of properly equipped teachers of the Law was acutely felt. To meet this need there arose a body of lay teachers who devoted themselves to the study of the Law and expended themselves on teaching it. It is important to emphasize the fact that these teachers were laymen. No doubt there were faithful priests who assisted this movement. Thus for some seventy or eighty years—from about 270 to 190 B.C.—there seems to have been a break in authoritative teaching. The text of the Law and the study of it were preserved during this interval by the piety of individual teachers, both priests and laymen. About

190 B.C. or a few years earlier or later, it is probable that this state
of things was brought to an end by the organization of the Sanhedrin, an authoritative body consisting of priests and lay
teachers, which was able to regulate officially the religious affairs
of the people. It was their task to harmonize the laws of the
fathers with the life of their own times; and this task had become
exceptionally difficult because the new religious customs that had
grown up among the people had now (owing to lapse of time) come
to be regarded by them as traditional, and meanwhile, also, the
text of the Law had become rigidly fixed. It was no longer possible
to introduce slight verbal modifications, as the earlier Soferim had
done. How was the problem to be solved? It was apparently in
connexion with the circumstances raised by this difficulty that
that division took place in the Sanhedrin which later led to the
secession (or dismissal) from that body of those who came to
be called 'Pharisees', i.e. as explained above, 'seceders'. But
before this critical state of affairs was reached, a long period
of discussion and controversy apparently took place. The priestly,
at that time the most powerful, element in the Sanhedrin wished
to maintain the sacred and obligatory character of the written
Torah, as apart from the new religious customs. According to
Lauterbach, they wished to give authoritative recognition to the
latter by special decrees issued and modified from time to time, to
suit varying circumstances, by priestly authority in accordance
with Deut. 17$^{8-13}$. These decrees were not to be put on a level with
the sacred text of the written Law, but were to be regarded as
authoritative so long as they remained in force. On the other hand,
the Chasidim, or members of the pious party, largely represented
by the lay teachers in the Sanhedrin, would not accept this solution. They were unwilling to recognize any such extension of
purely priestly authority and contended that their own authority
as teachers was equal to that of the priests and that all authorized
religious customs must be based directly upon the Law or its
equivalent. 'Acknowledging the Law of the fathers to be the sole
authority, these lay teachers now had to find all the decisions and
rules necessary for the practical life of their time contained or
implied in the Law. They also had to devise methods for connecting with the Law all those new decisions and customs which were

now universally observed by the people, thus making them appear a part of the laws of the fathers.'[1]

This oral law was later developed on a large scale and was regarded as of equal authority with the written Torah. On it the Pharisaic teachers developed the whole system of Rabbinical Judaism. The age-long conflict between the Sadducees and the Pharisees was the most important factor in the development of Judaism. At first, the oral law was quite independent of the written Torah. On the other hand, the Sadducees, who were the priestly party, and included the nobility who supported the Maccabean princes, were the champions of the old conservative positions of the priesthood and inherited the traditions of the older scribism. The 'scribe' as he is depicted in Sirach (*circa* 190 B.C.) is a judge and man of affairs, a cultivated student of wisdom, well acquainted, of course, with the contents of the written law and a frequenter of the courts of kings. He belongs to the leisured aristocratic class and is poles asunder from the typical Pharisee and teacher of the Law, who was drawn from the ranks of the people. It was in the reaction against Hellenism that Torah-study among the people was born. The public reading and exposition of it in the Synagogue probably dates only from the Maccabean period. Both parties were compelled now to devote themselves to Torah-study in the new and exacting way demanded by the times, the Sadducees, because, in their view, the Law was the only valid standard for fixing juristic and religious practice, and the Pharisees, because it was necessary for them to adjust their oral tradition, as far as possible, to the written word. The first result of Pharisaic activity in this direction was the development of a remarkably rich and subtle exegesis. A further result was the evolution of new laws by exegetical methods.[2]

The Pharisees were thus essentially a democratic party, in the sense that they were themselves mainly drawn from the people and safeguarded the religious rights and privileges of the laity as

---

[1] Lauterbach, in *J.Q.R.*, new ser., vi. 578.

[2] The thirteen exegetical principles of R. Ishmael (developed from an earlier nucleus attributed to Hillel) are set forth in S. Singer's *Hebrew-English Authorized Daily Prayer Book*, London, 1914, p. 13. They are explained and illustrated in M. Mielziner, *Introd. to the Talmud*, Cincinnati, 1894.

against the aristocratic and exclusive priesthood. The reaction against the Hellenizing movement was largely strengthened by their work in succession to that of the earlier Chasidim; they democratized religion by making the scriptures the possession of the people and expounding these in the weekly assemblage of the Synagogue.

In marked contrast with those of the Sadducees, their judgements in questions of law were, as is well known, of a mild and compassionate character. When it is realized how they spent their energies without stint in the work of instructing the people in the Torah and in bringing religion to bear upon popular life, their enormous influence with the people generally, to which Josephus testifies, is explained. Josephus says that the Pharisees led the people, compelling even the priestly aristocracy to yield to them. 'Practically nothing was done by them [the Sadducees]; for whenever they attain office, they follow—albeit unwillingly and of compulsion—what the Pharisees say, because otherwise they would not be endured by the people' (*Ant.* XVIII. 1. 4).[1]

We had occasion to note the manifold *political* activities of the Pharisees, especially in the reign of Alexander Jannaeus. This was really an aberration from their true function. Primarily and essentially they formed a religious, not a political, party; but because of the opposition of the Sadducees they were forced to take political action. Like the party of Chasidim, or the 'pious', whom we have met in connexion with the reign of Antiochus Epiphanes, they were cold towards the popular ambition for political independence and national expansion. They regarded alliances with the heathen world as treason to Jehovah. Paradoxically they combined conservatism in politics with a democratic and progressive attitude in religious matters.

Their supreme aim was to bring religion into the everyday life of the people—they objected to priestly privilege and invested the home with the sanctions of religious life. The Passover became essentially a home feast, when the father of the home acted as a sort of priest. They were always ready to adapt religious customs and usages to the requirements of life. Among their great

---

[1] For the later developments of Pharisaism and its importance in the first two centuries of the Christian era see the article *Pharisees* in Hastings, *E.R.E.*

The importance of the Synagogue. The reconstructed north end of
the Roman synagogue at Capernaum

achievements was the creation and development of the Synagogue and its services, and the popularization of the Bible. They extended knowledge of the Torah among the people by a system of education connected with the synagogue and in manifold ways expended themselves in instructing the masses of the people. They laid the foundations and built up the system of Judaism as we know it that has lasted down to the present day.

(g) The Jewish Diaspora

'The first and most remarkable phenomenon presented by Judaism during the Graeco-Roman period is its dispersion along the shores of the Mediterranean.' So writes Th. Reinach.[1]

The existence of scattered Jewish communities outside Judaea was no new thing. The two deportations to Babylonia in 597 and 586 B.C. resulted in the establishment of a very important Jewish community in that part of the world, which exercised great influence through many centuries. But perhaps the most important of these settlements was that in Egypt, where a small Jewish Diaspora was formed as far back as the time of Jeremiah; cf. Jer. 24[8], 26[22], 40–44. When Ptolemy I evacuated Syria many Jews voluntarily followed him. The same thing happened in 198 B.C., when Palestine passed for good under the control of the Seleucids. Under Ptolemy VI Philomitor, the son of the High Priest Onias, disappointed of his expectations, betook himself with a considerable number of followers to Egypt, and there set up a rival temple to that of Jerusalem (Josephus, Ant. XIII. iii). During the wars of the third and second centuries B.C. thousands of Jews were made captives and reduced to slavery, passing from owner to owner and from country to country until enfranchisement. The Jews thus freed, instead of returning to Palestine, usually remained in the land of their former slavery, and there in conjunction with their brethren in the faith established communities. According to Philo, the Jewish community in Rome owed its origin to released prisoners of war.

We have already seen how important a centre of Jewish colonies Egypt was under the Ptolemies. A settlement of new communities of Jews in that country was facilitated by the fact that during the Persian period Jewish communities had established

---

[1] Article, *Diaspora* in *Jewish Encyclopaedia*; cf. Jn. 7[35].

themselves there. These colonies preserved their individual character as Jewish settlements and were not absorbed into the surrounding populations. As we have already seen, in Alexandria they possessed their own quarter, a quarter entirely Jewish; and they also had their own ethnarch, who in coming to important decisions summoned to his aid a council of assessors, who numbered after the Mosaic pattern seventy elders.

We learn that in the region of Heliopolis a large district was exclusively possessed by Jews. Further, in the district of Memphis there existed a self-contained Jewish colony.

In Thebes, in Upper Egypt, evidence has come in the form of a number of documents, connected with the royal tax revenue, of the existence of Jewish officials. A surprisingly large number of Jewish names is revealed of the holders of offices in this department of the government service.

In countries connected politically with Egypt, such as Cyrene and Cyprus, the Jewish element became very strong. According to Josephus, the first Ptolemy, when he annexed Cyrene, established a Jewish Colony; and a similar proceeding is ascribed to Antiochus the Great, who is said to have ordered the transportation of 2,000 Jewish families from Babylonia to Phrygia and Lydia. As Schlatter[1] remarks, the disturbances in Judaea, which resulted in military intervention by the Romans (Pompey, Gabinius) and involved the siege and capture of Jerusalem, resulted in many Jews being taken prisoners of war. The markets were full of Jewish slaves, who would in course of time be bought out of slavery and freed by co-religionists. Perhaps the Synagogue of the Libertines mentioned in the Acts of the Apostles 6[9] belonged to emancipated Jews of this kind.

Other causes also contributed to swell the Jewish Diaspora. There was a strong impulse—in many cases an overmastering impulse—on the part of individual Jews to wander from country to country. The Jews early discovered that they could maintain themselves in foreign lands, though perhaps less securely than in their homeland. Jerusalem with the Temple as its centre acted as a magnet to which the Jews who lived in the dispersion were inevitably drawn. So powerful and binding a force as the Jerusalem

[1] *Geschichte Israels* (1925), p. 30.

Temple could not exist in any foreign land. To the Temple a constant stream of pilgrims was always flowing for the great festivals.
On the other hand, from the second century B.C. and even earlier,
the Synagogue acted as a powerful binding force wherever Jewish
communities were congregated. After the destruction of the
Temple the power of the Synagogue was even more conspicuous.

Another remarkable and important development in the Jewish
Diaspora was concerned with the question of language. Naturally,
the Jewish communities learned the language of the country
where they dwelt. In what was considered the civilized world
during the Hellenistic period, Greek was the common language.
This was conspicuously the case in such a country as Egypt. Here
the Jews adopted Greek not only as the language of everyday life
but used it in their services and read the Bible in Greek (the LXX).
One further result, at any rate in Egypt, seems to have been that
the Jews lost all knowledge of their original language, Hebrew.
The preface to the Greek translation of Ecclesiasticus makes it
clear that, at the time when the translator wrote, the Greek Bible
was exclusively used by the Jews in Egypt. The Greek Bible itself
bears witness to this fact by the way in which it treats the text of
certain later books, such as Proverbs, Job, Esther, and Daniel,
where certain substantial additions of purely Greek origin have
been inserted into the text without being detected as such.

A Hebrew book could count on readers in such circles only if
it were translated into Greek. Pseudonymous books like the
Wisdom of Solomon, which is a purely Greek composition, could
circulate without the fact being recognized that there was no
corresponding Hebrew original.[1] It is evident from Philo's own
explanations of the divine names that he knew no Hebrew.

Even in Palestine knowledge of the Hebrew language was confined to the learned; the generality of the population was, however, bilingual, the two languages commonly used being Aramaic
and Greek. It is a striking fact that in the New Testament period,
and for some considerable time before,[2] the lections from the Bible

---

[1] Of course, it is not suggested that nobody in Egypt knew Hebrew; the
mere fact that translations were made is sufficient to prove the contrary;
but such knowledge was comparatively rare, and as time went on grew rarer.

[2] Probably from at least the second century B.C.

read in the Synagogue services in Palestine were read both in
Hebrew and an Aramaic Targum or translation, the latter being
necessary in order to make the lesson intelligible to the people.[1]

Farther east, in Babylonia, Greek did not play so prominent
a part. The language used in those regions at this time was a

Jewish astrology. Part of a mosaic in the ruins of the synagogue at Ain
Duk, north-west of Jericho. The female figure represents one of the
Seasons (teḳūphah); below her are the Hebrew names dāgūn (Pisces) and
ṭāleh (Ariel)

dialect of Aramaic, differing somewhat from the Aramaic spoken
in Palestine. Thus for the Jewish communities scattered throughout the world during the Hellenistic period two languages sufficed
—Greek and Aramaic; and it would be possible for a Jew to make
himself understood in one or other of those tongues in any part of
the civilized world.

[1] It is worth noting that the historian Josephus, who studied and wrote in
Greek, knew Aramaic as his mother tongue and wrote a version of the
Jewish War in that language for the benefit of Jews living in the East.

The principal seats of the Jewish Diaspora in the Greek-speaking world during those centuries were Alexandria and Antioch. The Jews were strong also in other important cities, such as Ephesus. In these places the Jews were influential enough to secure citizen-rights; in some cases during the Roman Hegemony they even attained to Roman citizenship—a highly prized and much sought-after privilege. They were sometimes able to take an influential part in the affairs of government.

We have already seen how the Maccabean princes were admitted to the highest ranks of the king's friends at the Syrian Court; and at a later time important offices were held by Egyptian Jews in the service of the State.[1] It was through the Diaspora that Judaism came into most intimate contact with the outside world. We have already noticed some phenomena of this kind as shown by the profound influence exercised on Judaism by Greek ideas and Greek institutions. Another stream of influence flowed from the east. Some effects of this factor during the period which we are considering have been pointed out by Schlatter.[2]

A new emphasis is now laid upon astrology. Abraham is represented as an astronomer, a pioneer who discovered the science of the stars; Solomon, too, was an astronomer; and Philo pictures Moses as having been instructed by Assyrians and Egyptians in that science, and similarly Enoch. Closely connected with this development was the growth in the belief in demonology and the control of man's fate by celestial agencies. The beginning of the New Year, as had long been the case in ancient Babylon, was the time when fate was determined for the next year.

One important result of contact with the Greek World was the assimilation of the Jewish communities to city life. Greek civilization was essentially *urban* in character; agriculture was no longer, to the Hellenized Jews, as in Judaea, their main occupation. In Alexandria they were engaged in commerce as well as, to some extent, agriculture. They were largely employed in the mechanical trades. When they assembled in the Synagogue they were grouped

---

[1] Tiberius Alexander, a nephew of Philo, was for a short time *procurator* of Judaea; the Jewish High Priest of Leontopolis took a prominent part in state affairs, even heading military expeditions.
[2] Op. cit., p. 34.

according to their respective handicrafts. The great Synagogue of Alexandria, a building of vast dimensions, is thus described:[1]

R. Jehudah says: Whoever has not seen the basilica-synagogue of Alexandria has never seen the great glory of Israel. It is something like a large colonnade with porches within porches, and accommodating sometimes double the number of those that followed Moses from Egypt. There were seventy-one Golden chairs therein, corresponding to the seventy-one elders, and each of the chairs was worth twenty-five myriad talents of gold. In the centre was a wooden dais, and the sexton stood upon it with a scarf, and all the people answered Amen. The people were not seated together anyhow, but the goldsmiths were by themselves, the blacksmiths by themselves, the embroiderers by themselves; so that when a poor man came in he joined himself to his fellow tradesmen, and in this way was enabled to obtain means of livelihood.

We learn from the inscriptions that the Jews in Hellenistic centres included among them weavers, tent-makers, dealers in purple, butchers, tavern-keepers, singers, comedians, jewellers, physicians, and even poets and men of letters as well as preachers, lawyers and theologians.

The glorious days of Judaism in Egypt were under the Ptolemies; from the ranks of the Jews in this period came forth soldiers, such as farmers of the revenue and generals. At a later date the Jewish community was not so prosperous and distinguished, and Hadrian could find among them only soothsayers, astrologers and charlatans. The Alexandria which produced a Philo and, indirectly, a Josephus was a thing of the past.[2]

The Jewish Diaspora, however, played an all-important part as an agent for extending the knowledge and practice of Judaism among non-Jews. Theoretically, the intercourse of the Jews with the pagans was confined to commercial relations mainly, and even these were greatly trammelled by the laws of purity. The Jews lived apart, most frequently in separate quarters, grouped around their synagogues. The pious Jew could neither dine at the table of a pagan nor receive him at his own table. He was not permitted to frequent the theatres, the circuses, the gymnasia, nor even to read

[1] Tos. Sukkah, iv. 6 (Greenup's translation).
[2] T. Reinach remarks that scarcely ever before the Middle Ages are the Jews referred to as money-lenders, bankers, or usurers.

a secular book 'unless it be at twilight'. Mixed marriages were prohibited under severe penalties. These rules, however, were not by any means always rigidly adhered to. The Jews were profoundly affected by their environment in many ways. The influence of Greek culture told heavily upon them—as the Judaeo-Alexandrine literature eloquently attests. They used Greek even in their religious services—they read the Bible in Greek, and they adopted Greek names and to some extent Greek organization in their commercial institutions. Above all they were animated by an intense missionary zeal to win over the pagan population to the higher monotheistic religion of which they were the chosen representatives.

Thus the oldest part of the Sibylline oracles [1] predicts that the Jewish nation shall become very powerful and be 'guides of life to mortal men' (III. 194 ff). The Jews of the Diaspora were possessed with the conviction that they were destined to realize the prophetic word *I have set thee for a light of the nations.* (Isa. 49[6].)

In spite of obstacles—prejudices and hatreds on the part of the old pagan world—this over-mastering missionary enthusiasm of the Diaspora-Jew was ready to overcome all obstacles. He was possessed with the conviction that Moses and the Prophets must win in the end. As the Sibyl has it (III. 710 ff.): *And then shall all the islands and the cities see how much the immortal God loves Israel, for all things help them in conflict and deliver them.*

Then the cry goes up from the pagan world:

Come falling on the earth let us all pray the immortal King, the great Eternal God

. . . .

Since he alone is Lord and let us all meditate on the law of God most High which is most righteous of all laws on earth. For from the path of the Immortal we have wandered and with senseless soul we honour works made by hand and wooden images of dead men. [2]

---

[1] Book III, 97–829. According to Bleek this is the work of an Alexandrine Jew, who may have flourished in the Maccabean period, 170–160 B.C. Other scholars assign it to the year 140 or 124 B.C. A convenient edition is that edited by H. N. Bate, *The Sibylline Oracles*, Books III–V. S.P.C.K., 1918.

[2] Cited from the translation (in blank verse) by Milton S. Terry, *The Sibylline Oracles* (New York, no date).

The Nile delta in time of flood. Part of the Palestrina mosaic, which gives a vivid and realistic idea of the aspect of Egypt in Ptolemaic and Roman times

This propagandist zeal was probably no new thing in the Diaspora. Its beginnings go back to the beginnings of the Diaspora
itself. In fact, the Greek translation of the Bible—the LXX—
doubtless owes its existence to zeal in converting the heathen
world. So Philo (*vita Moysis*, ii. 136) expressly says: 'Some held it
unfitting that the laws were known only to a part of the human
race, and that a non-Hellenic part, the Greeks knowing nothing
about it; therefore they hastened themselves about a translation
of it.'

An eloquent witness, too, to the energy and success of this
propaganda is to be seen also in the fierce opposition it provoked
from heathen writers.[1]

Some of the earliest attacks came from Egypt. Thus Josephus
(*c. Apion*. i. 25) says: 'now the Egyptians were the first that cast
reproaches upon us. When they saw us approved by many, they
were moved with envy.' Again (v. 40), 'for even if we were able
ourselves to understand the excellence of all our laws, yet would
the number of those who desire to imitate them induce us to plume
ourselves greatly upon them.'

Thus we see the Diaspora Jew fired with unquenchable zeal to
convert the heathen world to his own pure, ethically severe and
monotheistic faith. All the Graeco-Roman world was his field of
operations; and over all this world a number of forces was operat-
ing to make the missionary's message at once timely and welcome.

'It must be admitted', says Reinach, 'that Judaism lacked
certain of those attractive features which drew the multitude to
the cult of Mithras and of the Egyptian deities. Its physical
exactions repulsed those wanting in stout courage; its cult, devoid
of imagery and sensuous rites, presented only an austere poesy
separating its adepts from the world and cutting them off, to some
extent, from communion with the cultured. But the practical and
legal character of its doctrines, furnishing a rule of life for every
occasion, could not but appeal to a disorganized society. The
purity and simplicity of its theology captivated the high-minded,
while the mystery and quaintness of its customs, the welcome
Sabbath rest, the privileges enjoyed at the hand of public authori-

[1] Apollonius Molon of Rhodes, 90 B.C. Poseidonius of Apamea, 70 B.C.
The Alexandrine Charemon, 50 B.C.

ties, recommended the Jewish faith to those more materialistically inclined.'[1]

The large increase in the numbers of the Jewish Diaspora can be accounted for only when the missionary propaganda is taken into account. The impression produced by this is vividly reflected in

The cult of Mithras. A Roman bas-relief found in Germany representing Mithras killing the bull at the bidding of Ahuramazda

the Hellenistic writers who represent the whole world as rushing towards Jewish observances. No doubt, there is a certain amount of exaggeration; but even when full allowance is made for this, it is clear that the propaganda was remarkably successful, and that it resulted in a large addition of Gentile proselytes. Such were drawn both from the upper, middle and lower classes of society. No doubt a large amount of increase was due to the fact that vast numbers

[1] T. Reinach: article, *Diaspora* in *J.E.*

of Jews passed through the state of slavery and afterwards emerged as free citizens who joined the Jewish communities.[1]

Another point that it is important to remember is this. The Jews of the Dispersion were not too exacting in their demands upon the new converts. The complete adoption of the Jewish law with all its obligations was not insisted upon, at any rate, all at once. 'The neophyte was at first simply a "friend" to the Jewish customs, observing the least enthralling ones—the Sabbath, and the lighting of a fire on the previous evening; certain fast-days; abstention from pork. His sons frequented the synagogues and deserted the Temples; studied and contributed their oboli to the Temple at Jerusalem. By degrees habit accomplished the rest. At last the proselyte took the decisive step; he received the rite of circumcision, took the purification bath, and offered, doubtless in money, the sacrifice which signalised this definitive entrance into the bosom of Israel. Occasionally a Hebraic name was adopted.'[2]

Diaspora Judaism knew how to commend itself to the Greek world by very clever literature, largely apologetic, which was clothed in a Greek garb and assumed a classical form. The thought of Israel as the chosen nation received a lofty interpretation. Israel was chosen to be a priestly nation for the whole world. To Philo the Jewish people is 'above all the nations beloved of God, one that has secured the priesthood for the whole human race' (*De Abrah.* ii. 15).

As Moriz Friedländer has pointed out (*Das Judenthum in der vorchristlichen griechischen Welt*, Vienna, 1897, pp. 20–46), the three great instruments which were employed to forward the propaganda were the Synagogue, the Greek Bible, and the Sabbath rest.

The importance of the Synagogue in the Hellenistic world can hardly be exaggerated. Philo represents the Synagogue as the great centre for religious teaching. In his time synagogues abounded.[3] They stood open to the heathen world and proved a

---

[1] The following are examples of distinguished adherents: the Chamberlain of Queen Candace (Acts 8[26]) and the Royal family of Adiabene and other kings. (Josephus, *Ant.* xx. vii. 1. 3.)   [2] T. Reinach, *ut cit. supra.*

[3] The success of the Diaspora synagogues in winning converts from heathenism gave rise to the famous remark of Seneca (quoted by St. Augustine, *De Civ. Dei.* vi. 10): 'usque eo sceleratissimae gentis consuetudo convaluit ut per omnes iam terras recepta sit: victi victoribus leges dederunt.'

great attraction to many earnest-minded heathen. Their origin, even in the first century of our era, appeared so venerable that it was traced back to the time of Moses (cf. Acts 15²¹).

The second great instrument of propaganda was the Greek Bible. The language used in the synagogues of the Dispersion in public services was Greek—at any rate, for the discourses. This must have been the case because of the large numbers of proselytes and

A representation of a small synagogue, from a fifth-century mosaic known as the 'Capitoline Plan' at Rome

adherents of the Jews who frequented them. The use of the Greek Bible—the LXX—is just as certain. When Philo says that the fame of the laws handed down by Moses has penetrated all inhabited lands and has been spread abroad to the ends of the earth, we are not left in any doubt as to whether he is referring to the Hebrew or to the Greek Bible. For he goes on to remark, 'originally the laws were written in the Chaldaean language and their beauty being unknown to the rest of mankind... some thought it unfitting that the laws should be known to a portion of mankind only. (This necessity brought about a translation of them.) For this reason there is still held yearly a great festival on the island of Pharos, in which not only Jews but also many others take part, in honour of the place where the translation originated, and to thank God for the old yet ever new deeds of good will' (*Vita Moysis*, ii. 137 fb.)[1]

The third great instrument was the *Sabbath rest*. The Sabbath was the regular time for the assemblages of the Jewish community to take place. The seventh day thus acquired great significance and importance not only in the Jewish community but also in the Gentile world generally. Philo says that God singled out for special honour the seventh day, because it is the festival not merely of a town or district, but of the world and is alone worthy of being called the birthday of creation.

The observance of the seventh day as the day of rest by the Jewish community made a great impression upon the heathen world. In time it came to be respected by the Roman authorities in their dealings with Jews; e.g. they were not forced to contribute taxes on the Sabbath. And even heathen scholars sometimes found it convenient to hold their lectures on the Sabbath. We must remember that many of the heathen were accustomed to visit the Synagogue on the Sabbath day. The boon of such an institution came in time to be widely recognized, and was a potent means for attracting converts.

In manifold ways the Jewish Diaspora, especially in the Hellenistic world, was a fact of immense importance. As we have seen, it exercised profound influence on Judaism itself, even in its most pure and unadulterated forms. But it also affected Judaism in a larger way. Through it all sorts of elements were coming into contact with Judaism from the outside world. But we must be on our guard against over-estimating these facts. Essential Judaism possessed within itself a vitality and vigour which enabled it to maintain its central core unimpaired. The mere fact that it could assimilate so much without sacrificing its identity is a mark of power, and in this respect Judaism has more than vindicated itself.

(h) The decline and fall of the Maccabeans (69–63 B.C.)

It must be remembered that the closing years of Queen Alexandra's reign, though peaceful, were marked by some significant indications of fresh internal conflict. The queen had allowed herself to back the Sadducees led by Aristobulus, who seized the

[1] Petronius read the Jewish Bible in Greek.

opportunity to occupy seventy-two of the fortresses of the land. His elder brother, Hyrcanus II, had been appointed High Priest, but, owing to his somewhat indolent disposition, he would have been content probably to have been left to himself with this dignity and to allow his younger brother to assume the functions of king. But now a sinister influence appeared on the scene, and brought about a conflagration in the affairs of the realm. It will be

Restoration of the Pharos at Alexandria, built by Sostratus of Cnidos in the third century B.C.

remembered that John Hyrcanus had forcibly converted the Idumaeans to Judaism. A prominent Idumaean in the person of Antipater, whose father had been appointed governor of the country by Alexander Jannaeus, was a born intriguer. He saw in the rivalry between the two Jewish brothers an opportunity of pushing his own interests at their expense. He suggested to Hyrcanus that his rightful role was that of king and that he ought to assert himself against his younger brother. Hyrcanus was persuaded to flee to Petra and seek the alliance of Aretas, the Nabataean king, who marched against Aristobulus and forced him and his followers to take refuge in the Temple at Jerusalem. The Jews were now divided into two hostile camps and a bitter civil war began to rage. This situation brought about Roman intervention. Pompey in 66 B.C. was engaged in a successful campaign against Mithridates, and also against Tigranes, king of Armenia. The Roman policy aimed at conquering the country as far as the Euphrates. With incredible folly the two brothers appealed to Pompey's lieutenant Scaurus. The Arabians were ordered to withdraw. Aristobulus was left in possession. In the spring of 63 B.C. Pompey came to Damascus. There came to him there three embassies, one representing the cause of Aristobulus, another that of Hyrcanus, and a third the Pharisees, who requested that the Romans should assume the political control of Palestine and leave them unmolested to practice their religion. Aristobulus was now a prisoner in Pompey's hands, but his followers were still entrenched in the Temple area and were only overcome after a siege. Aristobulus and his family were deported to Rome to grace Pompey's triumph and the request of the Pharisees was granted. From this time forward the political control of Palestine was in the hands of the Romans and was exercised by them either directly by a procurator or indirectly through a subordinate king or monarch.

The Maccabean rule had lasted for a little over a century, 165–63 B.C. It collapsed for various reasons. In its earliest stages it enlisted the religious enthusiasm of the best elements among the Jewish people. But with military success its aims became mainly secular; after Simon its representatives grew more and more worldly. The inevitable alienation of the religious party produced a breach which resulted in bitter civil strife which ultimately brought about the collapse of the Jewish State.

Nevertheless its effects on Jewish life and religion were marked and permanent. The Jewish realm was at once expanded and consolidated. Judaism became self-conscious and aggressive. One immediate result was the growth of a feeling of hostility between Jews and their Gentile neighbours. This extended also to the Samaritans, who, after the destruction of their Temple on Mount Gerizim (c. 109 B.C.), became intensely embittered against their Jewish neighbours. The fact that the Samaritans themselves were half Jews and that the conflict was more or less domestic in character, intensified mutual hatred.

Of the religious effects the most important was the intensification of devotion to the Law. This became the hall-mark of

Judaism; copies of the Law were multiplied, and the study and the teaching of the Law were extended. Another important development was the growth and organization of the Jewish parties. These in their conflicting forms, stimulated the evolution of Judaism in its most characteristic later developments. Another highly important feature, which was ultimately connected with the experiences of the Maccabean struggle was the emergence of the belief in the Resurrection—a belief which was ultimately accepted as an integral part of the creed of orthodox Judaism.

The real significance of the Maccabean movement is to be seen in the gradual and clear definition of two factors, which it proved difficult if not impossible to harmonize, and which were constantly in conflict. These were the feeling of nationality and bound up with it racial self-consciousness and pride; and the claims of the Jewish religion. When the deputation from the Pharisees presented their case before Pompey at Damascus, they clearly stated that what they desired was the abolition of the Maccabean kingship and all that it implied; they demanded religious freedom, and were fully prepared, if this condition were granted, to leave the control of secular affairs in the hands of the Romans. This issue has never been fully decided. At the present time there are large numbers of Jews, the Zionists, who emphasize the importance of the racial side, and believe that there can be no real Judaism apart from it. Others again maintain that Judaism is a form of religion quite independent of a racial basis—or at least is not bound up in essence with such a basis.

Some words of a distinguished representative of the former class —Rabbi Joseph Klausner—may be cited in this connexion:[1]

The Maccabeans built up a Jewish Palestine; the Herodian kings destroyed it. . . . These defeated cities (of non-Jewish Palestine) were all compulsorily Judaized or repopulated by Jews, and those few places which refused to accept Judaism were mercilessly destroyed. From the moral side, needless to say, it is impossible to justify such forcible conversion at the hands of kings and rulers whose forefathers had endured such religious persecution, persecution which itself had compelled the Maccabeans to resort to arms. But only by such methods were the Jews able to secure their position beyond the con-

[1] *Jesus of Nazareth* (English translation), pp. 135 ff.

fines of Judaea and lay the foundation of a considerable kingdom such as should stand in no fear of the heathen who surrounded those believers in the unity of God, and those who preserved the moral teaching of the Prophets. But for the heroism of the Maccabees the heathen must, finally, have swallowed up the Jews. Only by such conquests and forced conversions could Judaism be established in its ancestral home and become a power, strong politically and socially, so that even the Romans, great conquerors though they were, were forced to take them seriously; otherwise the Jews must have remained a negligible quantity both in religion and civilization. Such, then, constitutes what the great Maccabean conquerors accomplished for Judaism, and, therefore, for the whole of humanity—as well!

(i) Some characteristic aspects and developments of Judaism in the Greek Period

In studying Judaism as it developed during the Greek period it is important to note how wide and free Jewish thought remained. It has been well said, 'Liberty of thought as well as speech was from the first characteristic of Israel's life and thought.' This tendency was, if anything, deepened by close contact with Hellenic life and thought during the Greek period, and is reflected in the O.T. literature. Side by side with the somewhat narrow ecclesiasticism of the Chronicler (3rd century B.C.) who looks at everything from the point of view of an ardent devotee of the Temple service and ceremonial we have writings which still reflect the spirit of the great prophets, e.g. the psalms 50 and 51. Such a psalm as 46 reveals a faith such as Isaiah preached but a faith which had become an integral part of the piety of the Psalmist, and influenced the most secret sources of his spiritual life. Referring to this psalm Dr. C. F. Kent remarks: 'In the background one hears the march of the multitude armed by Alexander for world-conquest and the din of conflict as army met army; but over all stands Jehovah, protecting his sanctuary and people, supreme in the lives of men and nations. The narrow, nationalistic, Messianic hopes have long since been abandoned, and instead Jehovah is recognized as the one supreme being whose kingdom or dominion includes all the nations of the earth. In imagination these disciples of the prophets saw the time in which rich and poor, Jew and Gentile, should bow before Jehovah and be united in loyalty to him. Then arose that highest conception of the kingdom of God which is the foundation of Jesus' teaching.' [1]

One of the most remarkable expressions of a broad and universal outlook is the book of Jonah, which probably belongs to the Greek period. It is a noble-minded protest against the narrow and exclusive type of Judaism which was only too often fostered by devotion to the Law. In its freedom from particularistic bias this little book is unique in the O.T. On the other hand, the book of Ecclesiastes, whatever view may be taken of its interpretation (see pp. 149 ff.), reflects a rather different spirit; especially the spirit of scepticism brought about by Greek philosophy. It has been described as 'an essay on the value of life'—more especially it would seem of life organized apart from God.

Thus Judaism during the Greek period is many-sided, and presents many facets. This is particularly apparent in the literature of the Jewish Diaspora, especially in such books as the *Book of Wisdom*. It was indeed at Alexandria that Judaism came into closest contact with Greek thought and culture. Nor must we omit to mention in this connexion the formation of the ancient Synagogue Liturgy, the oldest parts of which belong to these centuries. A Liturgy is perhaps the surest criterion of a peoples' piety. [2]

Attention has already been called to the fact that the most characteristic mark of Jewish piety at this period was devotion to the study of the Law. Already in the early post-exilic period we have reflected in the Psalter (cf. especially Pss. 27, 84, 85, 122) the deepest devotion and joy in the religious activities of the Temple as the source of spiritual satisfaction. A different note is struck in Ps. 1, the second part of 19, and 119. Here every line breathes devotion to the Law; and all this is but the expression of a profound conviction that God has chosen to make the supreme revelation of Himself and His requirements in the Divine Law, and that man is sanctified by the Divine Law, which is the very principle of his perfection.

The Law thus becomes supreme in Judaism, and devotion to

[1] Kent, *Makers and Teachers of Judaism*, p. 174.
[2] The most convenient edition of the Synagogue Liturgy for ordinary purposes is Dr. Israel Abraham's *Authorized Daily Prayer Book, Hebrew and English Annotated Edition* (Eyre and Spottiswoode, 1914).

it pervades all forms of Judaism.[1] The transition to the study of it as the principal occupation of students and teachers was easy, and the teaching of it by professional teachers became the absorbing occupation of the Rabbis. Though the stately ceremonial of the Temple went on in its full splendour for well over a century after the last of the Maccabees, the real centre of gravity in Judaism was no longer the Temple and its cultus but fidelity to the Law as such, and especially the study of it; so that when the ruin of the Temple came in A.D. 70, the reorganization of Judaism on the basis of the Law was effected without difficulty. Devotion to the Law and the study of it as such determined the character of later Judaism.

Bousset[2] has pointed out that in the time of Jesus the features in popular piety that He attacked are the sins to which the legalistic type of religion is specially prone, viz. undue emphasis upon the external observance of the Sabbath, the importance attached to the distinction between clean and unclean, the hypocritical assumption of special holiness in prayer, almsgiving and fasting. On the other hand, of exaggerated estimation of the sacrifices of the cultus His invective takes little account. His opponents are the Pharisees and the teachers of the Law, not the priests, the Law and not the cultus. Jesus indeed was possessed by a holy zeal for the Temple of Jehovah and its purity.

The following passage attributed to R. Meir and printed as an appendix to Pirqe Aboth will illustrate the attitude of the Rabbis towards the Torah study:

Rabbi Meir said, Whosoever is busied in Torah for its own sake merits many things; and not only so, but he is worth the whole world: he is called friend, beloved: loves God, loves mankind: pleases God, pleases mankind. And it clothes him with meekness and fear, and fits him to become righteous, pious, upright and faithful: and removes him from sin, and brings him towards the side of merit. And they enjoy from him counsel, and sound wisdom, understanding, and strength, for it is said, Counsel is mine, and sound wisdom: I am understanding; I have strength (Prov. viii. 14). And it gives him kingdom, and dominion, and faculty of judgment. And they reveal

[1] An interesting study, *Law in the Apocrypha*, by Ralph Marcus has been published by the Columbia University Press, 1927.
[2] *Die Religion des Judentums im neutest. Zeitalter*, p. 129 f.

to him the secrets of Torah; and he is made, as it were, a spring that ceases not, and as a river that flows on increasing. And he becomes modest, and long-suffering, and forgiving of insult. And it magnifies him and exalts him over all things.

Greater is Torah than the priesthood, and than the kingdom; for the kingdom is acquired by thirty degrees, and the priesthood by four

A stone relief of a wheeled coffer found at Tell Ḥum (Capernaum) in the ruins of the synagogue. It represents a portable Torah shrine, containing scrolls of the law

and twenty, and the Torah is acquired by forty and eight things. And these are they, by learning, by a listening ear, by ordered speech, by discernment of heart, by dread, by fear, by meekness, by cheerfulness, by pureness, by attendance upon the wise, by discussion with associates, by the argumentation of disciples, by sedateness; by Scripture, by Mishnah; by little traffic, by little intercourse, by little luxury, by little sleep, by little converse, by little merriment; by long-suffering, by a good heart, by faith in the wise, by acceptance of chastisements; he that knows his place, and that rejoices in his portion, and that makes a fence to his words, and does not claim merit to himself; he is loved, loves God, loves mankind, loves righteousness, loves uprightness, loves reproofs; and retires from honour, and puffs not up his heart with his learning, and is not forward in decision; bears the yoke with his associate, and inclines him to the scale of merit, and grounds him upon the truth, and grounds him upon peace (i. 19); and settles his heart to his study; asks and answers, hears and adds thereto; he that learns in order to teach, and that learns in order to practise; that makes his master wiser, and that considers what he has heard, and that tells a thing in the name of him that said it. Lo, thou hast learned that whosoever tells a thing in the name of·him that said it, brings redemption to the world, for it is said, And Esther told it to the king in the name of Mordekai (Esth. ii. 22).

Great is Torah, which gives life to those who practise it in this world and in the-world to come, for it is said, For they are life unto those that find them, and health to all their flesh (Prov. iv. 22); and it saith, It shall be health to thy navel, and marrow to thy bones (Prov. iii. 8); and it saith, She is a tree of life to them that lay hold upon her: and happy is every one that retaineth her (Prov. iii. 18); and it saith, For they shall be an ornament of grace unto thy head, and chains about thy neck (Prov. i. 9); and it saith, She shall give to thine head an ornament of grace; a crown of glory shall she deliver to thee (Prov. iv. 9); and it saith, For by me thy days shall be multiplied, and the years of thy life shall be increased (Prov. ix. 11); and it saith, Length of days is in her right hand; and in her left hand riches and honour (Prov. iii. 16); and it saith, For length of days, and years of life, and peace, shall they add to thee (Prov. iii. 2).

INTRODUCTION AND NOTES TO SELECTED PASSAGES

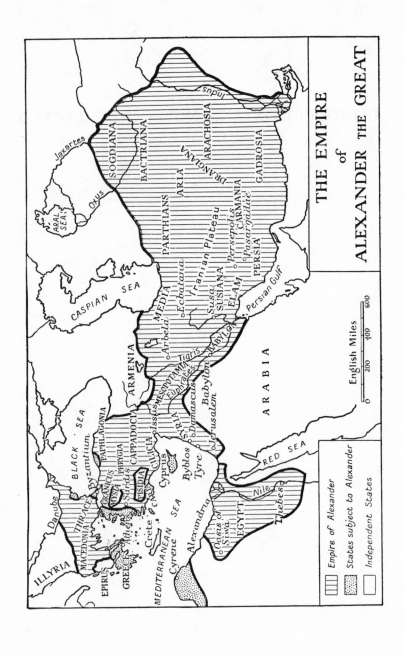

THE EMPIRE
of
ALEXANDER THE GREAT

Indus

SOGDIANA
BACTRIANA
ARACHOSIA
ARIA
DRANGIANA
GADROSIA
PARTHIANS
CARMANIA
Persepolis
Pasargadae
PERSIA
Iranian Plateau
Ecbatana
MEDIA
Susa
SUSIANA
ELAM
ARMENIA
Ar-bela
Tigris
MESOPOTAMIA
Euphrates
Babylon
BABYLON
Persian Gulf

ARAL
SEA
Jaxartes
Oxus

CASPIAN SEA

BLACK · SEA
Byzantium
PAPHLAGONIA
Danube
CAPPADOCIA
THRACE
PHRYGIA
GRANICUS
Sardis
ISSUS
PISIDIA
CILICIA
Issus
SYRIA
Damascus
Jerusalem
Tyre
Byblos
Cyprus

ARABIA

RED SEA

MACEDONIA
ILLYRIA
EPIRUS
GREECE
Crete
MEDITERRANEAN SEA
Cyrene
Alexandria
Nile
Oasis of
Siwa
EGYPT
Thebes

English Miles
0   200   400   600

Empire of Alexander

States subject to Alexander

Independent States

INTRODUCTION

IN addition to passages selected from Old Testament books proper and passages from the Old Testament Apocrypha, it will be necessary, in order to illustrate our period, to include select passages from non-canonical books such as the so-called Ethiopic Book of Enoch (1 Enoch), the book of Jubilees, the *Testaments of the Twelve Patriarchs*, and the Psalms of Solomon.

Convenient editions of these books (in English) are published by the S.P.C.K. Full Commentaries will be found in the Oxford Corpus edited by Dr. Charles (*Apocrypha and Pseudepigrapha of the Old Testament*, two volumes; Oxford (Clarendon Press). It will suffice for our purpose if we confine this selection of non-canonical passages to 1 Enoch and the Psalms of Solomon.

It will be necessary also to say a word here about *Josephus and his Sources*, because his writings are one of our chief sources—or contain such—for the external events of the Greek period.

Josephus himself belongs to the first century of our era. He was born in A.D. 37 and lived on until nearly the close of the century. He belonged to a well-to-do priestly family, and according to his own account joined the Pharisees at the age of 19. The Pharisees at this time were the dominant party in Judaism. It is significant, that though originally they were a party of *laymen*, constantly in collision with the Priesthood, yet at this time distinguished members of the Priesthood found it expedient to join their ranks. In the year A.D. 64 Josephus, then a young man of about 26, visited Rome, in connexion with the trial of certain Jewish Priests. On his return to Judaea he found the country seething with revolt, and soon found himself involved in the insurrectionary movement against Rome. At the age of 29 he was given an important commission in Galilee, where he assumed supreme command of the Jewish insurgents. His own story of what happened is given in the *Jewish War*, and in his *Life*. He was besieged in the town of Jotapata, and finally capitulated to the Romans (July, A.D. 67). He made himself a *persona grata* to the Romans, especially to Vespasian, and when the latter was proclaimed Emperor (July, A.D. 69) he was released from captivity, and accompanied the Emperor to Alexandria; thence he returned with Titus, the Emperor's son, to the siege of Jerusalem, and was present at the fall of the city A.D. 70.

After this tragic event he lived in Rome, basking in the favour of the Imperial Court. There he died soon after A.D. 100.

During this latter period of his life he was actively engaged in producing a number of books which we know in a Greek form. The earliest of these is *The War*, which in its first form was written in Aramaic for the benefit of the Jews who lived in Upper Syria (i.e.

Mesopotamia on the eastern frontiers of the Roman Empire). This version has not survived. It may have been intended as a political manifesto warning the Jews of this remote region against the danger of fighting against Rome. We know this work in its Greek edition, which includes a long Introduction carrying the story back to the time of Antiochus Epiphanes. The work, which appeared in parts, was published towards the end of Vespasian's reign (before A.D. 79). It was written in Greek with the aid of collaborators, and with full access to official documents in the Imperial Archives.

Some sixteen years later he produced another elaborate book, *The Antiquities*. This work, divided into twenty books, embraces the Biblical and post-Biblical history of the Jews. For our purposes the latter division, dealing with the period from the exile to Antiochus Epiphanes, is the more important. Two other works were produced in the last years of his life—*The Vita* and *The Contra Apionem*, the former being issued as an appendix to a later edition of *The Antiquities*.

Josephus is specially important because he cites ancient authorities; chief among these are Nicholas of Damascus, the historian of Herod, and Strabo, and Polybius.[1]

For the period from Ezra and Nehemiah to the death of Simon Maccabaeus Josephus has besides the Biblical sources (in the LXX), a Greek legendary history of Alexander the Great, the letter of Pseudo-Aristeas, and probably a history of the Tobiads, as well as 1 Maccabees; he seems not to have known 2 Maccabees. He also employs Polybius (down to 143 B.C.) and other historians; while he had access to such official documents as the Genealogy of the High Priests. This section of the work extends from XI. 7 to XIII. 7 of *The Antiquities*.[2]

---

[1] Among the non-Biblical authors cited by Josephus in the first eleven books of *The Antiquities* are the following: Berosus, Hieronymus the Egyptian, Minaseas, Manetho, Mochus, Hestiaeus, Hesiod, Hecataeus, Hellanicus, Acusilaus, Ephorus, Menander, Dion, Herodotus, Megasthenes, Diocles, Philostratus. Many of these quotations were probably derived from the works of Alexander Polyhistor, Nicholas of Damascus, and Strabo. Nicholas was born about 64 B.C.

[2] A collection of citations from ancient authors which occur in Josephus has been made by Th. Reinach, *Textes d'Auteurs Grecs, &c.*, Paris, 1895. A convenient edition of Josephus in Greek and English is being published in the Loeb Classical Library (edited by Dr. St. J. Thackeray). A good edition of Whiston's translation, revised by Prof. D. S. Margoliouth, was published by Routledge, 1906. The works of Josephus owe their survival, like those of Philo, to the Christian Church. They were widely read by the Christians, because of their historical importance for the N.T. period. An excellent essay by Dr. St. J. Thackeray on Josephus is included in the volume *Judaism and the Beginnings of Christianity*, Routledge, n.d., based on lectures delivered in 1923.

A. ALEXANDER THE GREAT

[For the story of Alexander's visit to Jerusalem (*Ant.* XI. viii. 4-5) see Additional Note III, p. 225.]

THE career of Alexander made an enormous impression upon the ancient world, and we should naturally expect to find some reflection of this in the O.T. literature.

1 MACCABEES 1[1-9]

1. *And it came to pass, after that Alexander the Macedonian, the son of Philip, who came out of the land of Chittim, and smote Darius king of the Persians and Medes, it came to pass, after he had smitten him, that he reigned in his stead, in former time, over Greece.*
2. *And he fought many battles, and won many strongholds, and slew the kings of the earth,* 3. *And went through to the ends of the earth, and took spoils of a multitude of nations. And the earth was quiet before him, and he was exalted, and his heart was lifted up,*
4. *And he gathered together an exceeding strong host, and ruled over countries and nations and principalities, and they became tributary unto him.* 5. *And after these things he fell sick, and perceived that he should die.* 6. *And he called his servants, which were honourable, which had been brought up with him from his youth, and he divided unto them his kingdom, while he was yet alive.* 7. *And Alexander reigned twelve years, and he died.* 8. *And his servants bare rule, each one in his place.* 9. *And they did all put diadems upon themselves after that he was dead, and so did their sons after them many years: and they multiplied evils in the earth.*

Questions of Introduction as regards 1 Maccabees will be dealt with when we come to discuss the Maccabean period. The above extract is given because it affords an excellent illustration of the impression made by Alexander on the Jewish people. The author of 1 Maccabees has grasped the world-significance of Alexander and expresses this summarily in an admirable manner.

NOTES ON 1 MACCABEES I. 1-9

1. *Chittim*: i.e. the people of the islands and coast-lands of Greece (Jer. 2[10], the isles of Kittim). The name Chittim is derived, apparently, from Kition, the chief town of Cyprus = Larnaca. Originally colonized by Phoenicians, it ultimately came to possess a Greek population.

2. *Darius*: i.e. Darius III Codomannus (335–331).
3. *he reigned in his stead*: cf. Dan. 8²¹.
4. *and his heart was lifted up*: cf. Dan. 11¹².
5. *he fell sick*: at Babylon, 323.
6. *his servants*: i.e. his generals, the most famous of these, who afterwards established dynasties, were Seleucus and Ptolemy.

7. *and divided his kingdom*: this is legendary, and has no basis in fact. For several years the empire nominally remained intact under a single monarch, and was governed in the name of Alexander's posthumous son.

8. *And his servants . . . place*: this is part of the legend. It was only after a long struggle that the division of the empire became fixed.

B. A MODERN VIEW OF THE BOOK OF HABAKKUK

THE generally accepted view about this little book is given in volume iii of this series, pp. 186 f. It regards Habakkuk as a contemporary of Jeremiah and assigns his date to 605 B.C. The alternative view, first put forward by Duhm, is well stated by Prof. C. C. Torrey in an essay published in the volume dedicated to Karl Marti (*vom Alten Testament*, 1925, ed. Karl Budde) entitled 'Alexander the Great in the O.T. Prophecies'. Prof. Torrey remarks: 'It is becoming more and more generally understood that the writings of the Hebrew Prophets were collected and redacted chiefly in the third century B.C.

'Among the writings thus collected and edited, either as separate books or as component parts of more extended collections, there are not a few which give plain evidence of an origin later than the time of the great conquest. In this later period, especially, were composed many oracles taking express account of foreign nations and their doings; often in the garb of prediction, but also in the form of poetic exhortation or dramatic exposition based on well-known facts of past history. It would be very strange indeed if Alexander and his armies had not frequently been taken as a subject of discourse in the Hebrew "prophecies" of the late fourth and early third centuries.'

He regards the little book as 'a highly poetic and very impressive meditation on the conquest of Alexander and his Greek invaders'.

NOTES ON THE TEXT

In 1⁶, for *Chaldeans* (Heb. *Kasdim*) read *Kittim*. The invading armies that came from Kittim were those of Alexander (cf. 1 Macc. 1¹, above, and 8⁵). According to this view the writer of Habakkuk was a contemporary. Cf. 1⁵.

I. **9.** *gather captives as the sand*: this would fit Alexander's swift and overwhelming victories.

10. *he derideth every strong hold; for he heapeth up dust, and taketh it*: an allusion to Alexander's siege of Tyre and the famous mole, by which he eventually took the city.

II. **5–10.** Here again the description fits Alexander exactly.

Wine is a treacherous dealer, a haughty man. 'Wine' is hardly a suitable epithet to apply to the Conqueror. A simple emendation (altering the Heb. *hay-yayin* to *hayewāni*) produces the sense 'the Greeks'—this is almost certainly right.

C. OTHER POSSIBLE JEWISH LITERATURE OF ALEX-ANDER'S AGE

IN the same connexion Torrey assigns the prophecy on Tyre in Ezek. 26, which in the present text is made to refer to Nebuchadnezzar's age, to the early Greek period.

Torrey points out that the siege of Tyre by Nebuchadnezzar was not successful and refers to Ezek. 29¹⁸ff., which states expressly that Nebuchadnezzar did not succeed in capturing Tyre. 'Son of man, Nebuchadnezzar, king of Babylon, caused his army to serve a great service against Tyre; and every head was made bald and every shoulder peeled; yet he had no wages, *nor his army from Tyre*, for the service that he had served against it. Therefore, thus saith the Lord God: I will give the land of Egypt unto Nebuchadnezzar . . . and it shall be the wages for his army. I give him the land of Egypt as his recompense for which he served.' This accords with what is known from history. The long siege of Tyre by the Babylonian king was a failure.

According to this view, the words in 26⁷, 'Nebuchadnezzar king of Babylon' are to be deleted as an insertion. The original words were: 'Behold I will bring upon Tyre from the north the king of kings.' A vivid description of the siege follows. Note the reference in 5⁸ to the building of a mole and a causeway ('Cast up a mount against thee'), over which the chariots of the victorious army were driven into the streets of the city. This description exactly fits Alexander's capture of the city.

THE BOOK OF JOEL
INTRODUCTION

Whether the book of Joel belongs to the age of Alexander is uncertain; according to Torrey, it does, and a good case can be made out for this view.

Nothing can be gathered from the title of the book as to its age; nor is anything known of the prophetic author except his name (Joel, the son of Pethuel). The theme with which the book deals is a simple one. It dwells upon the approach of the 'Day of Jahveh', the precursor of which the author sees in a terrible plague of locusts, which, accompanied by drought, is causing the severest distress.

The prophecy falls into two parts, viz. (a) 1^{2-17} and (b) 2^{18} to end. In (a) the occasion of the prophecy (a visitation of locusts) is vividly described (1^{2-7}); the prophet proceeds to exhort the people to fasting, supplication and mourning, for the present visitation suggests the approach of the 'Day of Jahveh' (1^{15}), which is to be ushered in by a visitation even more terrible (2^{2-11}). In (b) Ch. 2^{18} to end, the result of the prophet's warning is set forth in narrative form: the people, apparently, repented; Jahveh graciously changed his purpose and responded to the people's prayer. The language here is largely eschatological.

The question of date

There has been a great variety of opinions regarding the date of the book. Older scholars (e.g. Delitzsch) put the book very early, during the minority of Joash; others dated it in the reign of King Josiah; but modern critical opinion concurs in making the book post-exilic. A number of indications confirm this view; the dispersion of the Jews among the nations is presupposed (cf. $3^{1-3,\ 17}$); no king appears, priests take the lead. The Temple is in existence and a public fast is held there. According to 2^9 Jerusalem is a walled city; this would point to a date subsequent to the age of Nehemiah.

One view that has been put forward regards the book as a combination of two distinct parts. Joel has taken an earlier poem which dealt with a plague of locusts and a merciful deliverance from it. This may have dated from the first century after the exile. By adding the announcement of the coming of the Day of Jahveh and predicting the destruction of the eschatological foe from the

north, and finally by appending 2^{28} to 3^{21}, he transformed the book
into an apocalypse. Here he may have been working on older
material.

According to Sellin, 'the locusts are suggested by the armies
and are mainly figurative; though the actual plague, which was
familiar enough, is naturally referred to in the passages dealing
with agricultural prosperity; the description of the warriors
reminds us of that in Habakkuk'.

NOTES

II. 20. *the northern army*: render *the northerner*—a standing
description of Alexander and his armies. Cf. Ezek. 26^7 (as corrected
above).

28–32 (= Heb. 3^{1-5}): the outpouring of the spirit. This famous
passage is cited in the N.T. by St. Peter as having been fulfilled on the
Day of Pentecost (Acts $2^{17ff.}$). It has been described as a compendium
of eschatology, summing up what the post-exilic Jewish community
had received and believed on the subject.

In the opening verse 28 notice the introduction 'And it shall come
to pass afterward', a formula for introducing such material. Cf. the
similar phrase of Isa. 2^2, in an eschatological connexion.

28. *I will pour out my spirit upon all flesh.* The gift of God's spirit
was a permanent equipment which seems to be based on the promise
of a new heart first given by Jeremiah; this forms the basis of a true
knowledge of God (cf. Jer. 24^7, 31^{33}, and 32^{29}; cf. also Ezek. 11^{19}; cf.
further Ezek. $36^{26, 27}$ and 39^{29}; Isa. 32^{15}, 44^3; Zech. 12^{10}).

upon all flesh. The meaning of the phrase in its original connexion
is restricted to Israel.

29. *the servants and the handmaids*: i.e. the Israelite slaves male and
female (cf. Neh. 5^2).

my spirit: LXX (cf. also Acts 2^{17-18}) for dogmatic reasons translates
of my spirit in order to indicate that *all* the divine spirit was not
poured out.

30 ff. *wonders in the heavens, &c.*: a regular feature in eschatological descriptions of the end. These portents are regarded as
heralds of the coming of the Day of Jahveh.

blood and fire, &c.: these point to war (cf. Ezek. 38^{22}; Matt. 24^6;
Mark $13^{7ff.}$).

30. *The sun, &c.*: this verse enumerates the signs in the heavens (as
contrasted with those on the earth. Cf. Amos 8^9; Isa. 13^{10}, 34^4;
Ezek. $32^{7ff.}$; Matt. 24^{29}).

32. *whosoever shall call on the name of the LORD*: i.e. those who are
true believers in Jahveh and who acknowledge him before the world
would be delivered in the day of Judgement.

Calling on the name of Jahveh refers to the Jewish worship as organized in the cultus. Thus the verse contains a promise of the deliverance of the Israelites on the great day.

for in mount Zion, &c.: those who are dwelling in Mount Zion : such will not be touched by the judgement; a similar conception underlies Isa. 4² ('them that are escaped').

and among the remnant, &c. No doubt the faithful Jews among the Diaspora are intended to be included in this phrase. Cf. Isa. 66¹⁹ᶠ·, 27¹²ᶠ·—in the latter passage Jahveh is represented as gathering together the Israelites of the Diaspora after the judgement. Cf. also Joel 3⁷.

Chapter III. The previous chapter describes how the Israelites are rescued in the world-judgement. This section amplifies the previous prophecy, explaining in detail how the world-judgement affects Israel's neighbours and the heathen peoples who dwell afar off.

III. 1–8. This section describes the gathering together of all peoples in the valley of Jehoshaphat, and the judgement effected on the Phoenicians and Philistines.

2. *the valley of Jehoshaphat*: i.e. not the valley where King Jehoshaphat won a great victory over the Moabites and Ammonites. Later tradition identifies it with the Kidron valley. This cannot be correct, though there is an element of truth in it in so far as the valley in question is thought of as near Jerusalem. Ezekiel depicts the world-judgement as being consummated before Jerusalem. Cf. Ezek. 38ᶠᶠ·. Cf. also Zech. 9¹⁴⁻¹⁶, 12¹⁻⁹; Dan. 11⁴⁵. The valley of Jehoshaphat is not an actual proper name of a place but a symbolical name (= Jahveh judges). Cf. also the second name, 'valley of decision'.

parted my land: the reference is to the plundering and seizing of the land by the Chaldaeans.

4. Note the apostrophe of the Phoenicians and Philistines.

5. *my silver and my gold*: this may refer to plundering of the Temple treasure, though it is possible to interpret it more generally.

your temples: or the word may be rendered *palaces*.

6. *the sons of the Grecians*: here referred to as slave-merchants who buy Jewish captives. The mention of Greeks suggests some part of the Greek period. Cf. 1 Macc. 3⁴¹; 2 Macc. 8¹¹.

9–17. After the digression about the Phoenicians and the Philistines there follows a description of the judgement on the heathen nations in the valley of Jehoshaphat.

10. *plowshares into swords, &c.*: reversing the promise of the Messianic Age, Isa. 2⁴; Mic. 4³.

17. *then shall Jerusalem be holy, &c.*: cf. Ezek. 39⁷· ²⁸ᶠ·; Zech. 9⁸, 14²¹.

18–21. These verses describe the felicity of the land of Israel in the time of the end, and the desolation of Egypt and Edom.

18. The wonderful fruitfulness that will characterize the Messianic Age is a favourite theme in such connexions; cf. Hos. 14⁶⁻⁸; Amos 9¹³.

18. *a fountain shall come forth, &c.*: the original passage on which this idea is based is Ezek. 47$^{1-12}$; cf. also Zech. 14^8.

the valley of Shittim. Possibly a symbolical name for the desert of Judah, east of Jerusalem, which in the Messianic time will be watered and made fruitful by the stream issuing from the Temple.

19. *Egypt . . . Edom.* The hatred of Edom by the Jews of the post-exilic period is well known; cf. Amos 1$^{11ff.}$; Obad. 5$^{6ff.}$; Mal. 1$^{2-5}$. Edom became a symbolical name in Apocalyptic for Rome, cf. 2 Esdras 6^9. But why is Egypt mentioned in this connexion? Possibly because, though she had been the first to oppress Israel, she had not yet received a proper punishment like Assyria and Babylon.

21. The first part of this verse may be a gloss.

ZECHARIAH 9–14

INTRODUCTION

That these chapters do not proceed from the Prophet Zechariah, who was the author of chaps. 1–8, is now generally recognized. They have separate headings (9^1 and 12^1), and are markedly different in style from the chapters preceding them. All the remarkable and peculiar characteristics of 1–8 disappear, and new features of a peculiar character emerge.

They contain two distinct prophecies, viz. (1) ch. 9–11, with which 13$^{7-9}$ should probably be reckoned; and (2) 12^1–13^6 and 14.

(1) Chapter 9 depicts a judgement as about to fall on various parts of Syria and Palestine (Damascus, Hamath, Tyre and Sidon, and the principal cities of the Philistines); this leads to the conversion of the remnant of the Philistines and their incorporation into Israel. These events prepare the way for the advent of the Messiah and the Messianic age. Chapter 10 begins with a warning against trusting in teraphim and diviners, and unworthy rulers. Judah and Ephraim under new leaders will gain a decisive victory over their enemies. Chapter 11 gives a picture of war bursting over the north and east of the land. An allegory, in which the prophet and the people are mainly concerned, follows. The people are represented as rejecting the divine guidance, and suffering the consequences (dispersion and ruin). A purified remnant will constitute the faithful people of God (13$^{7-9}$).

(2) Chapter 12 opens with a picture of nations (including Judah) advancing against Jerusalem. Their forces are routed and Jerusalem is delivered. The population of Jerusalem have, apparently, been guilty of a judicial murder, but, seized with compunction, they mourn long and bitterly over their crime. Jerusalem hence-

forth (13^{1-6}) is permanently cleansed from sin. In ch. 14 Jerusalem
is pictured as again assaulted by the nations. The city is captured
and half its population carried into captivity. Jahveh intervenes
to rescue the remnant, and the Messianic age begins. The nations
who survive acknowledge Jahveh by coming up yearly to the
Feast of Tabernacles. The material embodied in these chapters
(Zech. 9–14) has some puzzling features, and this fact has led
scholars to form the most various estimates as to their date and
origin. The tendency of recent criticism has been to place their
composition in the early part of the Greek period (shortly after
the time of Alexander the Great). Duhm and Marti, however,
would bring the date down to the Maccabean period. On the other
hand, older scholars like Dillmann defend a pre-exilic date; while
others (e.g. Steuernagel) argue that chs. 9–11 are to be assigned,
in the main, to a pre-exilic date, and chs. 12–14 to the post-exilic
period. Another most interesting view is that of Sellin, who now
regards these chapters as emanating from an Apocalyptic writer of
the third century B.C., 'Who, however, wrote in the character of
a pre-exilic prophet'. Of the features that point to a pre-exilic
date the following may be noticed: $9^{1\text{ff.}}$ seems to imply that
Damascus is an independent kingdom; and in the same chapter
(9^{10}) reference is made to war-chariots and horses in Jerusalem and
Ephraim; the existence of the northern kingdom is pre-supposed
(9^{13}, 10^{6-7}, 11^{14}); in $12^{7,\,8,\,10,\,12}$ it is assumed that the Davidic
dynasty is still reigning; that idolatry is still rampant ($13^{2\text{f.}}$).
Indications of a post-exilic date may be summarized as follows:
the yearly pilgrimage of all nations to Jerusalem to the Feast of
Tabernacles in 14; the announcement of the termination of prophecy and its expulsion together with the spirit of uncleanness,
13^{1-6}; in 9^{13}, the heathen world-power appears in the guise of
Greece, the independent position of the 'House of Levi' beside the
'House of David', &c. Probably some part of the Greek period
(after 331) is indicated by such passages. There is a strong
apocalyptic tinge and the writer (or writers) appears to have been
steeped in the older literature of the Old Testament.

NOTES ON ZECHARIAH 9–14

IX. 1–10. *The establishment of the Messianic Kingdom with the
Prince of Peace in Sion.*

1. *upon the land of Hadrach, &c.* Jahveh should be inserted at the
beginning; then render: *Jahveh is in the land of Hadrach, and
Damascus is his seat*; the land of Hadrach according to the Assyrian

inscriptions lay to the north of Lebanon, and in the same region *Hamath* is to be located; these places constitute the ideal boundary of the Davidic Kingdom in the north, cf. 1 Kings 8[65]. Damascus is within the free boundaries of Jahveh's realm.

for the eye of man . . . LORD. The present text yields no satisfactory sense; the context requires a continuance of proper names, and by a slight emendation this can be secured; read *for Jahveh's are the cities of Aram* (omit *and of all the tribes of Israel*).

Lebanon. A distant view of the range with the village of Angil in the foreground

2. *Tyre and Zidon, &c.* The misplaced wisdom of Tyre was the cause of her downfall, cf. Ezek. 18[1-10]. For 'because' substitute 'although'. The northern foe indicated in this description is the Macedonian Greek empire.

3–4. In spite of her strength and wealth Tyre is doomed; Tyre's wealth is alluded to in the clause 'heapeth up silver as the dust', &c. A graphic picture of Tyre's commercial prosperity and power is given in Ezek. 27. The word rendered *power* would be translated better by *substance* or *riches*; or by a slight emendation *rampart*.

5. *Gaza also . . . sore pained*: there may be an allusion here to the five months' siege of Gaza by Alexander in 332 B.C. This and the following verses describe the conquest of Philistia. In v. 7 *as a Jebusite* means 'as an inhabitant of Jerusalem'.

9–10. Here we have a description of the advent of the Messianic king, who enters his capital in triumph as the Prince of Peace.

9. *having salvation*: better *victorious*; the Messiah has behind him the power of Jahveh; *lowly*, the word constantly met with in the Psalms to denote the afflicted pious: it characterizes the Messiah 'as belonging not to the worldly or godless party dominant in Jerusalem, but to that of the oppressed pious'. (Cited by Driver.)

sitting upon an ass: another mark of humility; the Prince of Peace comes seated upon an ass, not a war-horse like a military chief; note the fulfilment Matt. 21⁵; John 12¹⁵.

10. *the weapons of war will all be destroyed.* For the picture cf. Isa. 2⁴.

That vv. 1ff. belong to the Greek period is clear enough; but to what part of it? Some indications suggest that the Seleucid Epoch is the period referred to (between 197–142 B.C.). Prof. Kennett summarizes vv. 1–8 as follows: 'The judgement of the Lord is now coming upon the cities which have been strongholds of the rule of the Greek Syrian kings, and therefore antagonistic to Israel. Tyre, strong as she is, is doomed; Philistia also may tremble for her safety; Gaza will lose her king; the population of Ashkelon will be annihilated; the mongrel race, half Philistine, half Greek, will be driven out of Ashdod. Indeed the Philistine as such will no longer exist, for the Lord, acting through Israel, will enforce the observance of the law of Israel even in the Philistine towns. There will be no more eating with the blood, or other abominable food; for the Philistines will be incorporated with Israel in such a way that henceforth an inhabitant of Ekron will be regarded as a native of Jebus, i.e. Jerusalem (cf. Ps. 87). Moreover, as the result of the Judaizing of Philistia—since the Syro-Greek government has given up the hope of conquering Egypt—Judah will no longer be menaced by the presence of vast armies on her flank. It will be as though the Lord Himself were encamped as a garrison to protect Jerusalem, and no exaction of tribute will trouble her any more. The prophecy is almost certainly later than Jonathan's victorious campaign in Philistia (c. 148) and may be as late as 143–142, when Demetrius granted the Jews full exemption from all taxes or tribute to the Syrian government.'[1]

11–12. The Jewish nation is told that Jahveh is now releasing those of its members who are now confined to waterless dungeons. They are bidden to return to the stronghold of Judah, where they will be safe. They shall receive double compensation for all their suffering. If the prophecy dates from 332 the reference may be general, cf. Isa. 27¹³. There may, however, be a more particular reference. The Jews settled in Greek cities after Alexander's conquest. Thus, Ptolemy transferred many Jews under compulsion to Egypt. Others migrated of their own free will. Seleucus Nicator also planted Jewish colonists in Antioch (312–280 B.C.).

[1] Peake's *One Volume Commentary on the Bible*, p. 580.

12. *prisoners of hope*: i.e. prisoners who may now at length nurse the hope of deliverance.

double: i.e. double compensation.

'The corners of the altar.' A stone altar found at Gezer with protuberances ('horns'?) at the four corners

13–16. These verses describe the great deliverance effected for the Jews with Jahveh's help. This victory over the Greeks inaugurates the Messianic age.

13. *I have bent Judah, &c.* The warriors of Israel are pictured poetically as arrows in Jahveh's hand. Judah is his bow and

Ephraim his arrows. Note the reference to Ephraim, i.e. the Northern Kingdom, who is to participate in the return.

13. *I will make thee*: i.e. O Zion.

14. In the crisis of the battle Jahveh will himself appear above the combatants, helping Israel. The imagery seems to be based on the idea of a storm; then the arrows are compared to the lightning. *with whirlwinds of the south*: the imagery is again suggested by the storm, though Kennett thinks there may be a reference to a Maccabean campaign against Edom.

15. *they shall devour, &c.* The text may be emended so as to read 'And they shall prevail and tread down the sons of [?].' Perhaps the term rendered *sling* may hide a word descriptive of their foes.

they shall drink, &c.: better read with LXX *they shall drink their blood as wine*.

they shall be filled (with their blood) like bowls: the bowls referred to are the sacrificial bowls in which the blood was collected and dashed against the sides of the altar.

like the corners of the altar: this again is derived from the ceremonial of the sacrifice. The corners of the altar would receive the blood. The victorious Jews are pictured as drenched with the blood of their enemies, just as the sacrificial basins are full of blood when an animal has been slaughtered for sacrifice, and the blood so collected is dashed on the sides of the altar. The verse reveals a feeling of passionate hatred against their heathen oppressors.

16. *as the flock of his people*: read *His people as a flock, &c.* *they are stones* (i.e. jewels) *of a crown glittering on his head*: the general sense is, Jahveh will deliver his people and tend them like a flock, because they are as precious to him as jewels. The text, however, is suspicious and seems to be in confusion.

17. This verse describes the abundant fertility of the land and the felicity of the people after the great deliverance.

how great is his goodness . . .: better with R.V. margin, *their goodness = their beauty*.

X. 1–2. An isolated section, out of connexion with what precedes and what follows. According to Prof. Kennett this probably dates from the time of Antiochus Epiphanes. The Jews are urged to ask Jahveh's help, not to resort to heathen divines and divination.

2. *the teraphim*: probably the household gods: they survived for a long time in ancient Israel. Cf. Judges 17⁵, 18¹⁴; Hos. 3⁴. The superstitious among the people would be inclined to resort to them in times of crisis in a later age.

they go their way like sheep: i.e. they move from place to place like sheep; lacking divine guidance they wander about restless and unshepherded.

3–12. Godless foreign rulers are denounced and their fall is described. Jahveh is about to visit his people and deliver them from foreign rulers. Instead, native rulers are to be set up, and once again Israel shall be strong enough to vindicate her cause against the heathen. The Ephraimites will return from exile. Egypt and Assyria will be humiliated. The restored nation will rejoice before its God.

3. *shepherds, he-goats*: these terms denote here foreign rulers, as v. 4 makes plain.

hath visited: i.e. will certainly visit. He-goats = rulers. Cf. Isa. 14^9; Exod. 34^{17}.

4. *from him*: i.e. from Judah, *the corner stone*, a metaphor for princes or leading men. Cf. Judges 20^2.

the nail, or better, *tent-pin*: another figure for the one who stays or supports.

exactor: ruler or governor, one in authority.

5. *the riders on horses*: i.e. the foes of Israel. Cf. Ezek. 38^{15}.

6–7. Note the mention again of the northern Israelites.

they of Ephraim: i.e. the ten tribes now in exile (also referred to as the house of Joseph. Cf. 9^{10-13}).

8–9. These verses describe how the gathering in will be effected.
8. *as they have increased*, they shall again be as numerous as they were in the past. Cf. Ezek. 37^{10-11}.

9. *And I will sow them among the peoples*. The context is speaking of the Israelites from exile and their gathering in. Probably there is something wrong with the text. Read *And though I scattered them among the peoples, yet in far countries they shall remember me* with the implied thought that they will turn to Jahveh again with penitence.

they shall live with their children: read *shall nourish*.

10. The reference is still to the ten tribes. The old names Egypt, Assyria, probably denote the later empires of the Ptolemies and the Seleucids.

place shall not be found: room will not be found for their overflowing numbers. Cf. Isa. 54^3; Obad. 19ff.

11. *And he shall pass through the sea, &c.*: i.e. Jahveh. The imagery is suggested by the passage of the Red Sea, and is probably intended symbolically.

12. *walk up and down in his name*: i.e. conduct themselves freely, as acting under the authority of Jahveh. But perhaps the LXX supplies a better text: *and in his name shall they make their boast.* Cf. Ps. 34^2.

XI. **1–3.** These verses picture a fire as devouring the cedars of Lebanon and the oaks of Bashan. And the shepherds bewail their desolated pastures.

The interpretation of this passage is not without difficulty. Probably there is a certain amount of symbolism. By the shepherds may be meant the rulers of the heathen nations. They are here depicted as lamenting the desolation and destruction of their strongholds.

Kennett understands the reference to be to the strongholds of the Syro-Greek empire, who are taunted with the failure of their power.

1. Note the poetical allocution. Lebanon is bidden to open its doors in order that the enemy may enter and fire its cedars. The same fate will overtake the fir-tree, and the oaks of Bashan.

3. *A voice*: render '*Hark*' the pride of Jordan is spoiled or laid waste. By the phrase *pride of Jordan* is meant the luxuriant, thick growth of trees which fringe its banks and in ancient times were the haunt of young lions. Cf. Jer. 12^5 and 49^{19}.

4–17. The people's rejection of the good shepherd. Driver describes this prophecy 'as the most enigmatic in the Old Testament. It is obviously an allegory, the imagery, like that of 10^3, being based upon Jer. 23$^{1-4}$ and Ezek. 34, in both of which passages it is taught how Jahveh will overthrow Israel's unworthy shepherds and appoint in their place one or more true shepherds (Jer. 23^4; Ezek. 34$^{23ff.}$; cf. 38^{24}).' The passage describes how a worthless shepherd was substituted and the consequences which followed. Israel has suffered at the hands of selfish shepherds, i.e. rulers, who have misused their position to oppress the people for their own ends. The prophet now describes what under these circumstances has been done, under divine direction. First of all, he himself played the part of a good shepherd who rescued the flock from its oppressors; but he is rejected by the people. Now he assumes the part of a worthless shepherd, making havoc of the people, but showing how ultimate retribution will come. The sequel follows in 13$^{7-9}$. The actions ascribed to the prophet could not actually have taken place, but the narration of them brings home the moral.

The allegory, however, is not interpreted, nor is it clear. The author alludes in figurative language to various historical events of the past, which presumably would be understood by the first readers, but which to us are highly obscure. In particular our knowledge of the inner history of the Jewish community from the time of Nehemiah to the rise of the Maccabees is very defective. It may, however, be taken as certain that the period referred to is either the Early Greek or the Maccabean. Stade fixed the historical background in the period when the world was convulsed by the wars of the successors of Alexander the Great (the Diadochi). This view is confirmed by 11^6, which runs (corrected text): *For I will no more pity the inhabitants of the earth . . . but lo! I am delivering every one into the hand of his Shepherd and of his King: and they shall shatter the land, and out of their hand I will not deliver them.* As Stade argues, 'the expression would well suit the period *c.* 320–300 B.C. when Alexander's generals were contending for the possession of the countries conquered by him.'

Cornill[1] agrees with this view, which he thinks is supported by 10^{11}, where it is prophesied that in the 'Messianic time the pride of

---

[1] *Introd. to the Canonical Books of the O.T.*, pp. 370 f.

Assyria, i.e. of the Seleucid Empire, and the sceptre of Egypt, i.e. of the Ptolemies, shall cease; this feature transports us into the interval falling between 301 and 198, when the Ptolemies were the rulers of the land in Palestine'.

Cornill would not deny that individual passages may belong to the Maccabean period, but these he prefers to regard as later insertions.

Shepherds with their flocks at one of the gates of Jerusalem

A good deal depends upon the interpretation given to 'the three Shepherds' in v. 8. Are the three shepherds heathen kings (e.g. Antiochus Epiphanes, 175–164 B.C.; Antiochus Eupator, 164–162; and Demetrius I, 162–150) who all met their death within a period of thirty years (symbolized by the 'one month' = thirty days)? Or do they symbolize Jewish High Priests? A variation of the latter view is strongly upheld by Prof. Kennett,[1] who says: 'the three Shepherds may well be the sons of Tobias, who according to Josephus (*War* I. x)

[1] Op. cit., p. 581.

were expelled from Jerusalem by Onias . . . it is certain that the language of Zech. 11 is entirely applicable to him on the assumption that the course of events was as follows: By his expulsion from Jerusalem of the unscrupulous sons of Tobias, Onias incurred the hostility of the great Jewish families: whereupon being slandered to Seleucus by Simon, he was compelled to leave Jerusalem in order to defend himself before the king, Seleucus IV, at Antioch. Upon the accession of Antiochus Epiphanes immediately afterwards, Onias was deprived of the High Priesthood, which was conferred first upon Jason, then upon Menelaus, who contrived to have Onias murdered at Antioch, a crime which in the opinion of many required expiation before national restoration could come. If, therefore, the author of this section speaks in the role of Onias, we can explain the details. Onias had received a commission as High Priest to shepherd the helpless Jewish people, whose position was like that of a flock sold to butchers for slaughter. The "buyers" are the Jewish nobles who farmed the taxes for the Syro-Greek Government, and whose extortion was unpunished (render "are not held guilty"); the "seller" (read the king) of the sheep is the Syro-Greek king, who has no respect for the law of Israel and says, "Cursed be the Lord and (not 'for') let me be rich". ("Blessed" is a euphemism for "cursed", cf. 1 Kings 21[10, 13]; Job 1[5, 11], 2[5, 9].) The sheep's "own shepherds" are the Jewish nobles, and apparently are not distinguished from their buyers.'

4. *Feed the flock of slaughter*: better *shepherd the flock, &c.*, i.e. the flock exposed to slaughter as explained in v. 5. The prophet was to act the part of the shepherd.

5. The flock is done to death by buyers and sellers and receives no pity from its own shepherds, who are the buyers and sellers. According to Prof. Kennett they are the Jewish notables who oppress and grind down their poorer countrymen especially by farming the taxes; the sons of Tobias were especially prominent in this connexion during the domination of Palestine by the Ptolemies, and the view would identify them with the Ptolemies and Seleucids between whom the community of the Israelites were exchanged and bartered in the struggle for possession between the rival Powers. Actual barter in this case is not implied.

possessors: better *buyers* with the margin. *and hold themselves not guilty*, i.e. are not punished: slay them with impunity.

6. For this verse see the introduction above. As explained there it may refer to the confusion caused by the wars of the Diadochi.

7. *verily the poor of the flock*: read *for the traffickers of the flock*—the prophet had only fed the flock in order to hand them over to the traffickers.

two staves: the staves have a symbolical meaning, i.e. the two shepherd staves (cf. Ps. 23[4]), one a sort of club for beating off the attacks of wild beasts and the other a staff to assist the shepherd in walking.

The symbolical names are given to the staves 'much as a modern cartoonist represents Cabinet Ministers as carrying parcels inscribed with the names of the measures which they are promoting' (Kennett).

Beauty . . . Bands. The word rendered *beauty* literally equals pleasantness, graciousness. It refers here to the favour of Jahveh, which the prophet aimed at securing. Such favour would mean security for Israel against attack from foreign nations. The other principle of the good shepherd was summed up in the words 'bands or binders', i.e. *union.*

8. *three shepherds in one month.* See the discussion of this verse in the introduction to the section above. Wellhausen, who thinks the passage may have been written between 200 and 166 B.C., regards it as alluding to some of the high priests who just before the Maccabean outbreak followed one another in rapid succession. Marti thinks Jason, brother of Onias III, who acquired the High Priesthood by bribery, is referred to together with Menelaus and Lysimachus, brother and deputy of Menelaus, the 'month' would then signify a short period of time.

for my soul was weary, &c.: render *and I was impatient with them*: 'This and the next clause describe the failure of the good "Shepherd" impersonated by the prophet, in his mission, and the mutual antipathy which sprang up between him and the people, even after he had removed their evil rulers' (Driver).

9. The prophet leaves the people to their fate.

10. The breaking of the staff 'Graciousness' signifies that Jahveh's favour is withdrawn, and that the 'covenant' by which they were protected in the enjoyment of friendly relations with the neighbouring peoples was at an end. The 'peoples' referred to are the Philistines, Idumeans, Ammonites, and Arabs, who were a constant source of trouble to the small Jewish community in Judea during the post-exilic period. For 'covenant' used in a somewhat similar metaphorical sense cf. Hos. 2[18].

11. *and thus the poor of the flock*: probably we should read following: *and the traffickers of the sheep.* Those who had been watching the prophet narrowly now saw that he had been acting as Jahveh's agent. For *gave heed unto* render *were watching.*

12–13. In response to the prophet's demand for his 'wages' now that he has given up his office he receives from the people thirty shekels (a trifling sum equivalent to the money paid by way of compensation for an injured slave, cf. Exod. 21[32]). The prophet cast it into the Temple Treasury; in this way making it plain that the insult of offering so paltry a sum was directed against Jahveh Himself. The shekel was worth about 2s. 9d.

13. *Cast it unto the potter*, read, following the Syriac version, *into the treasury* (so R.V. margin). *the goodly price* or *the noble price that I was priced at*: the words are sarcastic. Several scholars would read *that thou wast priced at,* the *thou* being the prophet. Verse 13 is quoted in a slightly varied form in Matt. 27⁹ᶠ· where it is applied to the purchase of the potter's field.

14. The prophet now breaks the second staff 'union'. This signifies that the bond of brotherhood between Judah and Israel was broken. The mention of Israel in this sentence is remarkable. If the text be correct it seems to point to a renewal of party conflicts between North and South Israel. The old northern kingdom was now in the Greek period represented by Samaria and, as is well known, antagonism between the Jews and Samaritans after the Persian period became acute at various times. Could the prophet, writing in the Greek period, have contemplated the possibility of restoring union between North and South even if he had ultimately to abandon the idea? Wellhausen, however, regarded the text as incorrect and conjectured that 'Israel' was an error for 'Jerusalem', comparing 12²ᶠ· and 14¹⁴, from which passages it is clear that a certain amount of antagonism existed between the capital and the province in the post-exilic period.

15–17. The prophet is now bidden to assume the role of the 'foolish shepherd'. This presents to the misguided people a picture of the fact that having rejected the good shepherd they will now have to endure the rule of a foolish shepherd who will neglect the flock and use it for his own ends and so bring them to a state of misery.

15. *the instruments*: i.e. the garb and equipment. The word *instruments* is used in a general sense for anything connected with the work and equipment of a shepherd. Here it is implied that the shepherd's equipment is worn out and useless.

16. *those that be scattered*: perhaps we should read *that which is driven away*.

broken: i.e. *wounded*.

eat the flesh. Instead of caring for the sheep he will devour them.

tear their hoofs in pieces: perhaps by driving them over rough and stony places.

17. The doom on the foolish shepherd.

XIII. 7–9. This section forms a continuation of what precedes. It is clear, however, that this passage is closely connected with 11⁴⁻¹⁷; the figures are the same (shepherd and flock), and further 11¹⁵⁻¹⁷ gives the ground why the shepherd of 13⁷ is to be smitten. This view of the passage is generally accepted. The foolish shepherd will be smitten and the sheep who had rejected the guidance of the divinely appointed shepherd will be scattered; but a remnant will be left in the land and after going through much tribulation will be purified and become the people of God.

7. *my shepherd*: i.e. the foolish shepherd of 11¹⁵⁻¹⁷.

the man that is my fellow: this appears to mean the High Priest. The unworthy holder of the office is singled out as such by the honorific titles bestowed upon him. The words *I will smite the shepherd and the sheep shall be scattered* are quoted by Jesus in Matt. 26[31], where they are applied to the dispersion of the disciples after his betrayal.

I will turn mine hand upon the little ones or *against* the little ones, vv. 8–9. Here the figure of the flock is changed and the prophet speaks literally. Two-thirds of the people will perish in the tribulation, but one-third will survive and after purification will become the people of God. The doctrine of the survival of the faithful remnant was first formulated by Isaiah.

9. *I will say, &c.*: cf. Hos. 2[23], 12[1]–13[6]. A series of passages with an apocalyptic colouring. The theme is the deliverance of Jerusalem, which is threatened by the armies of the heathen; the penitence of the Jewish community for some great crime—a judicial murder; and the purification of the community from sin and uncleanness.

(*a*) XII. **1–9.** The prophet sees a number of nations which include Judah advancing against Jerusalem, vv. 1–3; they are smitten (v. 4) and fall into confusion and the leaders of Judah, recognizing that Jahveh is fighting for Jerusalem, turn against the other nations (v. 5 f.); they helped to save Jerusalem (vv. 7–9). The passage is essentially apocalyptic in character and develops the idea first formulated by Ezekiel of a massed attack by the combined heathen nations against Jerusalem (cf. Ezek. 38–9). This is part of the eschatological drama that ushers in the final act.

2. *a cup of reeling* or *bowl*: 'Jerusalem is figured as a vast bowl large enough for many to drink from at once' (Driver). The gathered nations are eager to drink, but after having done so reel and stagger overcome. The picture shows Jerusalem luring on the nations to their ruin.

and upon Judah also shall it be, &c. The text is difficult and uncertain. The margin has *shall it fall to be*, i.e. to be obliged to take part in the siege against Jerusalem. This probably expresses the real meaning; but it is best to correct the text with the help of the LXX and to read, *and there shall be a siege against Jerusalem.*

3. *the burdensome stone.* The meaning is a stone so heavy that those who attempt to lift it only lacerate themselves. According to Jerome a Palestinian custom existed for young men to test their strength by lifting heavy stones as high as possible.

4–9. The hostile forces are seized with panic. Judah seeing that Jahveh is protecting the city turns to help Jerusalem.

4. *open mine eyes upon*: i.e. look favourably to.

5. Judah is brought to see that Jerusalem ought not to be treated as a foe.

6. Describes how Judah works havoc among the other assailants with whom she was at first allied.

shall yet again dwell: i.e. yet again flourish as a populous city.

even in Jerusalem: omit. So nineteen MSS. of LXX.

7. Judah is entitled to the credit of having given the decisive blow which ended in victory. The House of David cannot arrogate to itself too much glory. There is here obviously an allusion to some historical event which cannot be exactly determined. A breach had opened between the country districts and the capital.

Kennett would refer the situation to the earlier days of the Maccabean struggle 'when Jerusalem was in the hands of the Hellenizers and the heathen while the Maccabees, who derived their forces from the country districts, were fighting against the Syro-Greek Government'. Later Jerusalem (with the exception of the Citadel) came under the complete control of the Maccabees.

the house of David: i.e. descendants of the Royal House.

8. The inhabitants of Jerusalem shall receive supernatural aid.

as David. David here represents the heroic type.

the house of David. Some scholars understand this to refer to the Government generally. Cf. Ps. 122⁵. These shall receive supernatural strength.

10–14. After this signal deliverance the nation gives itself up to great lamentation on account of a martyr 'whom they have pierced'.

10. *the house of David and the inhabitants of Jerusalem*: i.e. all classes of the population, the rulers and the ruled.

the spirit of grace and of supplication: i.e. is a spirit eager to obtain grace or favour (Driver). What the people desired was forgiveness of the great sin they had committed. *they shall look upon me whom they have pierced.* So the text reads. They will look with grief and penitence. The passage is startling, for as it stands the speaker is Jahveh; in a sense it is true that the Jews had, metaphorically speaking, pierced him, by their sin and rebellion. If the text is correct the original meaning must have been that Jahveh had been pierced through the murder of his representative. But could the prophet have spoken in this way? It is very difficult to think that he could. Several manuscripts read *him* instead of *me* and this seems to be required by the following clause; but even so the Hebrew is very peculiar. Some scholars have conjectured that some word, probably a proper name, has been omitted from the Hebrew text (*And they shall look unto . . . whom they have pierced*).

and they shall mourn, &c.: better, *wail*.

11. *and there shall be a great mourning*: better, *wailing, &c.* The reference to the wailing of Hadad-Rimmon in the valley of Megiddon obviously refers to some great public lamentation; Hadad-Rimmon, which does not occur elsewhere, may be the name either of a place or of a deity. It has commonly been taken as the name of a place. According to Jerome, a city near Jezreel in the plain of Megiddo where Josiah was bewailed after his death at Megiddo (2 Kings 23²⁹ᶠ·). According to the chronicler (2 Chron. 35²⁵) dirges in memory of Josiah were chanted even in his day, but Josiah was buried in Jerusalem, and it is very unlikely that a lamentation would be kept up for him anywhere else. Many scholars prefer to think that Hadad-Rimmon is the name of a deity. It is well known that Tammuz, known to the

The Plain of Esdraelon

Greeks as Adonis, was worshipped in Syria and Phoenicia. In the Greek legend Adonis, killed by a boar, is mourned by Aphrodite, and this gave rise to a cultus. 'The weeping for Tammuz' is referred to in Ezek. 8[14]. It has been suggested that Hadad and Tammuz, who were both worshipped in the city of Byblus, may have been fused or confused together, and there may have been wailing for Hadad-Rimmon analogous to that for Tammuz. It may be noted that the Babylonian and Aramaic god of the elements was sometimes called Rimmon (2 Kings 5[18]), sometimes Hadad (1 Kings 11[14, 19, 21]; 2 Sam. 8[3ff.]). It must be remembered that the only wailing for a god known to the O.T. is the weeping for Adonis already mentioned. Cf. Jer. 22[18].

Megiddon: in the south-west corner of the plain of Esdraelon.

12–14. The lamentation will be universal, but it will be carried out with a due order, every family grouping itself separately and the sexes sitting apart. The family of the house of Nathan were probably descendants of David through the son mentioned in 2 Sam. 5[12].

13. *the family of the house of Levi*: i.e. the priestly family.
the family of Shimei: another branch of the family of Levi.

Who was the martyr whose death caused such a strong revulsion of feeling? His name is not given, but 'since the guilt involves the whole land', says Dr. Kennett, 'the murdered person must be the head of Judaism, i.e. the High Priest'. He thinks Onias III is intended, who, however, was murdered at Antioch, not at Jerusalem, and the whole community may in a sense be said to have been involved in the guilt of the murder, because they had failed to give proper support to Onias. According to Sellin, on the other hand, 'the martyr whose fate forms the subject of 11[4-14], 13[7], 12[10ff.], is, in reality, none other than Moses'. (Cf. Sellin, *Moses*, pp. 113–24.)

It is noteworthy that the prophet depicts the lamentation described in vv. 12–14 in the monotonous style of the dirge; the whole population is involved. Sellin [1] points out that it is significant that the whole population does not mourn together but in groups separated according to generations, as in the family cultus (cf. 1 Sam. 20[6]); for the differentiation of the sexes in connexion with such rites cf. Ezek. 8[14].

XIII. 1–6. A fountain for purification from sin will be opened in Jerusalem and permanently available for the whole population; all vestiges of idolatry and the discredited and degraded prophets will be eliminated. The passage is eschatological in character.

1. *there shall be a fountain opened*. The Hebrew means 'shall be permanently opened', cf. Ezek. 36[25]. In the older eschatology the idea is expressed that in the good time coming a life-giving stream will once again flow: cf. Ezek. 47[1-12]; Joel 3[18]; Ps. 36[9ff.]; here this idea is modified and takes the form of a prediction that a fountain will be opened which will wash away all sin and uncleanness (cf. Zech. 3[10]).

2. With the advent of the time of salvation the rooting out of idolatry and of the prophets takes place; cf. 10[2]. As regards the prophets it is noticeable that no distinction is drawn here between true and false prophets; all the prophets are regarded in the lump as repre-

[1] *Commentary on the Minor Prophets*, pp. 524 ff.

sentatives of the unclean spirit. This means that when the author wrote he knew only of the degraded forms of prophesying. Our author paints a different picture of the Messianic age from that of Joel $3^{1ff.}$, where the outpouring of the spirit in the Messianic age is depicted as universal.

3. If any one comes forward in the character of prophet he will be utterly repudiated, even by those closely related to him, and put to death, it being assumed as a matter of course that he is an impostor: cf. Deut. 13^{6-10} and 18^{20}.

4. The prophets themselves will be ashamed at their own calling: cf. Mic. 3^7 (of the false prophets).

hairy mantle: this is a prophetic garb; cf. 2 Kings 1^8. John Baptist wore a garment of camel's hair, Matt. 3^4. Here the hairy mantle is worn by the professional prophet.

5. *for I have been made a bondman, &c.* The text is probably corrupt. Read with Wellhausen *for the land has been my possession from my youth.*

6. The prophet is forced to acknowledge that he bears in his lacerated hands the marks of his degraded calling. It is probable, however, that for 'hands' we should read 'breasts'; cf. 2 Kings 9^{24}. The prophets of Baal lacerated themselves in their frenzied endeavours to bring about a state of ecstasy; cf. 1 Kings $18^{28ff.}$, $20^{35.}$ and $^{41ff.}$; Hos. 7^{14}.

friends: the Hebrew word is not the usual word for 'friend'. It is sometimes used of paramours, and is taken by some scholars to refer to the false gods or Baals, as in Hos. $2^{5, \ 7, \ 10, \ 12-13}$. But the reference to idolatry in this context is rather forced. It seems better to understand the phrase of the prophet's friends who sought to kill him. Perhaps the Hebrew text should be emended, so as to read the usual word for friends.

XIV. Picture of Jerusalem rescued from the heathen and made the metropolis of the world. Another attack on Jerusalem is here described—this time the city is captured, and half its inhabitants go into exile. Jahveh now appears to rescue the remainder. An extraordinary event is described. He stands upon the Mount of Olives, which is divided in the midst by an earthquake, and through the chasm the fugitives escape.

1–5. The Messianic age now begins, and is described in glowing language. The mountain country round Jerusalem is reduced to the level of the plain, but Jerusalem itself remains in its former position, now at a great height, enhanced by the depression of the surrounding country; it becomes the centre of pilgrimage for the nations of the earth who go up annually there to the Feast of Tabernacles.

The prophecy has the character rather of a résumé of older Messianic passages fused together in a single picture. It forms a grand description of the final conflict and the establishment of Jahveh's sovereignty over the entire world. In a sense, it is a sort of doublet of chapter 12. Both passages deal with the deliverance of Jerusalem at the end of the age, but the character of the two passages is radically different; chapter 14 is pervaded by a different spirit from that which animates chapter 12. While chapter 12 envisages an inward change in the religious purification of Jerusalem after the great deliverance, chapter 14 merely concentrates on the external side—describing the wonderful changes that take place in nature and the relations of the peoples of the world to Jerusalem pictured as a result of Jahveh's sovereignty set up at the end. Some of the conceptions expressed in chapter 14 are different from and irreconcilable with those expressed in chapter 12; e.g. Jerusalem is pictured as being taken in 14$^{1ff.}$; contrast 12^6. Possibly chapter 14 was added independently to the previous chapters 9–13 and originally may have contained only verses 1–5+12+15–18, while verses 6–11, 13, 14, 20, 21 were written later; they may have been added by the original writer or by a later hand. Notice that they contain six oracles beginning with the formula 'On that day', possibly suggested by 14^1.

1. Render *Behold a day is coming for Jahveh*, i.e. a day of judgement.

thy spoil. The pronoun is feminine and apparently indicates that Jerusalem is addressed. The prophet plunges at once into a description of what takes place after the capture of the city. He does not describe the assault and capture in detail. Sellin points out that it does not follow that the prophet is writing under the impression received from a new capture of Jerusalem; it may be due to eschatological tradition that Jerusalem must first be captured before Jahveh can emerge and become king over the whole world.

2. *all nations*. This is the eschatological idea, and is not based on any historical event.

3. *as when he fought, &c.*: many such divine interventions would be recalled in the older history and prophecy; cf. Isa. 9^3, 10^{26}, 51$^{9-11}$; Exod. 15$^{3ff.}$.

4. *in that day*: omit with the Babylonian Codex.

which is before Jerusalem on the east. This is intended to emphasize the idea that the final salvation comes from the east.

the mount of Olives shall cleave, &c. This is pictured as the result of an earthquake which takes place at the theophany. Similarly elsewhere, Judges 5^5; Mic. 1$^{4, 8}$; Nah. 1^9; Hab. 3^6; Ps. 97^5.

Through the cleft made in the ridge, the survivors in Jerusalem will make their escape.

5. *ye shall flee by the valley of my mountains*. The LXX Targum and the Oriental MSS. of the Hebrew text read instead *and the valley of my mountains shall be stopped up*. In this way the repetition of *and ye shall flee* is avoided. Wellhausen suggests reading *and the valley of Hinnom shall be stopped up*. For the valley being stopped at one end cf. Ezek. 39[11]. The valley of Hinnom always played an important part in the eschatological scheme. Cf. Jer. 7[32], 19[6].

unto Azel: a locality which cannot be identified if the text is correct. It presumably lay not far from the Mount of Olives.

the earthquake, &c. This evidently made a great impression and was long remembered. Cf. Amos 1[1]. It must have taken place about 750 B.C.

and the LORD my God, &c.: read at the end *with him* instead of *with thee*. The Holy Ones are the angels: Ps. 89[5, 7]; Dan. 4[13], 8[13]. Apparently Jahveh, accompanied by his army of angels, now enters Jerusalem in triumph: cf. Deut. 33[3]; Ps. 68[18], &c.

6–7. An eschatological description of the glorious future. These and the following verses down to v. 11 picture the transformation in nature and the new Jerusalem and Judah which now become the seat of rule of the king of the whole earth. The transformation will exclude extremes of temperature and perpetual daylight will prevail. The idea is worked out in 2 Esdras 7[39-42]: cf. also Rev. 22[5]. It reflects earlier eschatological ideas: cf. Is. 4[6], 30[26], 60[20].

6. *the light shall not be with brightness and with gloom*: read *there shall be neither heat nor cold nor frost*; cf. 2 Esdras 7[41].

7. *but it shall be one day*: i.e. one long continuous day.

which is known unto the LORD: probably a gloss—the sigh of a pious reader who longs for the day to come.

not day, and not night: i.e. there will be no interchange of light and darkness.

8. A perennial stream flowing east and west will bring fertility to the whole land. In other words, a complete transformation of the country round Jerusalem will take place. It is now largely without water. In Ezek. 47[1-12] and Joel 3[18] the stream flows to the east, into the Dead Sea, into which it brings life. Here it flows both east and west simultaneously.

the eastern sea: i.e. the Dead Sea.

the western sea: is the Mediterranean.

in summer and in winter shall it be: i.e. the stream flows all the time.

9. *in that day shall the LORD be one, &c.* The entire earth will worship the one god; monotheism will be universal. The one name of the true god will be recognized, not many names. All false gods will disappear from the whole earth.

10. The transformation that will take place in the territory of Judah. This is largely mountainous in character and descends precipitously to the Dead Sea. Jerusalem itself shall be elevated to an even greater height. The writer is evidently influenced by Isa. 2[ff.]. All other mountains in the country will disappear. Notice the writer deliberately fixes the boundaries of Judah in accordance with those of the pre-exilic kingdom of Judah: cf. 2 Kings 23[8]; 1 Kings 15[22]; he, however, fixed as the southern boundary-city not Beersheba but Rimmon; cf. Josh. 15^{32}, 19^7; Neh. 12^{29}.

As the Arabah: i.e. like the floor of the valley through which the Jordan flows.

Geba: six miles north-east of Jerusalem.

Rimmon: about nine miles north of Beersheba.

from Benjamin's gate, &c. Benjamin's gate lay in the north wall, in the eastern half of it. Cf. Jer. 37^{13}, 38^7. In Nehemiah's wall it cannot be traced. It is uncertain whether it ought to be identified with the later sheep gate. The other gates mentioned in this verse are also uncertain. The tower of Hananel, according to Neh. 3^1, 12^{39}; Jer. 31^{38}, lay in the north-west corner of the Temple Area.

11. *And men shall dwell therein*: wrongly divided. They belong to the previous verse.

The general sense of this verse is that Jerusalem shall never again fall under the ban.

12. We now hear how the war, the victorious results of which have already been detailed in vv. 3 and 5, was conducted by Jahveh; he does not fight with ordinary weapons but by means of demonic powers. A fearful plague falls upon them, and they become mouldering corpses.

13–14 describe how a great panic will break out among them, leading them to destroy each other. Thus wealth will become a spoil to God's people. For similar plagues in an eschatological connexion cf. Ezek. 38^{22}. The proper sequel of v. 12 is seen in v. 15. A similar plague will overtake the animals and beasts of burden.

14a may be regarded as a gloss, since the second part of the verse logically follows on v. 13. The content of the second part of the verse may be suggested by the episode described in 2 Kings 7$^{6ff.}$; cf. Ezek. 39^{10}.

16–19. The effect of the Divine judgement upon the survivors of the heathen nations is here described. They will become worshippers of Jahveh and come up every year to Jerusalem to celebrate the Feast of Tabernacles. The nation that neglects to carry out this duty will be punished, visited by drought or some similar misfortune.

16. *the King*, absolute sovereign of the entire world. It is noticeable that the author does not anticipate the utter annihilation of the heathen world. The remnant will be converted to the worship of Jahveh.

the feast of tabernacles: sometimes referred to as the Feast. It marks the culmination of the harvest. Earlier in the same month (Tishri) the Jewish New Year feast was celebrated, in which the kingship of Jahveh is a special feature.

17. *there shall be no rain.* The Feast of Tabernacles is a sort of Harvest Thanksgiving, and the neglect to observe it would appropriately be punished by cutting off the supply of rain. One of the central features of the ceremonial of the feast was the libation of water from the pool of Siloam, which was brought to the Temple and solemnly poured out at the base of the altar of burnt offering. This was associated with prayers for rain. Cf. John 5[7ff.]

18. Egypt not being dependent upon rain but upon the rise of the Nile for the fertilization of the land will not escape punishment if she neglects to come up to the feast. The same plague with which the nations were to be smitten will affect them.

For *neither shall it be upon them; there shall be, &c.*, read *upon them shall be the plague wherewith.* The whole verse may be a gloss on v. 19. Sellin suggests that the Glossator here in contradistinction from the author of vv. 17 and 19 has not in view the Egyptians proper but the Jewish colonists in Egypt, especially the community at Elephantine who by the erection of the Temple in Egypt were guilty of disrespect towards the Jerusalem Temple.

19. *This shall be the punishment of Egypt*: i.e. Egypt proper. The mention of Egypt in this sense may suggest that when the writer wrote Judah was still under the dominion of the Ptolemies.

20–21. These verses emphasize the holiness of Jerusalem—a feature often emphasized in the eschatological pictures of the ideal Jerusalem. All objects in the new Jerusalem shall be holy. To illustrate this two kinds of vessels are singled out, namely, the bells on the horses and the pots and bowls. The bells on the horses are selected because they stood furthest removed from the idea of serving in any sense the purposes of the Divine rule. The original purpose of the bells was to frighten away demons. For the use of bells see further Ezek. 28[33ff.]. These are to be inscribed with the same words as were placed on the High Priest's diadem, Ezek. 28[36], *pots . . . bowls.* These vessels were already holy because of their sacred use. What is meant by the text in this part of the verse? It has been suggested that so great will be the pressure on account of the multitude of sacrifices that the ordinary vessels will not suffice; so all will be called in to serve the need. This idea does not suit the context, which emphasizes the thought of holiness. Sellin regards 20*b* as a gloss to 21*a*, the meaning being that in the new Jerusalem all secular vessels will in future be holy; the pots will attain the rank of a sacrificial bowl, which latter, being used for the purpose of dashing the blood of the sacrificial victim against the altar, already occupied a comparatively high grade of holiness.

21. *they that sacrifice*: i.e. the pilgrims; for them all pots are now available in Judah and Jerusalem, not merely those confined to the Temple.

seethe therein: i.e. boil; for boiling of sacrifices see e.g. Lev. 6[28].

Canaanite: render with margin *trafficker.* Perhaps the idea is suggested that in view of the multitude of pilgrims it will no longer be necessary for them to purchase the vessels required for sacrifice in the Temple court. All vessels now being holy throughout Judah, the presence of traffickers with objects for sale to the pilgrims will no longer be necessary in the Temple court; cf. Matt. 21^{12}.

ISAIAH XXIII

This famous oracle on Tyre has usually been regarded as falling either in the age of Isaiah (the five years' siege by Sargon then being referred to) or in that of Nebuchadnezzar who besieged it (586–573 B.C.). On this latter view the difficult verse 13 is a later interpolation. It would be about contemporary with Ezekiel's prophecy with the same occasion in view (Ezek. 26–8). But, as we have already seen, it is doubtful whether Ezek. 26 really does refer to Nebuchadnezzar's siege. It more probably refers to Alexander's capture of Tyre in 332 B.C., and the same view may be adopted regarding this chapter, namely, Isa. 23. This is at least a possible view and may be conditionally assumed here. The poem is artistically constructed in metrical form, but the text is gravely corrupted in parts.

The chapter falls into two distinct parts: (*a*) vv. 1–14 in poetical form, and (*b*) vv. 15–18, which to all appearance are a later addition, in prose. The poem is concerned with the Phoenician cities, especially Tyre and Sidon. The poem takes the form of a dirge on the destruction of the cities, which is assumed to have already taken place. The ships of Tyre are addressed, and in their long voyage throughout the whole length of the Mediterranean they are pictured as meeting with desolation wherever they touch. It is on their journey home that this takes place. The sources of Tyre's commercial prosperity are referred to and especially Shihor (v. 3), which probably means Egypt. We know that Tyre carried on a trade in corn between Egypt and various Mediterranean ports. The proud city 'dispenser of crowns' (v. 8) is laid low.

Verses 15–18 picture Tyre as lying desolate for 70 years and then recalled to life and activity like a forgotten harlot.

NOTES

1. *for it is laid waste, so that there is no house.* Torrey reads *the house has been devastated so that none may enter; from the land of Kittim it has been laid bare.*

ships of Tarshish: this was the name given to the great merchant-ships of Tyre which journeyed along the whole length of the Mediterranean to Tartessus in Spain (Tarshish = Tartessus).

2. *the isle*: rather *the coast-land.*

3. *the harvest of the Nile*: read *whose harvest*; *Nile* is probably a gloss on *Shihor*.

4. *the stronghold of the sea, saying*: probably a gloss.

5. *When the report . . . Tyre*: probably a gloss.

8. *the crowning city*: render *the dispenser of crowns*.

10. *Pass through . . . any more*: the text is corrupt; read *Pass over to the land of Egypt, ye ships of Tarshish; there is no haven any more*.

12. *arise, pass over to Kittim*: Torrey would render: *Kittim, arise and pass on*; even there there shall be no rest for thee.

13. This verse is very difficult and corrupt. It is very probably a later editorial insertion by an editor who regarded the poem as referring to Nebuchadnezzar's siege of Tyre (586–573 B.C.). The student may omit it.

15–18. Tyre is evidently once again wealthy after a long interval. The piece was probably composed and inserted by a later redactor who may have interpreted the original prophecy as referring to Nebuchadnezzar's siege. For the figure of the harlot cf. Nahum 3[5, 6]; Ezek. 16[37], 23[10]. In v. 16 a citation is made from a popular ballad which may be rendered:

> *Seize lyre—walk up and down the street,*
> *O harlot by the world forgot!*
> *Twang well—sing many a ditty sweet*
> *To win a last forget-me-not!*

THE BOOK OF JONAH

This remarkable book enshrined in the collection of the Twelve Prophets is quite distinct from the other writings in the collection in style and character. It largely consists of a narrative in which the prophet Jonah plays the leading part. Jonah, the son of Amittai, of Gath Hepher in Galilee, was an historical person who actually lived in the reign of Jeroboam II in the eighth century B.C., and according to 2 Kings 14[25], he predicted to that monarch his successes. He was probably the contemporary of Elisha.

The story, as it is set forth in our present book of Jonah, represents Jonah as the recipient of a divine commission to go to Nineveh with a message of warning as to the consequences of its evil ways. The Prophet is unwilling to carry out this commission and attempts to evade it by embarking at Joppa on a ship for Tarshish in Spain. A storm sent by Jahveh frustrates his purpose. The events that now took place are described dramatically. The crew in a panic, after appealing for divine help, eventually decide by lot that Jonah is the guilty man, and as such the cause of their misfortune. Eventually, Jonah is cast into the sea (1[15]), the result being that the storm subsides and Jonah's God is recognized by the heathen sailors. Jonah is rescued from death by being swallowed by a great fish, specially prepared by Jahveh's Providence. After three days (1^{17}) he is cast out ($2^{1, 10}$).

The divine commission is renewed; Jonah now obeys, and undertakes the long journey to Nineveh, where he delivers his

Jonah in Muhammadan tradition. A miniature from an Arabic MS. of the fourteenth century A.D., showing Jonah resting under the gourd, with the whale in front of him

message—the result being that the city repents, all classes joining in a common penitence, and the divine anger is appeased (3^{1-10}). The final section (4^{1-11}) brings out the essential incompatibility between the divine purpose and Jonah's temperament. Jahveh rebukes him, and the passage ends with a striking phrase illustrating the universality of the divine compassion.

The story told in the book presupposes a time when the Assyrian Empire was at the height of its power and Nineveh might be regarded as the metropolis of the world. The prophet Jonah is an historical person and is referred to in 2 Kings 14^{25}, as we have seen. But the narrative cannot be regarded as contemporary—the character of the language makes it certain that the composition must be a comparatively late one. The historical Jonah is in fact made the hero of a late narrative dominated by a didactic purpose, rather in the style of the later Midrash. According to Budde, the book of Jonah has been extracted from a Midrashic work which is cited by the chronicler. The book appears to have been written as a protest against the exclusive spirit which more and more dominated official Judaism after the time of Ezra. Jonah is the type of his unspiritual fellow-countrymen who were disappointed because the heathen had not been exterminated by Jahveh. The lesson of the book seems to be that God, being not merely the God of the Jewish nation, but of all creation, extends His love to all His creatures; that He is concerned with the well-being of the heathen world; and that the heathen are ready to respond to the prophetic message about the true God, which it is Israel's duty to proclaim to the whole world.

The story may be treated allegorically, Jonah representing the Israelitish nation as a whole. Israel has a mission to bear witness to the entire world to the revelation of the true God but has failed to do so. As a consequence she is swallowed up by the world power Babylon (cf. Jer. 51^{34}). The sojourn in the fish's belly represents the exile; when this discipline has produced repentance the nation is disgorged (cf. Jer. 51^{44}). The main ideas of the book are dependent on Deutero-Isaiah (cf. Isa. 49^6), according to which Israel has a mission to proclaim the true God to the Gentile world.

The composition of the book must be assigned to a comparatively late date, probably to some time in the Greek period. This view is supported not merely by the character of the language, which is marked by late elements, but by the broad universalism of the book. Perhaps a date about 250 B.C. is plausible.

NOTES

II. 2–9. This is probably a later interpolation. It was intended to give the actual words of the prayer mentioned in v. 1; but actually the composition is a thanksgiving and is largely a mosaic of quotations from the Psalter (cf. Ps. 5^7, 18^6, 31^{22}, 42^7, 120^1, 142^3, 143^4). A more appropriate place for the psalm would be after 2^{10}.

IV. 5. This verse is clearly out of place. Its original position may have been after 3^4.

CANTICLES

To the pre-Maccabean Greek period may also be assigned perhaps the collection of marriage songs known as *Canticles* or the *Song of Songs.*

The general character and interpretation of this little book has been much debated. The subject of the song is love, and one school of interpreters assumes that it is dramatic in structure. It is, according to them, possible to detect in the poem not only changes in number and gender but also traces of dialogue and monologue— the whole being governed by a certain unity.

The form of the dramatic theory which will best bear examination is that which makes the dramatis personae three in number, viz. Solomon, the Shulamite maiden, and her country lover. Upon this construction the story embodied in the drama sets forth how a beautiful country maid of Shulam had been compelled by her brothers to watch the vineyard. She had fallen in love with a young shepherd. One day Solomon's courtiers, whom she met while walking in the garden, induced her to come to the King. The women of the court, 'the daughters of Jerusalem', make every effort to induce her to accept as her lover King Solomon—but in vain, and the king himself when he intervenes in person is equally unsuccessful. She will not break her troth. At last the king is so much impressed by her loyalty that he lets her return home. The culmination is reached in ch. 8⁶ᶠ· in a splendid poem in praise of true love.

It is doubtful, however, whether this theory can be maintained. It requires that there should be read into the poem the whole dramatic structure in Acts and Scenes and this means a great deal; the poem itself will hardly bear the weight of this elaboration. Moreover, the drama was not cultivated in Hebrew literature.

Another view has gained ground within comparatively recent years. Budde, partly reviving an older view, explains the *Song* by the customs of the East which have survived down to the present day. 'Among the Syrian peasantry the seven-day marriage festival is called "the king's week"', because on this occasion the young pair are looked upon as king and queen, and, sitting upon an improvised throne, are treated as such.' [1] There is a series of ceremonies which are gone through to the accompaniment of singing, playing, and dancing. Budde has shown that parts of Canticles agree with these songs. The 'king' is the young husband (called King Solomon, as the most fortunate of lords), and the 'Shulamite' is the young wife. The love referred to is conjugal love (after marriage). This theory necessitates the view that the songs have been redacted, and makes the interest culminate in the middle and not at the end of the poem.

---

[1] Cornill, *Introd. to the Canonical Books of the O.T.*, p. 460.

As has already been hinted, the composition of the book can hardly be placed earlier than the beginning of the Greek period. It is true the style of the Hebrew is generally pure, but Persian and Greek loan-words occur, and there are other marks of late linguistic usage.

Recent discussion has been directed to the question of foreign influences on the *Song*. Points of resemblance between certain parts of the *Song* and the Idylls of the Greek poet Theocritus (310–270 B.C.) have suggested that there has been direct influence on one side or the other. But this is at the best highly doubtful. It has also been pointed out that there are strong resemblances in the *Song* to the work of such poets as Meleager and Philodemus, and Nathaniel Schmidt regards the song as an anthology of love lyrics after the Greek model. There may even be older affinities, e.g. in the Liturgies of the early Tammuz cult. For some time—at least down to the time of R. Akiba, A.D. 132–135, and even later—the fitness of *Canticles* to form part of the Canonical scriptures was hotly debated; and it is a significant fact that the book was only admitted to canonical rank on the view that it was an allegory of the history of Israel from the Exodus to the Messiah (cf. Psalm 45). According to the Targum on the *Song* the congregation of Israel is represented by the bride, King Solomon representing God. A similar view has prevailed in the Christian Church, Christ being regarded as the Bridegroom and the Church as the Bride—this is the traditional interpretation.

NOTES

I. 9–11. The bridegroom compares the bride to a noble mare and her jewellery to the trappings of a royal steed. This comparison can be traced in Theocritus, Anacreon, and Horace.

III. 6–11. *the palanquin of King Solomon.* This song describes the rustic wedding procession; the bridegroom in his character as King Solomon goes to fetch the bride accompanied by his friends, three-score mighty men. The bride with her maids ('the daughters of Zion') is brought to the house of the bridegroom's parents. Cf. Matt. 25[1-12]; in 1 Macc. 9[37-41] the story is told how the bridal procession was turned into mourning. Cf. also Ps. 45[8-15].

6–8. The procession is seen approaching, 'as pillars of smoke', a reference to the clouds of dust that accompany the procession.

Who is this, &c.: better *What is this.* It is the sedan-chair of Solomon, i.e. the peasant bridegroom.

Perfumed with myrrh, &c.: cf. Prov. 7[17].

They all handle the sword, &c.: i.e. the three-score mighty men, the friends of the bridegroom, who protect the king against sudden attack. Such precautions were sometimes necessary, cf. 1 Macc. 9[37-41].

9. *palanquin*: Hebrew *'appiryon* = Greek φορεῖον so the LXX renders here. The word is a Greek loan-word and its presence in the text of our book is a mark of late date.

10. *the pillars thereof of silver, &c.* The pillars supporting the roof are covered with silver while the seat is of gold and the cushion is of purple. *The midst thereof being paved with love, From the daughters of Jerusalem*: for *love* read *ebony*, and delete *from the daughters of Jerusalem* as a gloss. The description of the palanquin may have been influenced by 1 Kings 10[18-20] (i.e. the description of Solomon's throne).

11. *the crown wherewith his mother hath crowned him, &c.* The custom of crowning the bridegroom apparently no longer survives in Syria; but it was evidently customary in Palestine at the time when Canticles was written and earlier, cf. Isa. 61[10], *as a bridegroom decketh himself with a garland.* It should be noted that the crowning of the bride and bridegroom is still part of the ceremonial of a Jewish marriage.

VIII. 6–7. A passionate declaration of the overwhelming power of pure love between man and woman. It forms an appropriate climax to the book.

seal. Either worn attached to a string around the neck, cf. Gen. 28[18] and [35], or as a ring on the finger, cf. Jer. 22[24]; Gen. 41[42]. *love is strong as death*: The association of love and death is common throughout all literature.

Jealousy is cruel as the grave: cf. Prov. 11[34]. The text may be emended so as to read *Its passion, &c.*

the grave: Heb. *Sheol*, i.e. the underworld, where the shades of the departed gather. For the insatiable greed of Sheol cf. Isa. 5[14]; Prov. 27[20] and 30[15f].

A very flame of the LORD: literally, *a flame of Jah*, the only occurrence of the divine proper name in Canticles. Perhaps something has fallen out. Or we might render: *its flames are flames of Jah*, i.e. lightning. The addition of the divine name in such a connexion intensifies the degree of the thing described, cf. Num. 11[1]; 1 Kings 18[38]. *The fire of the LORD*, i.e. intense fire.

7. Cf. Prov. 6[34f].

THE CHRONICLER

The books of Chronicles and Ezra-Nehemiah form a remarkable and peculiar group among the historical books of the O.T. In the first place they are not included in that part of the Canon which contains the other historical books (Judges, Samuel, Kings), but come at the very end of the books which form the third part of the Canon of the O.T.—the Hagiographa. This fact in itself is an indication of later origin and, as we shall see, the Chronicler's work is of comparatively late date. In the second place, while the contents of these books (or the greater part of them with the exception of Ezra-Nehemiah) run parallel with the earlier books and to some extent cover the same ground, the books themselves are distinguished by a very peculiar style, phraseology, and point of view. They survey the entire history from Adam to Nehemiah's second visit to Jerusalem (432 B.C.) from a standpoint which may be described as ecclesiastical and priestly. The entire work consisting of 1 and 2 Chronicles followed by Ezra-Nehemiah was originally one continuous whole compiled by an editor or redactor whom we may style the Chronicler.

This is made clear by various indications. The same very peculiar style, and the same standpoint from which the history is treated, prevail throughout. The same compiler's hand is, in fact, manifest all through. The fact that Ezra verbally continues the narrative of 2 Chron. 36 (cf. 2 Chron. 36$^{22, 23}$, with Ezra 1$^{1-2}$) is significant in this connexion. Thus the entire work (1 and 2 Chron., Ezra-Nehemiah), which forms a single continuous narrative from Adam to Nehemiah's second visit to Jerusalem in 432 B.C., was, doubtless, compiled by the Chronicler. That part of the Chronicler's work which supplemented the earlier historical books, viz. Ezra-Nehemiah, was detached and admitted into the sacred collection of Scriptures first; then, later, the rest. Hence the order in the Hebrew Canon: Ezra-Nehemiah and Chronicles.

It will not be necessary to deal in detail here with the book Ezra-Nehemiah. This has already been done in volume iv of this series;[1] but something must be said about the contents and character of 1 and 2 Chronicles.

THE BOOKS OF CHRONICLES

The contents of 1 and 2 Chronicles run parallel with those of the historical books from Genesis to 2 Kings. The whole work falls naturally into four parts:

(1) 1 Chron. 1–9 contains a series of genealogies (with short incidental notices scattered within it).

(2) 1 Chron. 10–29 contains the history of David. The reign of Saul is briefly referred to in 1 Chron. 10, and soon dismissed. In the account of David there are many omissions (e.g. incidents of David's youth, his persecution by Saul, &c.); most of what is

---

[1] *Israel after the Exile*, pp. 194 ff.

recorded in 2 Sam. 9–20 is ignored (as being of a personal or private nature).

(3) 2 Chron. 1–9: the reign of Solomon (with some omissions) and
(4) 2 Chron. 10–36: the history of the kings of Judah up to the Exile. After the division of the monarchy no account is taken of the Northern Kingdom (except where this is unavoidable, as e.g. 2 Chron. 22⁷⁻⁹). The interest of the compiler manifests itself especially in the ecclesiastical aspects of the history.

It is manifest that the compiler's interest throughout is concentrated on Judah and more especially on the Temple and its cultus. 'The whole work is dominated by Levitical and priestly ideals, and animated by the spirit of the Priestly Writing.' Over considerable portions of the book we can check the Chronicler's work by comparison with the earlier sources, the books of Samuel and Kings. He uses the material very freely, sometimes abbreviating, sometimes expanding; cf. e.g. 1 Chron. 17¹³ with 2 Sam. 7¹⁴.

THE DATE OF THE CHRONICLER

Ezra-Nehemiah contains many indications that it cannot have been composed until the end of the Persian period, i.e. 332 B.C. A date a few years later than 332 B.C. is therefore adopted by some scholars. But if, as there is some reason to believe, the Davidic genealogy in 1 Chron. 3¹⁹⁻²⁴ is brought down to the eleventh generation *after* Zerubbabel, we are brought down well into the Greek period—perhaps to a date between 300 and 250 B.C. —as the time when the Chronicler wrote.

There are some indications that in the Maccabean period the Chronicler's work underwent a certain amount of revision so that in its present form it may date from the second century B.C.

The evidence for this conclusion may be briefly summarized as follows:

In 1 Chron. 24⁷ Jehoiarib is mentioned as the first of the twenty-four priestly courses, whereas in the older lists (Nehemiah 10³⁻⁹, 12¹⁻⁷, ¹⁷⁻²¹) Jehoiarib is either not mentioned at all, or if mentioned is assigned a subordinate position. Now it is significant that the Maccabees spring from the family of Jehoiarib; and we may infer plausibly that the prominence given to this family in 1 Chron. 24⁷ is due to revision in Maccabean times.[1]

[1] See Keet, *A Liturgical Study of the Psalter*, p. 30. See further Dr. Keet's judicious estimate of the historical value of the Chronicler's work, op. cit., p. 31 f.

THE PERMANENT VALUE OF THE
CHRONICLER'S WORK

The work of the Chronicler is valuable not so much as a reconstruction of the history of the past as for the light it throws upon the age in which the Chronicler lived and upon his own special interests in the Temple and its cultus. He was especially interested in the musical service of the Temple and much valuable evidence regarding this may be gathered from his writing.[1]

It is interesting also to trace indications of his special religious interests; e.g. the way he stresses monotheism (1 Chron. 29^{10-19}); the wrongfulness of idolatry (1 Chron. 14^{12}; 2 Chron. $14^{3f.}$); he emphasizes in the characteristic priestly way the transcendental aspects of the conception of God, cf. 2 Chron. 16^9; 1 Chron. 29^{10-19}; but Jahveh is not credited with the idea of having provoked David to sin—according to the Chronicler (1 Chron. 21^1) it is Satan who 'moved David to number Israel', whereas, according to 2 Sam. 24^1, it is Jahveh himself who does this.

It is interesting also to notice the Chronicler's teaching on the circumstances which make war justifiable or successful or the reverse. Cf. 2 Chron. 13^{4-20}, 14^{9-15}, and 20^{1-30}, and on such a subject as worldly wisdom, i.e. Hellenism, cf. 2 Chron. 16^{12-14}. He insists much on the duty and efficacy of prayer, cf. 1 Chron. 17^{16-27}; 29^{10-19}, and 2 Chron. 6^{1-12}, 7^{1-3}. The general value of the Chronicler's work as history has been well summed up by Professor Sayce:[2] 'The consistent exaggeration of numbers on the part of the Chronicler shows us that from a historical point of view his unsupported statements must be received with caution. But they do not justify the accusations of deliberate fraud and fiction which have been brought against him. What they prove is that he did not possess that sense of historical exactitude which we now demand from the historian. He wrote in fact with a didactic and not with a historical purpose.'

[1] See further Keet, op. cit., p. 24.
[2] Cited in the *Abingdon Bible Commentary*, p. 440 f.

D. THE WISDOM SCHOOL AND ITS LITERATURE

It will be convenient at this point to consider the Wisdom literature; for though the various elements of which it is composed belong to different dates which go back in some cases to the pre-Greek period, yet the most characteristic products of the Wisdom School belong to a later epoch. We shall consider in this connexion the following books: (1) the book of Job; (2) the book of Proverbs; (3) Ecclesiastes; (4) Sirach (Ecclesiasticus); (5) the book of Wisdom. But before we approach the consideration of these books a word must be said about the Wisdom School generally.

THE WISDOM SCHOOL

Though this school became particularly prominent in the Greek period, it had its antecedents in ancient Israel. The typical wise man was Solomon; and 'Wisdom', as exhibited especially by skill in judgement, in interpreting riddles and dreams, was extolled. Joseph is termed 'discreet and wise' by Pharaoh. Edom was specially famed for 'wisdom' (cf. Obad. 8; Jer. 49⁷). 'Wise men' are mentioned in 1 Kings 4³¹; and it may be inferred from other references to them in the O.T. that they must have formed a distinct class or school, cf. Jer. 18¹⁸ [*For the law shall not perish from the Priest; nor counsel from the wise nor the word from the prophet*]; Prov. 1⁶, 22¹⁷, 24²³. In the earlier pre-exilic period 'the wise' tended to become secular in their interests and outlook. Their transformation into religious as well as secular teachers took place apparently after the destruction of Jerusalem.

The fundamental change in the conditions of Jewish life after the Exile profoundly affected Judaism generally. With the destruction of the old-fashioned life and institutions there came into existence a new balance of forces. The community was now reorganized on an ecclesiastical basis, and the High Priest became the dominant figure in Jewish Palestine. The old prophetic order began also to decline, and practically disappeared at the end of the Persian period. With the advent of Greek culture and civilization the disintegration of the old order was completed. One striking result of the new conditions was the rise of the individual into prominence. The old national interests fell gradually into the background. It is a striking fact that the name 'Israel' nowhere occurs in the book of Proverbs. The rights and needs of the individual were more and more emphasized; and it was to meet the demands created by this situation that the wise now turned their attention to problems affecting the individual primarily. These are largely concerned with questions of conduct and in the book of Proverbs, as well as in the later *Wisdom of Sirach* (Ecclesiasticus), take the form, to a considerable extent, of ethical maxims. It is true that the individual aspects of life are not alone considered; the cosmopolitan and universal aspects are not neglected, and the maxims apply to Jew and Gentile alike.

Another point must be borne in mind. As time went on the problems that confronted the individual tended to become more and more complex. This was especially the case during the Greek period, and perhaps the most characteristic product of the Wisdom School which mirrors this for the period in question is *Ecclesiastes*.

At this point a word may be said on the Hebrew conception of 'wisdom'. The Hebrew word *hokmāh* has as its dominating principle the fear of God. It is essentially practical—not speculative—in character. Hence its main energies were directed to questions of conduct. Practical sagacity in the conduct of the affairs of life, skill in judgement (Solomon) in interpreting riddles and dreams, earned a title to wisdom (cf. Gen. 41^{39}, e.g. where Joseph is termed 'discreet and *wise*' by Pharaoh). As Dr. Driver says,[1] 'the wise men took for granted the main postulates of Israel's creed, and applied themselves rather to the observation of human character as such, seeking to analyse conduct, studying action in its consequences, and establishing morality upon the basis of principles common to humanity at large. On account of their prevailing disregard of national points of view, and their tendency to characterize and estimate human nature under its most general aspects, they have been named, not inappropriately, the *Humanists* of Israel.'

The aims of the 'wise' may best be considered in connexion with the very remarkable Preface to the book of Proverbs (chs. 1–9), which probably belongs to the Greek period.

(1) THE BOOK OF JOB

The book of Job has been described by Sellin[2] as a tremendous work and may be considered the finest flower of the *Hokmāh* literature, although it is also a declaration of bankruptcy by a wisdom-teacher (ch. 28). The problem which forms its subject is:

---

[1] *Introduction to Lit. of O.T.*, p. 369.
[2] *Introd. to O.T.*, p. 212.

How can the suffering of a righteous man be reconciled with the existence of a righteous God?

The main body of the book is usually assigned to the Persian period. The book in its present form is the product of different writers and of different dates.

The poem proper is fitted into a prose introduction (chs. 1 and 2) and Epilogue (ch. 42$^{7-17}$). It is generally agreed that these sections embody a story which was probably current before the poem was composed. The book recounts how Job from the land of Uz— a pattern of piety and blameless virtue—meets with a series of unparalleled misfortunes. These are supposed to indicate some special sinfulness on his part by the three friends, Eliphaz, Bildad and Zophar, who arrive on the scene to console him. The friends demand from Job confession of his guilt and submission to God's righteous judgement. This confession Job feels himself unable to offer without making himself a hypocrite, and the book is mainly occupied with a debate between Job and his friends, in which the issues involved are thoroughly discussed. An Epilogue completes the account of Job's vindication. The hero of the prose-story, according to the old tale, has shown exemplary patience under a succession of dire misfortunes. God, according to the Prologue, permitted these misfortunes to fall upon Job in order to convince Satan that true service to God, apart from the hope of material reward, was possible. To prove this, Satan, who had not yet become the malignant spirit of later theology, was allowed to afflict Job to the utmost, but not to slay him.

Probably the poet has cut out the middle part of the old story, which doubtless enlarged on Job's patience under trial, and has inserted the poem in its place.

The Prologue thus lets the reader into the secret of Job's sufferings, which, however, is hidden from Job himself. The poet does not himself accept the common view that suffering is a sign of divine displeasure; and in fact raises the problem in its most acute form: Why do the righteous suffer?

The prose Prologue and Epilogue, though retained by the poet as a sort of text, is in no sense a composition of his own but is governed by radically different ideas. It is probably older than the poem. The main body of the book is made up of chs. 3–27, 29–31, 38^1, 40^{14}, 42$^{1-6}$.

The book in its present form has apparently been glossed at various points by later hands. The most considerable interpolation, according to the prevailing view, is the Elihu speech in chs. 32–7, which are held to have been written by an author or authors 'who wished to rebuke Job's seeming impiety and the failure of his friends to bring forth a satisfactory explanation of the suffering of the innocent'.

In its present form the book may then belong to the Greek period.

In an important paper on the earlier history of the book of Job the German scholar Buhl [1] argues that 'later hands have striven to tone down the fierce attacks by Job on God's ways and providence, and to bring the figure of Job nearer to the ideal description given in the prose narrative. In the original form of the poem the splendid speech of Job now given in chs. $27^{1ff.}$ probably formed the climax and turning-point, and led on immediately to the restoration described in the Epilogue'.

CONTENTS AND ANALYSIS OF JOB

The book consists of five parts, viz. (*a*) chs. 1–2, (*b*) chs. 3–31, (*c*) chs. 32–7, (*d*) chs. 38^1–42^6, and (*e*) 42^{7-17}.

(*a*) Chapters 1–2, the Prologue, written in prose. This furnishes the necessary information respecting the personality and fortunes of the hero of the poem. 'Without the Prologue the whole of the following speeches would remain suspended in the air' (Cornill).

(*b*) Chapters 3–31, written in poetry, set forth by a debate between Job and his three friends, Eliphaz, Bildad and Zophar. The section opens with a passionate cry from Job bewailing his birth and asking why life should be prolonged, when it can only mean misery (ch. 3). With ch. 4 the debate proper begins. The *first cycle of speeches* (chs. 4–14) is opened by Eliphaz (chs. 4–5), to whom Job (chs. 6–7) replies. Bildad (ch. 8) now takes up the discussion, and Job (chs. 9–10) in a tone of bitter irony replies. The debate is continued by Zophar (ch. 11), to whom Job replies (chs. 12–14). The friends all fail to offer Job any real satisfaction. In the *second cycle of speeches* (chs. 15–21) the debate is again opened by Eliphaz (ch. 15), followed by Job (chs. 16–17), who reproaches the friends for their empty solace. Bildad follows (ch. 18) and is replied to by Job (ch. 19), and again Zophar (ch. 20) joins in and Job (ch. 21). In the *third cycle of speeches* (chs. 22–8) the friends adopt a different line. They explicitly charge Job with great sins (in-

[1] In the volume dedicated to Karl Marti entitled *Vom alten Testament*, pp. 52–61.

humanity, avarice, abuse of power), which they *infer* from his calamities. Eliphaz again opens the debate (ch. 22); Job (chs. 23–4) declaims against the justice of God's providence. Bildad follows (ch. 25) in a short speech which practically concludes the friends' case. Job replies to all three in chs. 26–8. Chapters 27–8 are difficult to fit into the position of Job. Probably 27^{1-10} is the reply to 25^{4-6}, just as 26 is to 25^{2-3}; 27^{11-23} is probably 'directed to the friends whom Job confounds with their own words, in this way welding a piece of recantation . . . into a weapon against the friends' (Cornill). Budde would transpose v. 7 so as to follow vv. 8–10. In chs. 29–31 Job finally surveys the whole circumstances of the case, protesting (in ch. 31) his innocence and appealing to God.

(c) Chapters 32–7. The Elihu speeches, likewise poetical in form (except the introductory verses, 32^{1-6}). After Job's direct appeal to God, at the end of ch. 31, it might have been expected that God Himself would answer and vindicate His methods of action and providence. Instead, a new speaker appears (who is never mentioned elsewhere in the poem, nor in the Prologue or Epilogue). He is represented as a bystander, younger than the rest, and so only intervenes at the end. Elihu's discourse falls into five parts: the first (32^{6-23}) introduces the speaker; in the second (ch. 33), third (ch. 34) and fourth (ch. 35) Elihu criticizes Job's contentions; in the fifth (chs. 36–7) Elihu offers his own solution of the problem. Here he warns Job against being blinded by isolated cases of apparent injustice to the love and providential wisdom of God as exemplified in the regulated course of the world. Above all, he gives a teleological explanation of the suffering of the righteous. Suffering is an instrument of education in God's hand. Right recognition of this on man's part leads to infinite blessing; failure to recognize it to grave sin. In this way Elihu provides the one and only solution to the problem that is given in the book.

(d) Chapters 38^1–42^6. Here Jahveh appears and answers Job out of the whirlwind. 'He does not dispute: He displays a series of living pictures, and surrounds, stuns, and overwhelms Job with His animate and inanimate creation' (Herder).

(e) Chapter 42^{7-17}. The Epilogue (written in prose) describes the end of Job's trials and his restoration to prosperity.[1]

The majority of critics allot chs. 3–27^{10} to the original poem of Job; some would add chs. 29–31. Other suspected passages are

---

[1] The above analysis is taken from the present writer's *Short Introd. to Lit. of O.T.*, p. 132 f.

chs. 7, 12, 14, 16, 17, 24, 26, 27$^{1-10}$, besides the Elihu section. These results depend upon literary analysis.

Another view, however, is possible and has been defended by more than one scholar, and especially by Sellin. According to this view the original author of Job repeatedly worked over what he had originally written. He wrestled 'with his subject all his life long. On this view he originally composed only the dialogue between Job and his friends as a *glorification of the righteous man who proves himself in suffering*, while his fellowmen seek to brand him as a sinner. It would be at once a protest against the vulgar doctrine of rewards and punishments, and a poem in which the good man triumphs by his faith, refuses to allow the crown of righteousness to be torn from his brows, does not, even to his last breath, let go his hold on God, even though he can find no righteousness in Him, and he knows that finally, even though it be only in the hour of death, he will behold Him as the God who justifies him.'[1] After a time, as the result of further reflection, the poet modified his original view. Job had longed for the vision of God and this is now granted to him; the God who appears is not the vindicator of righteousness to whom the original hero of the poem had appealed, but the Incomprehensible and the Absolute who does not vindicate, but tacitly condemns (cf. 38^2, 40$^{1, 8}$, 42^6).

Further reflection led to the formulation of the problem: Why does God allow the righteous to suffer? In the original poem no definite answer is given to this question. The only real attempt at an answer is contained in the Elihu speeches, which work out the theory that the object of suffering is to cleanse the righteous from spiritual pride. On this view the author may be supposed to have composed the Elihu speeches as the ripe fruit of his own mature reflection and experience.

THE RELIGIOUS VALUE OF THE BOOK

The book of Job is a great monument not only of the poetic genius of its author—it is one of the greatest poems of the world—but it is also a work of profound religious value. In a strikingly original and powerful way the poet makes the speeches of Job reflect the varying moods of the sufferer—his intense feeling of God's injustice and his sensitiveness to well-meant but tactless speeches of his friends—all these are set forth by a master hand.

[1] Sellin, *Introd. to the O.T.*, p. 217.

Equal psychological skill is manifested in the way in which the friends' speeches are handled.

The main body of the poem may be regarded as an indictment of the currently accepted theology. The comfortable orthodox belief that righteousness would bring prosperity is shown to be irreconcilable with the experiences of life. But Job is not merely critical; he has something constructive to offer. As the poem advances the poet skilfully makes it apparent that Job's faith in God, so far from being overthrown, actually grows and develops—Job finds real and growing satisfaction in the sense of communion with God. It was owing to the false orthodox view which Job inherited that the first impact of his sufferings produced such a violent shock to his faith in God's providence (cf. $7^{12\text{-}25}$, $9^{21\text{-}2}$). The skill of the poet is shown when he gradually makes Job react against this mood of despair and almost involuntarily appeal to God for justice (Job $13^{15,\,16}$). This conviction that God is just, in spite of all appearances to the contrary, comes to sublime expression in 19^{25}. Very noteworthy are the passages where Job, without accepting it as certain, hints at the possibility of a future life (cf. 13^{22}, $14^{13\text{-}15}$, 19^{27}). One of the most remarkable features is the way in which the poet represents Job as gradually discovering 'the healing power of present communion with God'. The pathetic yearning of the sufferer to come face to face with God in the conviction that then he could vindicate his innocence is expressed in more than one passage; and nowhere more so than in ch. 13 (especially vv. 14 ff.); this rises to a higher level in 14^{15} and culminates in the great passage in which Job expresses the conviction that he will come face to face with God in a life after death, and then be vindicated ($19^{25\text{-}7}$). The conviction here expressed did not rise to complete certainty—it was apparently but for a moment, but is none the less significant. It points the way by which the great truth was painfully won in the agony of struggle, only after strong crying and tears. The final passage in this connexion is $31^{35\text{-}7}$. The great denouement follows when God appears to Job in the whirlwind ($38^{1}\text{-}42^{6}$). The effect upon Job is remarkable; everything appears under a different aspect. As Barton[1] points out: 'Life looked different when viewed from the divine point of view; new feelings of penitence and trust sprang up within him, and he made the unexpected discovery that the solution of life's paradoxes and travail are really to be found in present communion with God. One goes

---

[1] *Religion of Israel*, p. 223 f.

on happily, not because he knows the answer to life's riddle, but because he is conscious that he lives in the loving companionship of One who knows and will guide the feet of his child into the ways of peace.'

NOTES ON SELECTED PASSAGES

(a) JOB 3²⁻¹². *Job curses his birthday.*

2. *Let the day perish, &c.*: cf. Jer. 20¹⁴⁻¹⁸.

5. *the shadow of death*: the real meaning is *deep shadow. all that maketh black the day*: i.e. eclipses; an alternative rendering: *let all ominous darkness terrify it.*

7. *joyful voice*: i.e. the sound of rejoicing at a birth.

8. *Who are ready to rouse up leviathan*: Here Leviathan is the name of a dragon or monster, perhaps a sky monster who was supposed to swallow the sun. The first clause of the verse refers to the enchanters who, according to ancient ideas, had the power of making a day unlucky. An eclipse was regarded as inauspicious. As Leviathan was primarily a sea monster, it has been suggested that for *day* we should read *sea* (the two words are very similar in Hebrew).

12. *the knees*: i.e. the father's knees when he acknowledges the new-born infant.

(b) JOB 3¹³⁻¹⁵. *A picture of Sheol.*

13. For the picture of Sheol as a place where the shades of the departed remain in a state of quiescence—the negation of living—cf. Isa. 38¹⁸. It is significant that Job regards this dreary place of darkness as affording a haven of rest.

14. *With kings, &c.* Cf. the vivid picture given in Isa. 14 of the descent of the King of Babylon to Sheol and of his greeting by the shades of other departed kings.

Which built up waste places, &c., or *rebuilt*. This yields a rather poor sense; perhaps we should render *pyramids* for *desolate places.*

(c) JOB 4¹⁻¹¹: *The righteous are safe.*

2. *If one assay to commune, &c.* Render rather: *If one attempt a word with thee, wilt thou be impatient?* (Driver). *Grieved* should be *troubled*. Notice in this and the following verses (2–5) the apologetic tone adopted by Eliphaz. He mildly expresses surprise that Job, the righteous man, who has been a pillar of strength in the past to so many, should himself now succumb.

6–11. The speaker here enunciates the orthodox view; Job's righteousness ought to be the source of his confidence; it is the sinner who is brought down by calamity.

6. *thy fear of God*: i.e. *thy religion*; the same term is employed by Eliphaz in all his three speeches.

8. *they that plow iniquity, &c.* For the figures cf. Hosea 8[7], 10[13].

9. This verse explains wherein the harvest of trouble consists. For the phrase, *by the breath of God they perish*, cf. Ps. 18[15].

10–11. Here we have a figure illustrating the violent destruction of the wicked. Notice the five different words for 'lion'; even these violent and powerful beasts of prey are reduced to impotence; so it is with the wicked. The verses commented on above form the opening paragraph of Eliphaz's opening speech, which extends down to the end of ch. 5. It is marked by a tone of unmistakable assurance, but is also tactful and forbearing.

(d) JOB 7[12-21]: *A challenge to God.*

This section forms part of Job's reply to the first speech of the friends. The sufferer sees nothing but death in view; but before he dies he will utter his complaint without reserve. Why does God torture him and make him loathe his life?

12. *Am I a sea, &c.* The sea is the lawless element in creation, and has to be restrained and kept within bounds by a superior being; cf. 38[8]. It was symbolized by a monster—the monster of Chaos who, according to the primeval myth, had to be subdued before order could emerge—referred to as Leviathan (3[8]), Rahab (26[12]), or Tiamat; it is significant that, according to Rev. 21[1], in the future world 'the sea is no more'.

15. *strangling*: choking is said to be one of the symptoms of elephantiasis.

rather than these my bones: we should say rather *my skeleton*; a slight emendation would yield the sense *my pains*; cf. 9[28]. This may be right.

16. *I loathe my life*: better with the margin *I waste away.*

17–18. These verses form a bitter parody on Ps. 8[4]. The general thought is: is not man too mean a being for the Almighty to busy himself with the persecution of him? It is notable that Ps. 8 seems to be dependent upon P (*i.e.* the Priestly narrative in Gen. 1) and is thus comparatively late (later, presumably, than 400 B.C.).

17. *magnify him*: i.e. deem him of importance.

19. *look away from me*: cf. Isa. 22[4].

till I swallow down my spittle: i.e. for a single moment; an Arabic idiom.

20. *If I have sinned*: note the hypothetical form of the sentence.

O thou watcher of men: the word in Hebrew might be rendered *guardian*; here again the words of the psalmist (Ps. 121[5]) seem to be parodied—note the bitter irony.

21. If Job has sinned why does not God forgive him? Soon it will be too late.

(e) JOB 13¹³⁻²⁷.

In this section Job bids his friends to keep silence while he again pleads his case before God.

13. He desires passionately to speak, and to speak freely, whatever may be the consequences.

14. *Wherefore*: delete (the word has come into the Hebrew text by mistake).

take my flesh in my teeth: i.e. undertake something very perilous.

15. *Though he slay me yet will I wait for him.* The form which this verse assumes in the A.V. is well known: *though He slay me yet will I trust Him*; these renderings, which express pious resignation, are inconsistent with the context. Job is desperate and believes his end is near. The R.V. margin is in any case to be adopted for the first part of the sentence: *Behold He will slay me*; as regards the last part of the sentence the Hebrew original is ambiguous. In one form of it the word *not* appears—this may be rendered *I need not hope*, i.e. for respite, death is near at hand. Another possible rendering is: *I will not wait.* If the alternative reading be adopted it will run: *I wait for Him*, i.e. *I am waiting for Him to give me the death-stroke.*

16. *This also shall be my salvation, &c.* What is meant is that the fact that Job is able to appear before God and plead his cause is itself a proof that his conscience is clear; no godless man would be able to do this.

18. *ordered my cause*: i.e. set in orderly array the arguments and statement of his case. The term *order* in these connexions is a forensic one, cf. 23⁴.

19. *For now shall I hold my peace, &c.*: render *For then should I, &c.* 'Job challenges anyone to come forward and refute him; adding that, could he think that possible, he would at once be silent and die.' (Driver.)

20. Job asks two conditions if he is to appear before God; these are stated in the following verse.

21. God is asked to withdraw his heavy afflicting hand and not to overwhelm Job with His majesty.

26. *thou writest bitter things*: i.e. *thou prescribest bitter things*: perhaps Job has in mind bitter medicine. For *the iniquities of my youth* cf. Ps. 25⁷.

27. Job compares himself to a malefactor, one with feet set in the stocks, or one narrowly watched and unable to move beyond certain fixed bounds.

(f) JOB 14¹³⁻¹⁵: *Would that a future life were possible for man.*

13. *Sheol*: i.e. Hades; the abode of the departed, the common destiny of man. Job plays with the idea of a possible return to earth after death, when God might meet him in kindlier mood.

a set time: or *a limit*: i.e. a bound to the divine anger.

14. *If a man shall die, shall he live again?* This is too good to be true.

my warfare: or *my hard service*: cf. 7^1. The term is a military one.

release: viz. from the darkness of Sheol.

15. *Thou shouldest call, &c.*: Notice the pathetic yearning in Job's appeal.

(g) JOB 16$^{18-22}$ and 19$^{25-7}$: *The Witness in heaven.*

These two passages should be read together. The 'Witness' of 16^{19} is doubtless to be identified with the 'Redeemer' of 19^{25}. Who is this 'Witness'? According to the usual interpretation Job is appealing to God. Notice the double strain in Job's language—he complains that God is robbing him of justice. God hides Himself from him and will not permit him to plead his cause before Him. In spite of all this, however, he cannot rid himself of the conviction that in the last resort God is righteous, for on that faith the existence of the Universe depends. If God is unrighteous then human rectitude ceases to have any meaning. He is firm, therefore, in the belief that God will grant him justice sooner or later. If only he could come face to face with Him, all would be well.

Another view has been put forward by Mowinckel,[1] who argues that the 'Witness in heaven' is a heavenly being, divine in nature, who acts as a sort of guardian angel for each individual man. This being is referred to in the Elihu section (33^{23}). In that passage (vv. 23 ff.) a Guardian Angel is mentioned as a heavenly intercessor for the sick. It may be assumed that the sick person is regarded as a sinner who has duly humbled himself and offered the required sacrifices to God, thereby having put himself in a state of ritual cleanliness. In this case the angel now accomplishes his part and announces, either to God or to the destroying angels, 'I have found a ransom (for him)' (33^{25}). It is also part of the angel's duty to reveal to the man now recovered (by a dream) the reason for the misfortune that has befallen him and the means to be taken to ward off the danger in the future (cf. 33$^{14ff.}$). It is to be noticed that in 33$^{22f.}$ the angel is described as 'an interpreter' (Hebrew *mēlîṣ*). The real meaning of this term is *intermediary*; it describes the double function of the angel.

It should be added that Mowinckel reconstructs the text of 16$^{19-22}$ as follows:

---

[1] In the volume dedicated to Karl Marti already referred to, pp. 207 ff.

19. *So then I have also a Witness in heaven, even a Surety in the height.*

20. *Behold, my Intercessor shall be my friend, for him* (i.e. *my God*) *mine eye weeps;*

21. *He will maintain the right of a man against God, between a man and his opponent;*

22. *When a few years are passed and I tread the path whence there is no return.*

NOTES

XVI. 18. *O earth, cover not thou my blood, &c.*: the blood, which is regarded as the life (cf. Lev. 16$^{11\text{-}14}$) is represented as crying out for vengeance if it has been shed unlawfully (cf. Gen. 4^{10}), and can only be appeased by the avenger of blood (the *Goel*). If it is covered the cry for vengeance is stifled or dulled. Here Job rhetorically appeals to the earth not to cover up his blood till God has given him justice. 'Blood not covered by the earth was understood to have been violently shed, and was regarded as calling for vengeance on the murderer' (Gen. 4^{10}; Ezek. 24$^{7\text{-}8}$). (Driver.)

20. *My friends scorn me*: this is a very doubtful rendering; for an emended text see above.

21. *And of a son of man, &c.*: for *and of a son of* read *between a.*

XIX. 25–7: according to the usual view Job here confidently appeals to God as his vindicator at the last; the alternative view, which regards the *Goel* in this passage as identical with the witness in heaven, cf. 16^{19}, has already been explained above.

25. *redeemer.* The term here employed (*Goel*) is a technical one and originally meant 'vindicator', and more especially the next-of-kin whose duty it was to act as avenger of blood. The term later acquired an extended significance and as a verb applied to God came to signify *reclaim* from bondage or misfortune (cf. Exod. 15^{13} and often in Deutero-Isa., e.g. Isa. 41^{14}, 47^{14}). Hence *redeemer* here means not redeemer from sin as in Christian usage, but redeemer from afflictions and wrongs *not* caused by sin. *And that he shall stand up at the last, &c.* For *stand up* in the sense *interpose actively* cf. Isa. 33^{10}. The word rendered *at the last* is better translated *after man*, i.e. *vindicator*; literally *as one coming after*—and so, even when I am dead, able to attest my innocence (Driver).

upon the earth: lit. upon the dust, i.e. on which Job's body will be laid; cf. 17^{16} and 20^{11}.

26. The text of this verse appears to have been deeply corrupted; we cannot be sure of any rendering that can be based on the traditional text. As the text stands, the first clause in R.V. runs *And after my skin hath been thus destroyed* (lit. my skin which they have destroyed in this respect = *thus*). An alternative to this would be (2) taking

the word rendered *thus* above as = *even this* (pointing to himself): *and
after this my skin is destroyed*; or (3) and after my skin hath been
destroyed this (shall be) even (from my flesh shall I see God).

26b. *Yet from my flesh shall I see God*: *from my flesh* may here mean
away from my flesh, i.e. apart from or outside of the body; for the
Hebrew preposition *from* used in this negative sense cf. Job 11¹⁵,
21⁹; Jer. 48⁴⁵. In the O.T. *seeing God* is a privilege, and the point here
is that Job's being allowed to see God is a token of reconciliation; cf.
Ps. 17¹⁵. This explains Job's anxiety to find God. Cf. 23³, ⁸.

[As has been noted above the text of this verse appears to be hopelessly corrupt. Some scholars suggest reading at the beginning of
v. 26: *and afterwards my witness shall rise up*. The thought would then
be a parallel to that in 16¹⁹ff.]

27. *for myself*: the margin *on my side* is to be preferred. The
Hebrew preposition is often used in this sense; cf. Gen. 31⁴²; Ps. 56¹⁰.

And mine eyes shall behold, and not another. Others render the end
of the sentence *and that not as a stranger,* referring to God whom, he
says, I shall see not as a stranger, i.e. no more estranged or hostile.

My reins are consumed, &c.: the reins or kidneys are in Hebrew
psychology the seat of the deepest emotions or feelings; *my reins*,
i.e. my inmost feelings; cf. Ps. 7⁹, 16⁷.

[For the last two lines of this verse Mowinckel suggests: *When mine
eyes no longer see the light and my reins within me are consumed.*]

The general thought of these verses is usually explained as follows:
The witness or *Goel* is God, at last and firmly his friend, and Job is to
behold him vindicating that very accusation of God which he has so
constantly, daringly and often despairingly uttered. This is not an
assertion of the (later) doctrine of immortality; we cannot be sure,
from our actual Hebrew text, that Job expects by some miracle to
come to life again, but he is certain, now, that the final authority in
the world is moral (*appealing from man's God to God's God*) and that
death itself is subordinate to the real justice of God.[1]

(h) JOB 38¹⁻¹¹.

In 38–42⁶ we have the speeches of Jahveh and Job's submission
recorded.

Job had constantly appealed that he might be allowed to con-
front Jahveh face to face; and now his wish is granted, but with
very different results from those which he anticipated. Instead of
disclosures being made as to the cause of his suffering and as to the
nature of the sin or sins for which he is being punished, he is over-
whelmed with the mysteries of Jahveh's power in the universe
and feels himself so utterly reduced to insignificance that all he
can do is to submit.

[1] Lofthouse in *Abingdon Bible Commentary*, pp. 497 ff.

'When the morning stars sang together and all the sons of God shouted for joy.' One of Blake's famous illustrations to the Book of Job

It is impossible here to study the full text of this section; it must suffice to take one small specimen of only a few verses and to annotate these.

XXXVIII. **2.** *Who is this that darkeneth counsel?* By *counsel* is meant here God's orderly plan for governing the world. Job had attempted to reduce this to confusion by rashly impugning God's justice. The second part of the verse stresses Job's ignorance in the presence of the mystery of the universe. Cf. 2 Esdras $4^{1\text{-}11}$.

5. *Who determined the measures thereof, &c.*: cf. Prov. 30^4.

6. *Whereupon were the foundations thereof fastened*: margin, *sockets*. To be preferred. Notice the picture of the pillars. God as the Architect of the world was a familiar idea in the Wisdom literature. Cf. Prov. 8.

7. *When the morning stars . . . sons of God, &c.*: the *sons of God* are, of course, the angels; and the morning stars are also regarded as living organisms; they are pictured as rejoicing in song as men do when a great enterprise is successfully inaugurated.

8. *who shut up the sea with doors, &c.*: the sea, as elsewhere in Job, is pictured as a dangerous element, which has to be firmly controlled. Cf. Jer. 5^{22}; Job 26^{10}.

10. *brake for it my boundary*: so read for *prescribed for it my decree*.

[Barton regards the following sections as interpolations in the original text of *Job*: ch. 28 (the praise of wisdom); chs. 32–7 (the Elihu speeches) which were added by two hands; and $40^{15\text{-}41}$ (description of behemoth and leviathan). Barton also thinks that in chs. 24, 27 and 30 words of Bildad and Zophar are attributed to Job, to make his utterances seem more orthodox. See his *Commentary on Job*, pp. 19–37.]

The following commentaries on Job may be mentioned here: A. S. Peake (*New Century Bible*, 1905); G. A. Barton (Macmillan, N.Y., 1921); Cambridge Bible for Schools (Davidson), *The Book of Job* in the R.V. with introduction and notes by S. R. Driver (Oxford University Press, 1906); and the International Critical Commentary by S. R. Driver and G. B. Gray. See, further, *Job* in 'The Study Bible' (Cassell & Company, 1928).

(2) THE BOOK OF PROVERBS

Some interesting questions have recently been raised regarding the date and origin of the book of Proverbs. In particular, an Egyptian document has recently been put forward as a possible source of the Hebrew book. This Egyptian work was originally published by Dr. Wallis Budge in 1923 under the title *The Teaching of Amen-em-Ope.* This, it has been maintained, was known to and used by the authors of Proverbs. The Egyptian manual is perhaps as old as 1000 B.C., and, it is suggested, was read by an Egyptian Jew, possibly in the Persian period, and used by him in compiling a Hebrew collection. This is the view of the Egyptologist Erman. The subject has been critically discussed by Gressmann, who examines the alleged parallels in detail. These are closest and fullest in the case of Prov. 22^{17}–23^{11}. Gressmann argues that the traditional ascription to Solomon of proverbial wisdom is not to be rejected. There is more than one Solomonic collection in the book; in fact, three, viz. chs. 1–9, 10–22^{16}, and a third (chs. 25–9) compiled under King Hezekiah. An interpolated section (22^{17}–24) separates the second from the third collection. Gressmann argues that the usual dating for *Proverbs* is too late. He considers that chs. 10–30 may be assigned to about 700 B.C.; chs. 1–9 are somewhat later (in the Persian period), as also $31^{10f.}$ Thus the Prophets would have started from the thought of the groundwork of the collection, viz. the doctrine of rewards and punishments in this life. The Egyptian 'source' may, with some probability, be supposed to have been used in the interpolated section (22^{17}–24).

Gressmann[1] accepts the view that our present book of Proverbs is a compilation out of previously existing collections. It consists of six collections which once existed independently. These are: (1) 1^1–9^8; (2) 10^1–22^{16}; (3) 22^{17}–24^{22} + an appendix 24^{23-4}; (4) 25^1–29^{27}; (5) 30^{1-33}; (6) 31^{1-31}. Not all of these profess to contain proverbs of Solomon; (3) is headed 'Proverbs of Lemuel which his mother taught him'. The heading of (4) is noteworthy: 'Proverbs of Solomon which the men of Hezekiah, King of Judah, copied out.' As this statement has every appearance of credibility, Gressmann accepts it as certain that (4) was compiled in the reign of Hezekiah. His general conclusion is that the greater part of the book was produced during the later period of the monarchy. Parts (1) and (6) are regarded as post-exilic, and are assigned to the Persian period (fifth century).

A very interesting part of Gressmann's essay is devoted to the affinities of Proverbs and the other parts of the Jewish Wisdom literature to similar movements outside Israel. This is illustrated not only from the Egyptian manual already referred to—which was apparently widely diffused as a school manual in Egypt—but also with the Wisdom of Aḥikar, whose affinities are with the

---

[1] See *Israels Spruchweisheit im Zusammenhang der Weltliteratur.*

Babylonian-Assyrian literature. The wide diffusion of the latter—in the fifth century B.C. it was known in Babylonia, Assyria, Syria, Palestine and Greece—suggests that the leaders of the Wisdom literature formed a school which was international in character. Their status in Israel was probably that of the Scribes—not of the ordinary type who acted as mere writers and copyists, but the more important class who occupied the highest posts in the State as ministers and officers under the governing power. As such they would be brought into contact with the state officials of foreign empires; their outlook would be enlarged, and they would be affected by foreign culture. Aramaic played a great part as the language of diplomacy in the ancient East, and it is certainly significant that Hezekiah's grand vizier, Shebna, bore an Aramaic name. The type of wisdom cultivated in Eastern countries generally was similar to that of the Hebrew sages—practical and non-speculative in character. Gressmann emphasizes the dependence of the earlier type of Solomonic Wisdom on this international school, but rightly says that in its highest achievement as exhibited in the book of Job it reaches heights far transcending what can be found elsewhere.

Gressmann has rendered a service to criticism by emphasizing the antiquity of the Wisdom movement, as against the modern tendency to give a late date to the production of the whole Wisdom literature. As we have already seen, he considers the groundwork of the collection of *Proverbs* to have been written by 700 B.C. It should be pointed out, however, that a later *literary* date for the composition of our present *Proverbs* is not necessarily ruled out by these considerations. If a Wisdom movement arose after the period of the Great Prophets, it may well have produced a literature which, while based upon older traditional material and forms, was reshaped to fit the spirit of a later age.

We have already seen that *Proverbs* is a compilation. The component parts of which it is made up vary in style and character more or less. But, except in the first nine chapters, the apophthegms are placed loosely together without any close logical connexion. 'The different proverbs lie, for the most part, like marbles in a bag; they touch, but have no organic connexion.' They reflect a sound, wholesome, if sometimes unduly prudential morality; moreover, the basic principle of all the Wisdom literature of Israel is truly religious. This fundamental element is expressed in the watchword and key-note: *the fear of the Lord is the beginning or chief part of wisdom.*

It is clear that the youngest part of the collection is the Introductory discourse on Wisdom, chs. 1–9. This may very plausibly be assigned to the Greek period. Many scholars, indeed, would regard the entire collection as a post-exilic compilation. The case for this view has been well stated by Cornill: 'All the struggles which convulsed and dominated the prophetic period are over; Prophecy and Law (28⁴⁻⁹, 29¹⁸) lie behind the book of Proverbs as completed and closed, and the book itself, taking its stand on the pure and lofty plane of the religious and moral ideas attained by those two potent forces, mints the good metal of Prophecy and Law into current coin.'

THE RELIGIOUS AND HISTORICAL VALUE OF THE BOOK[1]

It is a noticeable fact that the conception of God in *Proverbs* is an exalted one; His creative power is emphasized (cf. 3¹⁹⁻²⁰). The great passage on Wisdom, 8²²⁻³¹, seems to have been influenced by Deutero-Isa. and the book of Job (cf. Isa. 40¹². ²¹ff., 44²⁴, 45¹¹ff., and Job 9⁵ff., 26⁷ff., 38⁴ff.).

The striking feature of the book is its lofty conception of the status of women. The book presupposes monogamy as the law of marriage, and woman's place in the family life is exalted (cf. 12⁴, 18²², 19¹⁴, 21⁹, 25²⁴), while the acrostic poem in praise of the virtuous wife, 31¹⁰⁻³¹, is famous. She is pictured as occupying a position of dignity which would be incompatible if rival wives were in evidence.

A further notable characteristic is the absence of all reference to the national life as such. It is striking to find that such words as 'Israel', 'Judah', 'nation' are conspicuous by their absence. It is difficult to find the background for these phenomena in the pre-exilic conditions of the national life. On the other hand, under the conditions of the dispersion which followed the exile we have exactly the medium in which the sages would find it possible and natural to teach their disciples in the way that characterizes the Wisdom books. The linguistic character of the book of Proverbs, which exhibits a considerable element of late words, further confirms this conclusion. But while this fact is plain it need not imply a denial that the Wisdom teachers worked on the basis of old material which they re-edited and to some extent transformed.

[1] See further E. B. Cross in the *Abingdon Bible Commentary*, p. 608.

NOTES ON SELECTED PASSAGES

(2) *Preface to the Book*: PROVERBS 1[1-6].

This section describes the purpose of the book as a whole.

2. *wisdom and instruction* or *wisdom and discipline*: cf. 15[33]. Wisdom, Hebrew *Hokmāh*, is the name given to the combined qualities which serve as the best means for attaining a definite end and which are under the control of a directing intelligence which knows how to use them. The skill of the handicraftsman is also styled wisdom; cf. Isa. 3[3], 40[20]. In the ethical sphere it denotes a capacity to attain health and blessedness in the conduct of life. The way for the attainment of such has been indicated in the sacred scriptures of the Law and the Prophets. In our Book of Proverbs Wisdom is the name applied to those who order their life in accordance with ethical requirements, and who, therefore, according to the opinion of the teachers, attain real success. Wisdom, therefore, from one point of view, is equivalent to religion.

3. *To receive instruction, &c.*: perhaps the sense could be brought out better by rendering *to receive the discipline* that causes one to understand what is righteousness, judgement and equity; judgement here means right expressed in right conduct: equity, i.e. uprightness, straightforwardness.

4. *To give subtilty to the simple, &c.*: *the simple*, i.e. the unsophisticated. The root-meaning of the word connotes standing open, i.e. open to every influence. Notice that *simple* here is parallel to 'young man'. Note that the word rendered *subtilty* is here used in a good sense. Elsewhere, it is often used in a bad sense, e.g. Josh. 9[4]. The word rendered *discretion* also occurs in a bad sense in Prov., e.g. 12[2]. Here in a good sense.

5. The previous verse refers to the instruction of youth; this verse will explain that instruction is also offered to the wise, in order that the wise man may increase his knowledge.

increase in learning. The word here rendered *learning* (Heb. *lekah*) connotes knowledge or science, literally what a man receives or takes from his teacher. It is one of the technical words of this literature. It is sometimes rendered *doctrine*, e.g. 4[2].

man of understanding, &c.: i.e. the man of discernment; the man who possesses a sharp and keen understanding is thereby enabled to give a right direction to this life. The word rendered in R.V. *sound counsels* literally means *rope-pulling*. It acquires a secondary meaning of direction, the art of a steersman. Another technical term of our book, where it is used in a good sense, except in 12[5]. It also occurs in Job 37[12], in the Kethib (written Hebrew Text).

6. *a proverb, and a figure* or *satire*.

This section (Prov. 1[1-6]) sets forth the aims of the wise and their programme of religious education. These may be summarized as follows:

(1) to know wisdom and understanding. Wisdom is a more comprehensive term than understanding. It connotes all the qualities which enable a man to practise to success the art of living in a manner pleasing to God. Note that with wisdom is also joined discipline, which has a double application, namely, the discipline imposed by the teacher and self-discipline. Discipline can never be dispensed with in life;

(2) to discern or understand the words of understanding. The word rendered discern connotes the actions of penetrating understanding, which sees through things to their underlying causes and significance;

(3) to receive instruction or discipline to enable one to understand righteousness and judgement and equity. An alternative rendering of v. 3 would be *to receive instruction in wise dealing, in righteousness, in judgement and equity.* The word rendered *judgement* (Hebrew *mishpat*) in later usage sometimes means 'religion'. If this sense be accepted here, wise conduct is interpreted as uprightness, religion, and righteousness;

(4) young and old are included in the purview of the book. An alternative rendering of v. 4 has been suggested:

To give shrewdness to the untutored,
To the young man knowledge and thoughtfulness.

As regards the mature the aim of the book is to assist them in adding to their store of learning. They can be learners all their life;

(5) verse 6 sums up the various literary forms used by the wise and states that one of the aims of education is to enable those who learn to understand them. They include difficult allusions and figures of speech; 'Proverbs' has a very wide range of meaning, including simile, figure, allegory, short and pithy saying, &c. An alternative rendering of v. 6 would be:

To understand poesy and parables,
The words of the wise, and their figurative style.[1]

The whole programme may be thus summed up: 'Mastery of life's fundamentals through discipline; the attainment of moral conduct; the development of intelligence in youth, and the perfecting of wisdom in the mature; the appreciation of the noble forms which truth assumes.'[2]

[1] E. B. Cross in the *Abingdon Bible Commentary*, p. 608.
[2] Barton, *Religion of Israel*, p. 225.

(b) PROVERBS I⁷⁻¹⁹: *An admonition to cultivate true religion and a warning against temptation.*

7. This verse stands in isolation both from what precedes and from what follows. It forms a sort of motto or text for what follows. In the same manner the Arabic poets are accustomed to put a motto at the head of their collections. Cf. also the texts set at the head of the Rabbinical proems prefixed to some of the Midrashim.

The verse contains the fundamental thought which dominates the first part of the book, chs. 1–9, and it is also repeated at the end of the section, 9¹⁰.

the beginning: if the meaning intended had been 'groundwork' or 'source', probably a different word would have been employed (e.g. 'root'; cf. Job 19²⁸). The man who possesses no fear of God is not even at the beginning of the acquirement of wisdom; cf. Ps. 111¹⁰. The man who neglects to acquire this foundation-truth is a 'fool', and a fool is a practical atheist; theoretical atheists are unknown to ancient Hebrew thought. A practical atheist was one who did not bother himself about God and His judgements; cf. Ps. 10⁴, 14¹. Wisdom is regarded as a gift of God, which He bestows upon those that love Him; cf. Prov. 2⁶, vv. 8–9: note that the disciple of the wise is addressed as son. For the general thought of the verses, cf. 4⁶⁻⁹; 6²⁰ff.

8. *the law of thy mother*: the margin *teaching* is to be preferred. Oral instruction is meant. If the disciple follows the admonitions of these verses, he will acquire much honour, symbolized by 'a chaplet of grace'; cf. 4⁹. According to the Talmudic interpretation *father* here is a metaphorical description of God and *mother* of the community.

10ff. The young disciple is warned against the enticements of those who are in a hurry to accumulate gain by violent means. The innocent referred to seem to be a persecuted party; the description reminds us of the persecuted Pious in the Psalms. Apparently the means contemplated do not stop short of murder.

11. *for blood*: read, by a slight textual emendation, *let us lie in wait for the upright*.

12. *Let us swallow them up alive as Sheol, &c.*: i.e. as suddenly and without warning as sinners have been swallowed up before, like Korah and his company, Num. 16³⁰, ³³. The word rendered *whole* (Heb. *tāmîm*) has both a physical and an ethical sense. Here it may denote those who are sound and healthy enjoying full vitality. For *and whole* we must read *and the whole*.

14. *all have one purse*: sharing alike the risk and the reward.

16. This is a gloss derived from Isa. 58⁷ᵃ. It is omitted in the best MSS. of the LXX.

17. The point of this verse is obscure. Two interpretations have been proposed: (*a*) the net of the allurements of the wicked is spread in vain when the victim is forewarned; (*b*) the net of retribution is spread in vain in the sight of the wicked, because they will not be forewarned. It is important to notice, however, that the Hebrew phrase rendered 'in the sight of' has a special meaning, as distinguished from combination with another preposition (Heb. *bĕ'ênê* as distinguished from *lĕ'ênê*). The former combination denotes 'in the opinion of'; the latter 'in the actual, physical sight of'. Applying this distinction of meaning to our text, the verse ought to mean 'In vain is the net spread in the opinion of any bird', i.e. the bird which is destined to be caught in the trap boasts to itself that however many of its comrades have fallen victims to the net in the past the present bird is much too clever to succumb. Taking the net to signify the net of retribution, this nuance yields an excellent sense here. The wicked know that the net of retribution is spread, but scorn the idea that they will fall victims by walking into it.

18. *They lurk privily for their own lives*: it seems best to connect with the LXX, *these who lurk privily for blood, lurk privily against their own lives*, i.e. they destroy themselves.

19. For *ways* read with the LXX *fate*.

(c) PROVERBS 8[12-31]: *Wisdom's power and gifts; her supreme place in creation.*

The first part of the book of Proverbs culminates in chs. 8 and 9. Here wisdom stands forth in her own person and admonishes mankind to pursue the path of rectitude and discipline. She extols her incomparable worth, her gifts and influence; she is the eldest among things created and stood side by side with the creator at the beginning of time. In ch. 9 wisdom and folly are contrasted.

12. *I wisdom have made subtilty my dwelling, &c.*: i.e. I dwell with; with the implied idea that she is also mistress over the dwelling.

13–16. Wisdom is the source of right government in the world. *The fear of the Lord is to hate evil*: cf. Job 28[28]. This is set forth as a well-known truth.

14. Cf. Isa. 11[2], which also contains a description of the equipment of the ideal king.

16. *judges of the earth*: several Hebrew MSS. and editions together with the Pesh. Targum Vulgate read *righteousness* instead of *earth*.

17–21. Here the rewards of those that seek wisdom are set forth. Cf. 1[28].

18. *durable riches*: perhaps *ancient* riches (margin) is to be preferred. Or it might mean 'stately'. Cf. Isa. 23[18].

19. Cf. 3[14], 8[10, 16].
My fruit. Wisdom is regarded as a tree of life; cf. 3[18].

20–31. Cf. with this section Sirach 1[1-10]. Wisdom here breaks fresh ground, and as a further reason why she should be listened to she displays her patent of nobility. She is the oldest of all the creatures of God, God's favourite before any act of creation took place;

moreover, she was present as Jahveh's master-worker at the creation. This passage has played an all-important part in the later theological controversies of the Christian church. Christian commentators referred it to the Logos—which may be defended as a perfectly legitimate application, seeing that the Logos is the link between the Transcendental God and His self-revelation in creation. It is noteworthy that the Rabbinical doctrine of the Divine character of the Jewish Law, Torah, assumed the form of a belief that the Torah had been created before the world. In Sirach, wisdom finds its most complete self-expression in the Torah. For the Christian application of the idea to Christ, compare Col. 1[15]. The whole passage may also be compared to Job 28.

22. *possessed me*: the older versions (Peshito, Targum, LXX) render *created me* (cf. R.V. margin): cf. Sirach 1[4, 9]; 24[8]. The later Greek versions (Aquila, Symmachus, Theodotion) render *possessed*; so also Jerome (*possidit*). In the Christological controversy the Arians appealed to the rendering of the LXX, while the followers of Athanasius pointed to the translation of Aquila.

In the beginning of his way: or, *as the beginning of his way*, or rather *ways*.

Before his works, or *as the first of his works of old*: cf. Ps. 93[2]. Wisdom was formed before the world.

24. *When there were no depths, &c.*: note the primitive conception of a watery chaos preceding the creation.

25. *settled*: lit. *were sunk*: for the old conception that the mountains had their bases in a subterranean ocean, cf. Ps. 104[8]. In the story of the Flood fountains of the great deep are represented to have broken up.

26. *the earth, nor the fields*: probably this means cultivated and uncultivated land. The Hebrew of the verse is suspicious.

the beginning of the dust of the world: for *beginning* substitute *mass*; cf. Ps. 139[17].

27. *When he established the heavens, I was there*: according to the ancient conception, God at the creation made a division between the different masses of water; cf. Gen. 1[6-7] and Prov. 8[25]. The water was partly concentrated in the deep places of the earth, partly gathered together in the heavens above. The waters were contained and confined within certain limits, partly by the surface of the earth and partly by the firmament, which was regarded as solid. Further, the earth's surface is surrounded on all sides by water. On this surrounding ocean God has rested the firmament; cf. Job 22[14], 26[10].

circle: perhaps *vault* would be a better rendering. The word *ḥûg* occurs only here, in Job 22[14] and Isa. 40[22].

29. This verse refers to the damming up of the water under the earth; cf. Job 38[8-11]; Jer. 5[22].

his commandment: cf. Eccles. 8[2].

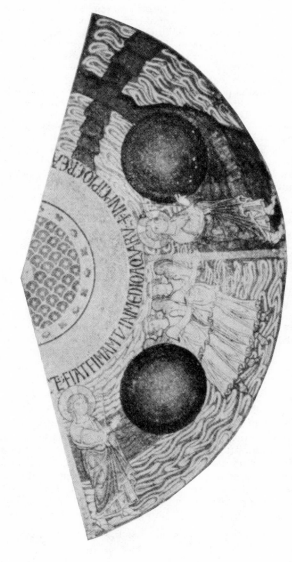

The Creation in tradition. Part of a 13th-cent. mosaic in St. Mark's at Venice which illustrates the first three chapters of Genesis. The scene on the right represents Gen. 1¹. That on the left represents the second day of Creation: 'Fiat firmamentum in medio aquarum'

30. *Then I was by him, as a master workman*: the word translated *master workman* is difficult—in a slightly different form in Canticles 7² it bears this meaning, but it is doubtful if the same meaning is suitable here. The expression used in the context (*by him*, i.e. by his side) implies intimate association 'but not necessarily architectonic activity' (Toy). The objection to this rendering is that the previous description implies that Jahveh Himself is the Architect, and in what follows Wisdom is represented as sporting or playing, not as working. If the Hebrew word is pointed here as it is in Lam. 4⁵, the meaning will be literally one brought up, cherished, *alumnus* or *alumna*, i.e. nursling or ward. This sense harmonizes with the context, and if adopted the various stages described in the preceding verses may be set forth thus: 'Wisdom is conceived (vv. 22–3); is born (vv. 24–6); is present at the creation (vv. 27–9); is as a young child at Jahveh's side under his care living a joyous life.'[1]

I was daily his delight: the Hebrew text has *I was daily delight*, which may mean *I experienced delight* or *I was a source of delight to God*. Perhaps the former suits the context best; *I was delight* = *I was full of delight*.

rejoicing: more exactly, *sporting*. The term shows how much wisdom delights in God's work.

31. *Rejoicing, &c.*: the same terms used in the previous verse are repeated here. Render *Sporting in the world of his earth*.

my delight was with the sons of men: the whole verse develops the implications of the previous verse. Wisdom was first of all by God's side, but afterwards she reveals herself as mediator of the divine creative activity on the earth and among the sons of men: cf. Wisd. of Sol. 7²²–8¹. Toy regards the second part of v. 31 as a gloss (*my delight was with the sons of men*). The author has already dealt with Wisdom's relations with men in the first part of the chapter and would hardly introduce the theme again in a half-verse.

[The remarkable picture of Wisdom given in the above section, Prov. 8²²⁻³¹, calls for some remark. The first thing to be noticed is the sharp personification 'approaching but not reaching hypostatization' (Toy). She is pictured as having been brought into being before the work of creation was begun; she was present when Jahveh established the heavens, the sea and the earth. She rejoices in all his work. Our author thus brings to a climax his picture of Wisdom. Noteworthy also is the picture of wisdom's function in the world; she is the source of sound knowledge in the conduct of life (vv. 5–11). She controls the government of society (vv. 12–16). She is the fountain of honour and the dispenser of noble rewards (vv. 17–21). She is anterior to all human experience, having been

---

[1] Toy, *ad loc.*, in *International Critical Commentary*: Prov., p. 177.

present at the creation of the world (vv. 22–31). Very remarkable is the universal character thus assigned to wisdom—there is nothing nationalistic in the picture, in marked contrast to the similar passage in Sirach (cf. ch. 24), in which Wisdom chooses Israel as her dwelling-place and is identified with the Jewish Law. Our passage is simpler than the corresponding ch. 7 in the Wisdom of Solomon; while Philo's Wisdom is more philosophical in form and is more of the nature of a hypostasis. Job, ch. 28, should also be compared, but there Wisdom is ethical, not cosmogonic.]

(*d*) Two extracts will suffice, perhaps, to illustrate the character of the main body of the Proverbs. Here we have no connecting discourse, and maxims are strung together loosely. The first extract is taken from

PROVERBS 14

This chapter brings in the figures of Wisdom and Folly and enunciates aphorisms for the moral government of the world.

Some Aphorisms psychological and moral: PROVERBS 14$^{13-16}$ + ^{34}.

13. *Even in laughter the heart is sorrowful, &c.*: here, as in v. 10 and v. 30, a psychological note is struck. As translated in the R.V., the passage says that joy always passes into sorrow. Toy would substitute *may be* in each line for *is*. He regards the absolute assertion as too pessimistic and out of harmony with the O.T. view of life. The verse more probably refers to the alternation of joy and sorrow which marks the ordinary experience of life.

14. The point of the verse is that deeds determine fate. Literally translated, the verse runs: *From his ways an abandoned man (backslider) is sated, and from himself the good man.* By a slight emendation we may substitute *his deeds* for *from himself*, and then render with Toy *The bad man reaps the fruits of his acts.*
The good man (enjoys) the outcome of his deeds; cf. Jer. 17^{10}. The general teaching of the verse is to enunciate the doctrine of retribution in its simplest and most absolute form; cf. Gal. 6^7.

15–16. Prudence and forethought are commended. They are the best safeguard against misfortune. For a similar thought cf. 27^{12}.
the simple or *simpleton*: i.e. the untrained, ingenuous; cf. 1^4, 22^3.
He is here contrasted with the *prudent man* or *man of sense*.

16. *A wise man feareth, &c.*: either in a general sense is cautious or in a narrower sense fears God and in consequence walks humbly.
and departeth from evil: i.e. in the concrete sense, misfortune; so, Toy, who renders *and avoideth misfortune.*
beareth himself insolently: the usual meaning of the word so translated is 'to be angry'. It might mean here 'passionately excited', but perhaps the R.V. rendering is better. Toy renders *is arrogant.*

34. *Righteousness exalteth a nation*: i.e. righteousness in a general sense, equivalent to moral integrity. *Exalts* to a position of prosperity and power. *Reproach*: the Hebrew word so rendered (*hesed*) occurs only here and Lev. 20^{17} in this meaning. The usual meaning is 'loving-kindness'. Toy renders *Sin is the disgrace of peoples*. The general meaning is, national righteousness follows on national loyalty to the divine law. The reference will be international—a noteworthy utterance. An interesting rendering of the couplet is given in the Talmud (T.B. *Baba-Bathra*, 10^b): *Charity exalteth a nation And the loving-kindness of peoples is a sin-offering.*
[*Righteousness* (Heb. *sedakāh*) in late Hebrew has the meaning *charity* or *almsgiving.*]

The second extract is taken from Prov. 16$^{10-15}$. It contains aphorisms about kings which may refer to the ideal king. In this case the verses may be regarded as parallel with Ps. 32, which contains a picture of the ideal king.

10. *A divine sentence* or *An oracular decision*: lit. divination. Resorting to divination was condemned by the prophets as inconsistent with loyalty to Jahveh. Here, however, the term is used figuratively. What the king delivers has the divine sanction. God speaks through him.
His mouth, &c.: judgement = legal decision. The king is the mouthpiece of the deity when he speaks officially and delivers judgement. The general sentiment of the verse is expressed in the aphorism 'The king can do no wrong'.

11. *A just balance and scales are the Lord's*: it is best to emend the text so as to read *are the king's*. The scribe may have interpreted 'the king' to mean God.
Weights and measures, which play so important a part in the affairs of a civilized community, depend upon the king for their integrity, the king being the fountain of justice. Doubtless, in the Persian and Greek periods, the Jews had a fully-developed system of stamp-weights, stone or metal.
All the weights of the bag. The travelling merchant carried his stone weights in a bag; cf. Deut. 25^{13}; Mic. 6^{11}. A merchant who falsified the weights transgressed the divine law; cf. Deut. 25$^{13-16}$; Lev. 19^{36}.

12. The true source of strength of the throne is the dispensation of justice. This applies to all kings, though the verse contemplates the monarchy under its ideal aspect. No greater boon could be bestowed upon a people than a just and beneficent law. This was the source of the Messianic hope; cf. Isa. 32^1; cf. also similar aphorisms in this book, 20^{28}, 25^5, 29^{14}.

13. Good kings value honest counsels and love not flattery.

14. The king has the power of life and death. His wrath has terrible consequences. It is mere folly to stimulate that wrath; cf. Eccles. 8^4

and Prov. 19^{12}, 20^2. The second line probably means *He who is wise will seek to pacify it, instead of braving it.* So Toy.

15. *In the light of the king's countenance is life*, or *when the king's countenance is favourable there is life*: cf. 15^{30}. Life here = happy life, prosperity.

And his favour is as a cloud of the latter rain: the latter rain = the spring rain, in March–April. This rain was essential for the ripening of the crops. Hence the cloud portending it was a symbol of blessing; cf. Jer. 3^3; Zech. 10^1; Job 29^{23}. The former rain falls in October, before the crops were sown. It is noticeable that the king in these verses is regarded as possessing absolute power of life and death. He is the arbiter of fate.

(e) PROVERBS 31$^{10-31}$: *In praise of the resourceful housewife.*

This famous section, forming part of an appendix to the whole book, is in form an alphabetic poem, which celebrates the praises of the resourceful housewife. Such alphabetic poems, which also are to be found in the Psalter, naturally do not represent poetry in its highest flights. The form imposes mechanical limits. The virtues of the ideal housewife are highly appreciated in our book; cf. 18^{22}, 19^{14}. The alphabetic structure is complete in twenty-two letters, as in Ps. 119. It is doubtless devised to aid the memory.

The passage has acquired a special place in Jewish home life because it has become customary for the husband to chant it on Friday evening on his return from the Synagogue. He and his sons on their return find the mother of the family with the table prepared for the celebration of Kiddush, i.e. the inauguration of the Sabbath day in the home. Before proceeding with the Kiddush ceremony the husband chants the praises of the resourceful wife in our passage.

10. *A virtuous woman*: better, *a resourceful wife*: cf. 12^4: *who can find?* i.e. one can very seldom find such; cf. 20^6.

her price: i.e. her worth. *rubies*, rather *corals*; cf. 3^{15}.

11. *The heart*: i.e. the mind. The reference is not to the husband's affection but to his reliance upon her capacities to manage the affairs of the house.

he shall have no lack of gain: the word translated *gain* is literally *spoil*. Elsewhere in the O.T. it means 'booty taken in war'. Here it means 'acquisition'.

12. *good*: i.e. in a material sense. She brings him financial prosperity.

13–15 describe the activities of the household in the production of useful works.

13. Cf. Ps. 78[72], where the *skilfulness of his hands* is referred to. For wool and flax compare Deut. 22[11].

14. Her resources are not limited to the use of merely local supplies. Toy omits the third line as a gloss. *meat = food* as in Ps. 111[5].

16–18. Her financial enterprise.

16. *considereth*: i.e. examines carefully and reflects. *she planteth a vineyard*: the culture of the vine was, and is, an important industry in Palestine (Toy); cf. 24[30]; Judges 9[27]; Neh. 5[1].

17. *She girdeth her loins with strength*: to gather up the robe with the girdle was a necessary preliminary for undertaking serious work; cf. 2 Kings 4[29].

18. *She perceiveth.* The verb so rendered means originally to taste. It suggests 'to find out by experience'.

Her lamp goeth not out by night: usually understood to refer to the indefatigable labour of the housewife even in the night. This, however, is doubtful. The expression really means 'prosperity rules in her house'. Lamp is used metaphorically. To put out the lamp means to bring to ruin; cf. Job 18[6]; cf. also 2 Esdras 10[1, 2]. Toy points out that in a well-ordered house the lamp 'burnt all night as a sign of life; its extinction marked calamity'.

19. *distaff*: 'distaff' is probably correct, though the meaning of the word so rendered is unknown to the ancient versions. Both 'distaff' and 'spindle' occur only here in this sense in the O.T.

20. Cf. 19[17], 22[9].

21. For snow in Palestine cf. 25[13] and 26[1]. *For all her household are clothed with scarlet*: the context desiderates the mention of some warm kind of clothing. A scarlet robe might be such, but not necessarily so. Possibly the order of the couplets should be modified, and following on v. 20 we should read 21*a*, then 22*a*, then 22*b*, followed by 21*b*. According to this arrangement, the coverlets (22*a*) are the protection against the cold and the scarlet (coloured garments) followed in the same couplet. In Palestine warm clothing was the only protection against winter cold. Windows were open to the air and unprotected. There were no fireplaces. Even in the winter palace of King Jehoiakim there was only a movable coal fire (Jer. 36[22]).

22. *carpets of tapestry*: or rather *coverlets*: cf. 7[16].

22*b* and 21*b*. Her clothing is fine linen and purple. For all her household are clothed with scarlet. 'Fine linen and purple', i.e. the finest clothing. Probably the linen referred to was of Egyptian origin. The purple was produced in Phoenicia. Garments dyed with purple were the mark of wealth and rank; cf. Judges 8[26]; Jer. 10[9]; Cant. 3[10].

23. *Her husband is known in the gates*: Toy renders *Her husband is distinguished in the council.* The 'gates' were the place where the elders of the city assembled and dispensed justice. The point of the verse is that her husband benefits from his wife's reputation; cf. 12[4].

24. *linen garments*: some fine linen undergarment is meant. The term occurs outside the present passage in the O.T. only in Judges 14$^{12\text{-}13}$ and Isa. 3^{23}.

and delivereth girdles unto the merchant: the girdles were probably of similar material; cf. Jer. 13^1. These she delivers for money to the merchants; cf. Tobit 2^{11}. Lit. *To the Canaanite*: i.e. Phoenician merchant. The term occurs in this sense elsewhere in the O.T.; cf. e.g. Zeph. 1^{11}.

25-7. Her wisdom and happy state.

25. *strength and dignity* : she has secured a well-established position and so *she laugheth at the time to come*. The future has no terrors for her ; she regards it without anxiety.

26. She is discreet. *the law of kindness*: better, *kindly instruction* for the benefit of her children, servants and friends. She is not domineering or harsh (Toy).

27. *She looketh well*: the Hebrew term suggests that she scans as a watchman.

ways: i.e. conduct, actions.

28-9. Her recognition by her own family.

29. *Many daughters*: notice the use of the word daughter as equivalent to woman; only here and in Cant. 2^2, 6^9.

virtuously: effectively, admirably.

30-1. The summing-up.

30. *Favour . . . beauty*: or comeliness and beauty; cf. 11^{22}. External beauty is not to be despised, but it must be accompanied by inner worth. The author obviously prizes domestic efficiency in the household.

that feareth the Lord: this is the sole reference to religion in the poem, which is confined to enumerating a woman's domestic character. Probably, we should read *A woman of intelligence*. There is some support from the Greek.

31. Let her share in the products of her own efficiency. It is noticeable that the woman is here contemplated as being a person occupying a position of her own and not merely an appendage to her husband.

in the gates: i.e. publicity, among the people.

[The picture of the resourceful housewife given in the poem is striking in many ways. The emphasis laid upon her capacity for business in the management of the home, on the amiable traits in her character as shown in her treatment of husband and children, is an attractive feature. Nothing, however, is said regarding intellectual interests, nor is there any mention of religion. Her sphere is the home, and there she is supreme. One consequence is that the husband is freed for public affairs and external business, and this is one of the reasons which redound to her honour.]

(3) ECCLESIASTES OR ḲOHELETH

Among the literary productions of the Wisdom School none is more remarkable than the book known as Ecclesiastes, or, to give it its Hebrew name, Ḳoheleth. The Hebrew title is rendered by the Septuagint *'Εκκλησιαστής* or *The Preacher*, latinized by the Vulgate into Ecclesiastes. In the body of the book Ḳoheleth occurs as a designation of Solomon. It should be noted that the word is feminine in form, which may imply that its original meaning is intensified. Hence the R.V. margin 'The great orator'. The writer, speaking in the name of Solomon, gives a sort of survey of life, mingled with his own personal reflections. He begins by declaring the vanity of all earthly things (1^{1-11}), the vanity of wisdom (1^{12-18}), of pleasure and riches ($2^{1-11ff.}$). In ch. 3^{1-15} he proves that God avenges all things, and that man is helpless before Him; men are like the beasts that perish (3^{16-22}); he depicts the misery produced by oppression, rivalry and toil (4^{1-6}), the advantages of companionship (4^{7-12}), and the hollowness shown in political life &c. (4^{17}–5^6). In 5^7–6^6 the vanity of riches is the principal theme; then the vanity of desire is touched upon (6^{7-12}). In the remaining chapters the ways of the wise (7^{1-24}) are described, the wicked woman, the advantages of wisdom in dark days and trust in God (8–9^2); a parable on the utility of wisdom is given in 9^{13-18}, which is followed by proverbs on the value of wisdom and the results of folly (10^{1-15}); the miseries endured by a land under an incompetent king are also described (10^{16-20}); benevolence is inculcated (11^{1-8}), and in 11^9–12^7 follows the song on the days of life and of death. The Epilogue (12^{8-14}) closes the book.

Ḳoheleth was written at the earliest about 200 B.C. and perhaps later still, after the Maccabean revolt. It contains what reads like a polemic against the doctrine of immortality (3^{19-22}). Many scholars, including Sellin, date it about 200 B.C., and as there is some reason to believe that Sirach was influenced by Ecclesiastes in some form it is safest to acquiesce in this date. The book reflects in a very marked degree the influence of Greek thought, which has had a disintegrating effect on the writer's religion. He has acquired the temperament of a sceptic, but has not entirely lost the Jewish faith. 'In head a Greek, in heart a Jew,' says Cornill, who regards the book as marking one of the greatest triumphs of O.T. piety. The book has certainly been glossed in order to make some of its remarks more acceptable to the orthodox. The best discussion of the way in which it has been influenced by

Greek thought is contained in Dr. Ranston's book *Ecclesiastes and the Early Greek Wisdom Literature*. Dr. Ranston, after a very careful investigation, arrives at the conclusion that 'the evidence strongly suggests that Ecclesiastes was not widely or deeply acquainted with the early Greek literature, i.e. he had not *read* much of it. Had his reading knowledge been greater, signs of it would have been more clearly apparent.' And further, that 'Theognis was the main source of the foreign aphorisms of Ḳoheleth's book'.

The commonly accepted critical view regards the book as having been elaborately revised and interpolated in order to make it acceptable to orthodox Judaism. The book was probably admitted to the Canon, it is assumed, on the ground of Solomon's authorship. But even so, the author's words had to be modified by two interpolators. According to Barton, one of these interpolators represented the orthodox Jewish standpoint and is responsible for the following additions: 2^{26}, 3^{17}, $7^{18b, 26b, 29}$, $8^{2b, 3a, 5, 6a, 11-13}$, 11^{9b}, 12^{1a}, 13, from the words 'fear God' and 14; the other was a representative of the Wise, who inserted a number of proverbs in the text, that sometimes interfere with the progress of the thought. According to Barton, this writer added 4^3, $5^{3, 7a}$, $7^{1a, 3, 5, 6-9, 11, 12, 19}$, 8^1, $9^{17, 18}$, $10^{1-3, 8-14a, 15, 18, 19}$. Possibly the latter writer acted as editor and furnished the book with editorial links, e.g. 1^1, *says the Preacher*; 1^2, 7^{27}, 12^8.

A fresh and striking interpretation of the book is provided by the German scholar G. Kuhn on the *Interpretation of the book Ḳoheleth*.[1]

First of all, regarding the puzzling name under which the author writes, Ḳoheleth—this word, although it is the name of a man, is feminine in form and indicates, according to Kuhn, that Solomon here speaks not as an ordinary man but as the representative of wisdom. Wisdom is often personified in the *Hokmah* literature as a woman. Here she appears in the person of Solomon himself. She speaks through him, and so the name Solomon is exchanged for that of the power which speaks from him. But how is the name Ḳoheleth to be explained? Kuhn suggests that owing to its connexion with *Kahal*, 'Assembly', the name is intended to indicate that Wisdom here speaks not as the mouthpiece of an esoteric and select circle of the elect but as she reveals herself in the assemblages and multitudes of men.

---

[1] *Erklärung des Buches Ḳohelcth* (Giessen: Töpelmann, 1927).

Another suggestion of the author is that the name Shulamith, Cant. 7^1, has a similar recondite meaning, and is connected with the root *Shalam,* and means the trusted or intimate one. The author of *Koheleth* was acquainted with Canticles and assumes knowledge of this work on the part of his readers; Kuhn thinks Canticles was from the first intended to be interpreted allegorically. Solomon means more than the king of that name. The union between Solomon and the Shulamite mystically indicates the union between the community and its divine king. There is a good deal to be said for this allegorical view, which can be traced in a consistent line of tradition both Jewish and Christian. The point about Kuhn's construction of *Koheleth* is that the author of the book speaks throughout not for the intimate circle of divine initiates, but for the multitude. He leaves on one side, or in the background, whatever would be beyond the reach of the multitude, namely, things of the unseen world. He does this deliberately, for he knows of their existence, as the name *Koheleth* in conscious opposition to *Shulamith* shows.

Another noteworthy characteristic confirming what has just been said is the phrase which so constantly recurs 'under the sun', e.g. ch. $1^{2, 9}$, &c. '*There is nothing new under the sun.*' Kuhn thinks this is intended with a certain emphasis to indicate that the author of the book is deliberately concerned with the things of this world, not of the next. The characteristic phrase, '*Vanity of vanities, all is vanity,*' sums up the character of everything under the sun and corresponds in meaning to the N.T. use of the word, e.g. 1 John 2^{16ff}. Rom. 8^{20-2}. Thus, a sort of curse lies on this world, so that whoever gives himself up to it must be disillusioned at last. The creation is not an end in itself, but may fulfil a good purpose if this fact is recognized. The grand error of the human race is that men toil in order to satisfy their desires, instead of finding their true satisfaction in communion with God. They pursue phantoms. Everything that man creates perishes. This is the case even with knowledge. Thus the author appears to take up a completely pessimistic position. The logical outcome of this would appear to be that it would have been well if man had never been born. But though there are passages that seem to suggest this, e.g. 2^{17}, 4^3, 7^1, it is not the author's last word. He is really rooted in the piety of Israel, the Law and the Prophets. Thus what he is striving to do in this book is primarily negative in character. It is not his task to teach men positive truth about God, but to overthrow those ideas which so continuously dominate their lives and are an obstacle to the knowledge of God. In order that they may find true happiness, he destroys with a pitiless consistency the false ideal of happiness which dominates them.

NOTES ON SELECTED PASSAGES

(a) ECCLESIASTES I¹⁻¹¹: *Prologue.*

I. 1. *the Preacher, the son of David, king in Jerusalem*: the word rendered *Preacher*, as has been pointed out above, is feminine in form, and is probably intended by the author to describe Solomon as here speaking in the character of embodied Wisdom and as revealing secrets of wisdom in a public capacity.

2. *Vanity of vanities*: the Hebrew is very expressive. The word translated *vanity* means 'emptiness', and the expression is equivalent to 'utter futility'. This verse forms the motto of the book.

3. This verse develops the meaning of the motto given in the preceding verse. There is no permanence in the results of man's labour. But there is an important qualification in the words *under the sun*. If Kuhn's interpretation is correct, the author intends by these words to hint that there is another aspect of the matter. This is accepted by Dr. Hugo Odeberg,[1] who paraphrases the meaning thus: '*There is another manner of work* (or perhaps *another way of living*) *than that designated by me as "labour under the sun"; that other way of living has permanent results; to that manner of living I want to direct the attention of thoughtful hearers by picturing vividly and emphasizing strongly the nothingness of the life lived "under the sun".*'

4–11. The life under the sun summed up. The verses form eight sentences illustrating this general conclusion of the futility of life under the sun. Four contain illustrations from nature and four from human life. 'The thesis propounded might be rendered thus: the sum total of the different moments or elements of sublunar reality never either increases or diminishes, and these elements or moments themselves can never be changed. . . . Nothing new is introduced.'[2]

4. 'The generations pass as they have passed,
      A troop of shadows moving with the sun.'

5. With a slight correction the verse reads: *The sun riseth, and the sun setteth, and to its place where also it riseth, doth it go.* The earth and the sun include all the phenomena referred to.

6. *The wind goeth toward the south, and turneth about unto the north; it turneth about continually*: even the wind is condemned to a monotonous round that never leads to anything new: *it returneth to its turning.*

7. *yet the sea is not full*: nothing is really added to the volume of the sea's waters.

---

[1] *Commentary on Qoheleth*, p. 8 f. (1929).   [2] Odeberg, op. cit., p. 9.

8. *All things are full of weariness*: better, *All things labour inces-santly.*

the eye is not satisfied, &c.: the eye and the ear are incapable of grasping the never-ending phenomena; the stream of events is con-tinuous but unchanging.

9. *That which hath been is that which shall be*: the past is not done with but will repeat itself in the future. And yet there is nothing really new.

10. 'If there be something of which one says "Lo, this is new"', (the truth is) it was already present in some one or other of the ages which precede ours' (Odeberg).

11. *There is no remembrance of the former generations*: the general meaning seems to be that the latest generation does not profit from the experiences and teaching of former generations. Each generation has to learn its own lessons afresh. This is another illustration that nothing is added, no real progress.

neither shall there be any remembrance, &c.: freely paraphrased, we may render 'And even with those who shall live last of all (if any "last" be imagined) there will be no profit from the experiences of the generations that come after us' (Odeberg).

(b) ECCLESIASTES 3¹⁶⁻²²: *Under the sun man's life is no better than that of the beasts.*

III. **16.** *in the place of Judgement . . . and in the place of righteous-ness* is the designation of the seat of authority occupied by the rulers.

17. All this does not take place without the divine cognizance. The time is coming when it will all be judged. This seems to be the general sense.

there is a time then for every purpose and for every work: the diffi-culties inherent in this clause are considerable. They are well dis-cussed by Lukyn Williams, *Ecclesiastes* (Cambridge Bible), p. 48.

18. This verse is full of difficulties. Odeberg translates it as follows: *I said in my heart: in regard to the sons of men (it behoves) them to seek God and to realize that they are beasts, they by themselves.* 'Men should seek God, that is, the higher attitude, and recognize that *by themselves* they are nothing but beasts (i.e. when life is viewed under the sun).'

19. Literally rendered, the first part of the verse runs: *For the lot of the sons of men and the lot of the beasts—one and the same lot there is for them; and there is one and the same life-breath for all of them.* They share the same breath; when the breath leaves them they share the same end—death. The R.V. margin renders: *For the sons of men are a chance, and the beasts are a chance and one, &c.* This is quite a possible rendering, and it may be compared with Solon's saying quoted by Herodotus: 'Man is altogether a chance.' So A. J. Grien in Peake's One-Volume Commentary; cf. Ps. 49¹²⁻²⁰, where, however, it is the unworthy man who perishes like the beasts; here men generally. But, according to the view given above, the author is regarding man's life here apart from God (under the sun).

20. *unto one place*: defined as the dust, i.e. the dust of the earth, to which the body is consigned at death. The grave is meant, not Sheol specifically. Sheol is mentioned in 9¹⁰.

21. *the spirit of man*: the Hebrew term here translated *spirit* is *ruᵃḥ*, which means rather the 'breath of life'. Only the breath of life is referred to. Nothing is said by Ḳoheleth regarding the soul or spirit (Hebrew, *nefesh, nĕshamah*): In 12⁷ the *ruᵃḥ* is said to return to God who gave it. But it is doubtful whether Ḳoheleth is the author of 12⁷.

whether it goeth upward: does this imply a conception of life after death in a region above the earth? 'Downward' would then imply a cessation of existence. This is the most natural meaning to assign to the phrase.

22. Let a man make the best of the life he has to live here. It has its limit, but within this it is the gift of God; cf. 3¹³.

who shall bring him back, &c.: i.e. to a moment beyond that which is allotted to him; cf. 6¹².

[Chapter 3¹⁹⁻²² at first sight seems to contain a polemic against the doctrine of immortality; but if it refers only to life under the sun the doctrine of a future life is not necessarily excluded. Notice the implied censure of Ḳoheleth's words in Wisd. 2¹², though what is there censured is a perversion.]

(c) ECCLESIASTES 8¹⁰⁻¹⁵: *The end of righteous and wicked.*

Lukyn Williams regards v. 9 as introductory to the section. This affords a suitable connexion. 'All this have I seen in concentrating my thought upon all work done under the sun during the time when one man lords it over another to his hurt.' For the rampant injustice and oppression which thus reigns there is, however, a term; wicked and righteous alike descend into the grave (v. 10).

10. The text of the verse is obviously corrupt. Various suggestions have been made, but none are really satisfactory. One emended form of the text may be translated *And further I have seen wicked men at worship, and they who have done so come in and go off on their ways from the Holy Place and boast of it—this also is vanity.* (Odeberg).

11. Delay in judgement encourages wickedness; cf. Theognis (203ff.) quoted by Ranston: *Ecclesiastes and the Early Greek Wisdom Literature*, p. 20.

12. The general sense of the verse is clear, though the Hebrew is not quite certain.

13. In contrast with what is stated regarding the righteous in the previous verse, it is here categorically asserted that the wicked man shall not prosper nor prolong his days. This doctrine accords with what was regarded as the orthodox view attested elsewhere; cf. e.g. Job 5²⁶, 15³²ᶠᶠ·, 20⁵⁻⁹, 22¹⁶; Prov. 10²⁷; also Wisdom 2⁵; 4⁸.

which are as a shadow: the phrase is difficult; cf. 6¹². It seems best to regard *as a shadow* as qualifying the predicate *he shall not prolong his days like a shadow*, i.e. he may prolong his days as v. 12 indicates, but, if he does so, he shall not do so in serene and quiet peace, as does the righteous. *Shadow* would then be a symbol of undisturbed enjoyment. As is hinted in the phrase that follows, the wicked is cut off from the real source of satisfaction, which depends upon communion with God, *because he feareth not before God*. This interpretation has the merit of getting rid of the apparent contradiction with v. 12. See Odeberg, *ad loc.*, and for a full discussion of other views Lukyn Williams, *ad loc.*

14. The absence of any effective working of the moral law in the ordinary world is here emphasized by Ḳoheleth. For the thought cf. Job 9²², 21⁷. Cf. also 3¹²ᶠᶠ·, 5¹⁸, 9⁷⁻¹⁰.

15. *for that shall abide with him*: the R.V. margin is to be preferred, *and that this should accompany him,* or rather *and this accompanies him in his labour.* Odeberg interprets the phrase as stating that 'the real joy of the nobler life assimilates with man, accompanies him every moment of his life'; cf. 5¹⁹. Notice the repetition of the phrase 'under the sun'.

(d) ECCLESIASTES 11⁷–12⁸: *Youth and Old Age.*

This section is probably interpolated. It is true that some of Ḳoheleth's terms recur in it but they are used in a sense alien to the author's.

XI. **7.** *Truly*: the Hebrew text has simply *and*. This may be interpreted as a contrast = *and yet*, or simply as additional = *and further.* Possibly, as Lukyn Williams suggests, the verse may originally have belonged to another context. He prefers the interpretation 'There is another point to be remembered as one thinks of work' (vv. 1–6); there is room for happiness. The verse, however, may be regarded as forming a fitting prelude to the section that follows, dealing with youth and old age.

8. *but let him remember the days of darkness*: the days of darkness presumably refer to the time that follows death.

All that cometh is vanity: the phrase is difficult. Most moderns interpret it to refer to things in the future, not to death. *Vanity* elsewhere in Ḳoheleth refers to the affairs of this life under the sun. It thus disagrees with the point of view of the real author, and may be ascribed to an interpolator.

9. Notice here that joy seems to be limited to youth. Odeberg

'The grinders cease because they are few.' Women in Palestine to-day grinding grain in a stone hand-mill

rightly points out that this contrasts with the rest of the book, where Ḳoheleth repeatedly asserts that '*real* joy belongs to *all the days of one's life*'; and, further, he enjoins attachment to God in the present life, leaving aside all fear of the coming judgement on the wicked who pursue the futile ends of the sublunar world.

10. Here again youth and the prime of life are pronounced to be vanity. A comment by a reader who found Ḳoheleth's teaching rather dangerous for the youths.

XII. 1–7 continues the description already begun in the preceding verses. The writer pictures the darker side of decrepitude and death.

1. *or ever the evil days come, &c.*: i.e. the years of old age with its suffering and illness.

2. This is the first simile. The burdens of old age or decrepitude are compared with the storm and darkness of winter weather. It is not necessary to press the details of the verse or to over-elaborate the allegory.

the sun, and the light, and the moon, &c.: cf. Isa. 13[10]; Ezek. 32[7ff.]

the clouds return after the rain: storm succeeds storm in the winter.

3ff. The application of the metaphors that follow has been much discussed, though a literal interpretation has also been advocated. Thus it has been suggested that vv. 1–7 should be regarded as a dirge for the dead, describing how the death affects the other members of a household. But it is more probable that the terms are intended to be taken metaphorically.

3. *keepers of the house*: i.e. servants, whose duty is to guard it. A metaphor for hands and arms, presumably. So *Aben-Ezra*.

the strong men shall bow themselves: the reference is probably to the physical strength of the body generally, or to the legs. For *bow themselves* substitute *get crooked*.

the grinders cease because they are few: the margin, *grinding women*, is preferable. In Palestine the women of the household grind the corn for the day's bread; cf. Matt. 24[41]. The simile is intended to suggest the teeth. *Cease* here means 'cease from work'.

those that look out of the windows be darkened: no doubt the eyes are referred to, implicitly compared to the ladies who in the East 'spend much time looking out of the lattices'.

4. This verse refers to the ears.

the doors shall be shut in the street; when the sound of the grinding is low: when there is much grinding to be done the doors of the house are opened, and there is much talk and merriment, but if there is little corn to be ground the doors are shut. What is the exact application intended is doubtful. Probably the ears are intended.

and one shall rise up at the voice of a bird: A reference to light sleep, from which those enfeebled by age are easily roused. The text is probably corrupt. One suggestion is to read *and the voice of the bird grows thin*, i.e. to the old man, becoming more and more enfeebled;

'In the East the women still carry (see p. 158) pitchers to the fountain.'
A scene near Samaria

the singing of birds becomes dimmer and dimmer. This applies either to the caged bird, or to birds in general.

and all the daughters of music shall be brought low: the reference may be either to women singers who had afforded pleasure to the master of the house in times past, or to the individual notes of the singer.

5. This verse pictures the old man first as regards his disability out of doors. He is afraid to go up and afraid to go out; and then it refers to his external appearance.

they shall be afraid of that which is high: they, i.e. old people generally. *That which is high*, either hills or stairs which led from the outside to the roof.

terrors shall be in the way: if the street is referred to it may be remarked that the Eastern street is highly dangerous for pedestrians, being narrow and without paths.

the almond tree shall blossom: this and the following two clauses are of doubtful meaning.

The almond tree blossoms early, about mid-winter, the petals being white. The meaning would then be, probably, that the 'signs of life's mid-winter are seen in the white hair of the old man' (Lukyn Williams).

the grasshopper shall be a burden: or R.V. margin, *Shall drag itself along*. The picture is that of a locust crawling along with difficulty. So the old man has lost all lightness of body and mind.

Even such a stimulus to appetite as the caper-berry fails to produce any effect at last upon the dying man.

man goeth to his long home: is going to his everlasting home; cf. Ps. 49[11] and Tobit 3[6]. The reference is, of course, to the grave.

the mourners: in the East mainly professional.

6–7. The imagery is resumed. The writer here speaks of death.

6. A description of death under four figures.

the silver cord be loosed: the R.V. margin *snapped asunder* is to be preferred. The metaphor is that of a lamp suspended by a silver cord. The burning lamp is a common symbol for life; cf. 1 Kings 11[36]; Prov. 13[9]; sometimes it symbolizes prosperity; cf. Job 29[3].

The 'golden bowl' is part of the lamp, being filled with oil and containing a floating wick.

or the pitcher be broken, &c: in the East the women still carry pitchers to the fountain to fetch water; cf. John 4[28].

or the wheel broken at the cistern: the cistern, i.e. into which the water was collected underground. Probably it refers to a wholly artificial cistern. There is a great divergence of opinion as to the detailed application of these figures. It will suffice here to say simply that the general conception illustrated by the figures is that of death. Regarding the *wheel broken at the cistern*, Levy's explanation is worth quoting.[1] 'A bucket hangs either on each end of the chain, or only on one

[1] See Lukyn Williams, *ad loc.*

'Or the wheel broken at the cistern.' A modern wheel-cistern in Mesopotamia, with a perpetual chain of buckets for irrigation

end, when there is a corresponding weight at the other. This last is
what we have in this picture of Ḳoheleth. The *cord* runs over a *wheel*
and carries at one end a bucket (= our *pitcher*), at the other end a
corresponding weight, a ball of metal (= our *bowl*). If one wants to
draw water one pulls the *bowl* down, then the *pitcher*, already filled,
rises up. If then the *cord* or the chain breaks and the *wheel* is rotten,
naturally *pitcher* and *bowl* fall both at once into the well and the *wheel*
falls in after them, and the machine is demolished—a fitting picture
of destruction by death.'

7. The sequel of death is the dissolution of the living man into two
elements, namely, the dust and the spirit, the former returning to the
earth, the latter to God.

to the earth: cf. Gen. 2⁷, 3¹⁹.

and the spirit, &c.: it seems clear that Ḳoheleth does not mean to
suggest that the spirit is absorbed into the divine being. The spirit
(Hebrew *ruᵃḥ*) must be taken as a separate entity, but it is doubtful
whether it was intended by the writer to represent a man's true self,
which will continue as a conscious personality, or whether it is simply
a statement describing the dissolution or separation between the two
elements in man's being. In any case, it is doubtful whether Ḳoheleth
was the author of this section.

8. This is the summing up following the conclusion of Ḳoheleth's
book.

[The verses that follow are later additions.]

[The latest commentator on *Ecclesiastes*, Dr. Hugo Odeberg,
regards the book as a unity. 'It is not', he says, 'composed from
different sources. . . The discrepancies are seen largely to be due
to the writer's peculiar ways of picturing vividly the two different
modes of life to their extreme consequences.' There are, he thinks,
however, interpolations and additions. The most obvious is the
epilogue; cf. 12⁹⁻¹⁴. Besides this, he regards the following passages
as interpolated: chs. 9¹⁷–10⁴, 10⁸⁻¹³, 11⁷–12⁷.]

(4) THE WISDOM OF JESUS THE SON OF SIRACH, OR ECCLESIASTICUS

Sirach is one of the most remarkable products of the Wisdom
literature. Belonging as it does to a comparatively late date, it
eloquently attests the persistence of the Wisdom school and its
influence. It is a piece of good fortune that the date of the book
can be approximately fixed with certainty. The book was
originally written in Hebrew but was translated into Greek by the
grandson of the author, who has prefixed an important preface to
the Greek translation, in which he states that he went to Egypt in

132 B.C. Probably, therefore, his grandfather wrote the original work some time shortly after 200 B.C., perhaps between 200 and 180 B.C.

The author of the book in his rapturous description at the end of the High Priest, Simon the Just (Ecclus. 50$^{1f.}$), makes it clear that he and Simon were contemporaries, and we know from other sources that Simon flourished between 200 and 175 B.C. A further indication of date may be inferred from the fact that there is not the slightest allusion to the Maccabean struggle. Thus, the writing must have been produced before 168 B.C. Probably he wrote somewhere about 180 B.C.

Ben Sira is himself aware that he occupies a comparatively late place in the tradition of Wisdom. Thus he says in four lines of poetry:

> 'I, indeed, came last of all
> As one that gleaneth after the grape-gatherers:
> I advanced by the blessing of God,
> And filled my wine-press as a grape-gatherer.'—(33$^{16-18}$)

One notable characteristic of the book is that our author develops the old-fashioned proverb by expanding it into a short essay. A good example is 38^{24}–39^{11}. Here the proverb taken as the text is 'The wisdom of the scribe increaseth wisdom, and he that hath little business can become wise'. This is expanded into a number of illustrations showing the need of leisure for the acquirement of wisdom. The essay concludes with a description of the ideal seeker after wisdom.

Though Ben Sira was not profoundly original and is dependent throughout on the O.T. scriptures, which he has thoroughly assimilated and with the phraseology of which he is saturated, yet he has a definite point of view and is no mere compiler.

The first part of his book consists of a series of essays on various themes. 'The same subject is often dealt with in many different settings (e.g. choice of friends, 6$^{5-17}$, 7^{18}, 12$^{8-12}$, 37$^{1-6}$). These brief essays are grouped together, and each group is provided with a brief introduction, usually in commendation of wisdom. Apparently the first half of the book consists of notes based on Ben Sira's early teachings. Each group of sayings may well represent his teachings on a given occasion. In ch. 42, v. 15–ch. 50, v. 24, is found the roll-call of Israel's spiritual heroes, beginning with a psalm in praise of Jehovah's majesty and power and concluding with the description of Simon the High Priest. This latter part of the book is clearly a pure literary creation, and was probably added by him as a conclusion to the collection of his wisdom teachings.'[1]

Ben Sira's book has had a curious history. Originally written in Hebrew, it was, as we have seen, translated into Greek by the grandson of the author some fifty years or so later than its original composition. The original Hebrew form of the book enjoyed for some time a considerable amount of popularity. Quotations from it occur in the later Rabbinical literature; but though it represented a point of view acceptable on the whole to Jewish orthodoxy it never became part of the Canon. This was doubtless due to the fact that it was known to be a comparatively late production. The consequence was that the Hebrew original for some long time was lost and has been recovered partially only in recent times. It is one of the romances of modern scholarship that about two-thirds of the original Hebrew text has come to light. On the other hand, the Greek text became part of the LXX O.T., and in the semi-canonical form, which books of the Greek Bible which are not included in the Palestinian Canon enjoy, has been handed down complete. Consequently, the official text of the book is the Greek text, and it is on the Greek text that our version in the Apocrypha is based.

The book is quoted in the N.T. several times, especially in the Epistle of James and in the Epistle to the Hebrews. It was also highly popular with the Church fathers, who quote from it even more frequently than from the other O.T. writings. As part of the Greek Bible it was accepted in the Canon of the Greek and Latin Church, though in the reformed churches it, in common with other books not recognized by the Palestinian Jews, was relegated to what we call the Apocrypha. It may be added that full account of the recovered Hebrew text is taken in the edition of Sirach printed in Charles's *Apocrypha*, published by the Clarendon Press. There, a reconstructed edition of the text based on the Hebrew and Greek is given. The book is interesting and valuable from several points of view. While it exhibits a certain amount of reaction against the influence of Greek ideas on Jewish life, yet it also exhibits unmistakably some of the permanent effects of Greek influence. Greek customs had long been affecting Jewish life in Palestine. Ben Sira refers to banquets, music and wine, and it is evident that Greek customs and Greek luxury had invaded Jewish life. But Greek influence was seen in deeper ways, latterly in the emphasis

[1] See Charles: *Apocrypha*: Introduction to the Book of Sirach, pp. 268 ff.

laid upon wisdom. Wisdom is the highest possession. On the other hand, wickedness is folly. Nevertheless, the old Jewish piety triumphed even here, and a fusion of the two conceptions took place. True wisdom was identified with the Law. Ben Sira gives glowing expression to this conviction in ch. 24, where wisdom finally makes her habitation in Jerusalem (v. 11) and is identified with the Torah (vv. 23–4).

Ben Sira's book is also significant in other ways. It reveals the transition from the earlier Wise to the later Scribes. In a famous chapter, 39^{1-11}, he gives a picture of the ideal wise man or scribe as he conceives him. These earlier scribes are men of leisure and form a cultivated class. They were very probably recruited for the most part from the priestly class, and not only copied and guarded the letter of the Law but were its interpreters, applying it authoritatively to the affairs of everyday life. It was from their ranks, as Kent points out, that there arose the martyrs who a generation later were ready to lay down their lives for the Law. These earlier scribes, however, belonged to a comparatively leisured and aristocratic class, and are to be distinguished in this respect from the later Rabbis.

The scribes of Ben Sira's age represent an early type of Sadduceeism at its best. The type of piety represented in Ben Sira exhibits Jewish orthodoxy in a very attractive guise. He sums up all that is best in the earlier teachings of Judaism. His conception of God is lofty—He is essentially the God of all mankind, omnipotent, just and merciful; it is through Israel that He had revealed Himself. Nor is this God merely transcendent—He can be addressed in the intimacy of personal communion as 'Lord, and Father and God of my life' (23^4). He had, however, no clear view or belief as to a future life for the individual; cf. 12^{2-4}, $38^{16, 23}$. Sometimes death is spoken of as punishment (7^{17}, 40^{9-10}); but there is nowhere any mention of punishment after death. It is only in one way, according to Ben Sira, that a man can be said to live after death, and that is by means of the wisdom he has acquired in his lifetime; cf. 39^9.

Ecclesiasticus is a compendium embodying the teaching of the Wise regarding the problems of life. It is a valuable thesaurus of moral maxims, but it is also important for the theology that it represents. It has much to say, e.g. concerning the origin of sin, which is important. Ben Sira inherits from the past; but he never leaves the subject with which he happens to deal exactly as he found it. Thus, he taught that the Law was eternal, a doctrine which is further illustrated by the way in which he identifies the Law with Wisdom, which was also eternal.

It is of special interest to note that the doctrine of the existence of the Law before the creation was taught long before Christian times. The doctrine also reappears later in Rabbinical literature.

Another important point concerning the Law is Ben Sira's teaching on the spirit in which legal ordinances should be observed. 'It might seem doubtful', says Toy, 'whether the introduction of the finished Law was an unmixed good from the ethical point of view. The code was largely ritualistic; it fixed men's minds on ceremonial detail, which it in some cases put into the same category and on the same level with moral duties. Would there not hence result a dimming of the moral sense and a confusion of moral distinctions? The ethical attitude of a man who could regard a failure in the routine of sacrifice as not less blameworthy than an act of theft cannot be called a lofty one. If such had been the general effect of the ritual law we should have to pronounce it an evil. But in point of fact the result was different. What may be called the natural debasing tendency of a ritual was counteracted by other influences, by the ethical elements of the Law itself, and by the general moral progress of the community. The great legal schools which grew up in the second century, if we may judge by the sayings of the teachers which have come down to us, did not fail to discriminate between the outward and the inward, the ceremonial and the moral; and the conception of sin corresponded to the idea of the ethical standard.' [1] Now the teaching of Ben Sira on the spirit in which the sacrifices prescribed in the Law are to be observed is a striking illustration of what is here so truly said: in $39^{18, 19}$ (Greek, 31^{21-3}) he urges:

> *The sacrifice of the unrighteous man is a mocking offering*
> *And unacceptable are the oblations of the godless,*
> *The Most High hath no pleasure in the offerings of the ungodly,*
> *Neither doth He forgive sins for a multitude of sacrifices.*

NOTES ON SELECTED PASSAGES

(a) ECCLESIASTICUS: *Prologue.*

By the law and the prophets and by the others that have followed in their steps: the well-known division of the Hebrew Canon into the Law, the Prophets and the Writings seems clearly indicated here,

---

[1] *Judaism and Christianity*, p. 186.
[2] See Introduction to Sirach in Charles, *Apocrypha*, i, p. 306.

though the third division is somewhat vaguely described. A third division was already, no doubt, in existence, side by side with the Law and the Prophets, and the vague language descriptive of it seems to indicate that it had not yet been formally delimited, and that it may still have been incomplete; cf. Luke 24[27], where the threefold division is clearly indicated.

instruction and wisdom: or, as one codex has it, *wisdom and instruction*, wisdom being the foundation and first principle. Israel is praised because it has made the Law the vehicle for imparting wisdom and the means of discipline.

readers . . . they that love learning: perhaps the teachers of the Law, i.e. the Scribes, are meant.

them which are without: probably the laity is meant.

by speaking and writing: oral instruction was an important department of the Scribe's activity. *Writing*, apparently a reference to the literary activity of the Scribes. Of extra-canonical works which show the influence of the Wisdom School may be mentioned the sayings of Ahikar; compare also the Book of Tobit.

to fail in some of the phrases. For things originally spoken in Hebrew: the younger Sirach was acutely conscious of the difficulties that beset the translation of one language into another. On the whole he is not an unsuccessful translator.

in the eight and thirtieth year of Euergetes. The date refers to the year in which the younger Sirach actually came into Egypt. Probably the thirty-eighth regnal year of Euergetes II is meant, i.e. 132 B.C.

continued there: the Greek word used seems to imply that he remained in Egypt until the end of Euergetes' reign, i.e. 117–116 B.C. The Prologue, therefore, was probably written between 132 and 116 B.C.

I found a copy: it is best to adopt another reading, which gives the sense, 'I found opportunity for no small instruction', i.e. the younger Sirach found plenty of opportunity in Egypt for instruction in the Wisdom of the Scribes. The synagogues in Egypt were essentially centres of instruction and discussion in learning, as Philo attests. Thus he says in one passage, referring to the synagogue assembly: 'The listeners sit in perfect order and absolute stillness, eagerly drinking in the most excellent doctrine. For here one of the most experienced puts forth the most perfect and most useful teachings by which human life can be adorned in the most beautiful way.'

[The importance of this Prologue for the history of the Canon is obvious. It is a document which can be dated within a few years exactly, and it shows the three stages by which the Canon of the O.T. Scriptures grew up in their original Hebrew form. The original work of Ben Sira himself is also important from this point of view, because he alludes constantly to the phraseology and sequence of the O.T. books, and it is possible to trace his knowledge of these books in detail as he proceeds.]

(b) ECCLESIASTICUS 6³²⁻⁷: *The disciple's pursuit of wisdom.*

The picture here given illustrates how the schools of the Wise anticipated in their character the later Rabbinical schools.

32. *if thou wilt yield thy soul*: i.e. if thou wilt set thy heart thereon, that is, give oneself whole-heartedly to the study of wisdom.

34. *in the multitude*: or assembly.
cleave thou unto him: cf. 13¹⁶ᵇ·

35. *discourse*: in late Hebrew the word here rendered *godly discourse* means *edifying discourse*. Cf. 8⁸, 11⁸·

36. *get thee betimes*: cf. 4¹²·

let thy foot wear out, &c.: cf. Prov. 8³⁴; and *Pirke Aboth* 1⁴ (*José, the son of Joezer, of Zeredah, said: Let thy house be a meeting house for the wise; sit amidst the dust of their feet, and drink their words with thirst*).

37. *the ordinances of the Lord*: the Hebrew text has *the fear of the Most High*. Perhaps we should read *the law of the Most High*. The disciple is to steep himself in the Law. If he does this he will be rewarded.

The picture here given is typical of an Oriental school. It was, of course, as all teaching down to the close of the Middle Ages, oral in character. There were no printed text-books, and the disciple imbibed from his teacher maxims and dicta which he stored up in his memory. There was much memorizing, and this fact has influenced the form in which these teachings have come down to us. They are couched in forms calculated to make memorizing easy. Further, in a large teaching centre, where many teachers and disciples assembled, classes were not held in separate rooms, but the whole assembly had classes going on all at once in the same large area. This was the case until quite recently in that typical Oriental University, the mosque of Al-Azhar at Cairo. Like all Oriental teachers, the Wise probably sat cross-legged with their disciples in a circle about them. The method of question and answer was used on a large scale.

(c) ECCLESIASTICUS 24: *In Praise of Wisdom.*

The hymn in praise of Wisdom contained in this chapter is a fine composition. It falls into six strophes, each containing six distichs. The main theme is that Wisdom is honoured in heaven and earth.

1. Wisdom is entitled to praise herself on account of her inherent excellence.

in the midst of her people: probably Israel is meant.

2. *In the congregation of the Most High*: Heaven is meant.

In the presence of his power: *hosts* would be a better rendering, i.e. the heavenly hosts.

3. Wisdom now speaks in her own proper person. For the personification cf. Prov. 8⁴ᶠᶠ·, and for the whole chapter cf. Prov. 8²², 9¹².

as a mist: Wisdom is diffused over the earth. Cf. for the phrase Gen. 2⁶. Wisdom is the spirit of God, and in later Jewish literature the identification is clearly made.

4. *in high places*: i.e. in the seven heavens, above the firmament, in the highest of which, 'Araboth, God dwelt.

pillar of the cloud: i.e. the Shekinah of later Jewish theology.

5. *depth of the abyss*: i.e. the watery abyss; cf. Job 36³⁰.

6. Wisdom pervades the entire creation.

7. *With all these*: i.e. with every people and nation. The thought is parallel with the later Rabbinic representation according to which the Law was offered to all the nations of the world, but Israel alone accepted it. So Wisdom sought among the nations a resting-place but found it only in Israel.

8. *Let thy tabernacle be in Jacob*: cf. John 1¹⁴. According to 1 Enoch 42, § 1, 2, Wisdom failed to find a resting-place at all on earth and was assigned one in the heavens.

9. *from the beginning before the world*: cf. Prov. 8²²⁻³, the classical text in this connexion.

to the end I shall not fail: the rendering of the Syriac is to be preferred: *the memorial of me shall never cease*. The Law, with which Wisdom is identified, is thought of.

10. *In the holy tabernacle*: where the Law was carried out into practice. Here the personified Wisdom can be said to have ministered before God.

in Sion: where the Temple later took the place of the tabernacle.

11. *the beloved city*: this descriptive term is not found elsewhere. Perhaps the Greek should be corrected and we should read *In the holy city* in accordance with O.T. usage.

he gave me rest: i.e. 'he caused me to rest'. Cf. Ps. 132⁸, ¹⁴.

in Jerusalem was my authority: Wisdom descended from her heavenly abode to dwell in the earthly Jerusalem. It is possible that this conception contributed to the evolution of the idea of a heavenly Jerusalem corresponding to the earthly; for this cf. 2 Esdras 8⁵²⁻⁵³ and 10⁴⁴⁻⁵⁹; and in the N.T. Gal. 4²⁶; Heb. 12²²; Rev. 3¹² and 21¹⁰.

13. *like a cedar*: cf. Ps. 92¹².

14. *on the sea shore*: a variant reading is *in Engedi*. This may be right. Engedi was famed for palm trees, which, however, do not flourish on the sea shore.

rose plants in Jericho: cf. 39¹³.

as a fair olive tree in the plain: they still grow luxuriantly in the plains around Jericho.

as a plane tree: some *codices* add *by the water*, perhaps rightly.

15. *aspalathus*: according to Pliny the root was used in making ointment (*H.N.* xii. 24).

galbanum: a gum used in the making of incense.

onyx, &c.: cf. Exod. 30³⁴. Stacte was an odoriferous gum.

as the fume of frankincense: or *as the smoke of incense*: i.e. something specially holy and pleasant.

16. *the terebinth*: the terebinth with its far-spreading branches is an apt simile for glory and grace.

17. *the fruit of glory and riches*: cf. Prov. 3¹⁶, 8¹⁸ᶠᶠ.

18 is omitted by the R.V. It has only slight textual authority.

19. *Come unto me*: cf. Prov. 9⁴ and Isa. 55¹.

20. *For my memorial, &c.*: cf. Ps. 19¹⁰ in reference to the Law.

21. Contrast John 6⁵⁸, 4¹⁴.

22. With this verse Wisdom concludes her speech.

they that work in me shall not do amiss: or rather, *they that serve me shall not commit sin*: i.e. those that are filled with wisdom will *ipso facto* be guarded against the commission of sin. For the thought, cf. *Ethics of the Jewish Fathers*, ii. 2, where Torah study is recommended in conjunction with worldly business. 'For the practice of them puts iniquity out of remembrance.'

23. *Even the law which Moses commanded, &c.*: Wisdom is here identified with the Law, and so in the following verses. For the phraseology here cf. Deut. 33⁴.

Notice that Ben Sira substitutes the plural *assemblies* for the singular of the Hebrew. So also the LXX, which has *synagogues*, suggesting the synagogues of the Dispersion.

24 is omitted by the R.V. on the same grounds as v. 18.

25. *Pishon*: cf. Gen. 2¹¹ᶠᶠ.

26. *in the days of harvest*: cf. Josh. 3¹⁵.

27. *That maketh instruction to shine forth as the light*: the Greek text depends upon a misreading of the Hebrew. Read with the Syriac, *Which poureth forth as the Nile instruction*.

in the days of vintage: i.e. in the autumn, September–October, when the river is in full flood.

29. *her thoughts are filled from the sea*: the Greek translation is due to a misunderstanding of the Hebrew. Render *Her understanding is more full than the sea, and her counsel is greater than the deep*.

30. *I*: i.e. the writer, who now speaks in his own person and continues the metaphor of the stream, comparing himself to a small canal supplied with water from the great river, Wisdom.

31. *I will water my garden*: i.e. by utilizing to the utmost the supply of wisdom. Cf. Isa. 58¹¹; John 7³⁸.

32. *afar off*: he has the Dispersion in mind.

33. *generations of ages*: 'eternal generations'.

34 recurs in substance in 33¹⁷.

(*d*) ECCLESIASTICUS 39^{1–11}: *The ideal scribe.*

1. *he that applieth his soul*: the Syriac adds, rightly, *to the fear of God.* For this description cf. Ezra 7¹⁰.

Olive trees near Jerusalem

the wisdom of all the ancients . . . prophecies: note that the source of the scribes' knowledge is defined as the Law, the Wisdom Books and the Prophets.

2–3. The other source of the scribes' knowledge seems to be oral, and to embrace proverbs, sententious sayings, maxims for the conduct of life and perhaps allegories. Cf. the description of Wisdom given in the book of Wisdom, 8⁸: *She understandeth subtilties of speeches and interpretations of dark sayings.*

4. *He will serve among great men, &c.*: the scribe as depicted by Ben Sira is a man of culture, who has access to royal courts. The high estimation of the value of foreign travel is interesting. The education of the scribe as here depicted is broad in character.

5. The note of true piety is emphasized.

6. Note the way in which the culture of the true scribe, even when the liberal conditions previously mentioned have been fulfilled, depends in the last resort on God's grace.

He shall pour forth the words of his wisdom: it is better to follow the Syriac and render *He himself poureth forth wise sayings in double measure*: i.e. he is not a mere conserver of tradition. He puts forth things of his own; for *in double measure* cf. 1²⁵.

9. *his name shall live, &c.*: cf. 38²⁶, 44¹².

10. For *nations* read *congregations*. Cf. 44¹⁵, 46⁷.

11. If a long life is granted him, his reputation is assured.

(*f*) ECCLESIASTICUS 44¹⁻¹⁵: *Praise of the fathers; Introduction.*

Chapters 44–49 form a well-knit and distinct division of the book, having for their theme the praise of the fathers of old. The heroes enumerated range from Enoch to Nehemiah (in a series of well-defined sections). The connexion with the preceding division is a natural one; God, whose glory is manifest in the mighty forces and phenomena of the natural world (ch. 43), is also worthy of praise both for and in the lives of the great heroes and pious men that shine through history. An appendix (50¹⁻²⁴) sets forth the praise of the High Priest Simon, who can hardly be reckoned with the fathers of old.

The whole forms an historical retrospect of Israel's history from the earliest age; cf. similar surveys in the O.T. in Ps. 78, 105, 106, 135, 136, and Ezek. 20; in the apocryphal literature, Wisdom 10 ff., 1 Macc. 2⁵¹⁻⁶⁰; and in the N.T. Heb. 11, &c. The subject throughout is Israel, regarded as the chosen and truly representative race. All that is best and highest in humanity is reflected in the Israelitish race and comes to glorious expression in the long line of patriarchs, pious kings, heroes, prophets and teachers, which stretches from the beginnings of history.

Ben Sira lays special emphasis on the duty and privilege of the community to remember the pious of the past (cf. 44⁹, ¹³, ¹⁵, 45¹, 46², 49¹, ⁹, ¹³). He also lays stress upon the splendour of the cultus as the visible expression of Israel's unique relation to God. Thus Moses is subordinated to Aaron in importance, and David's greatest glory is that he was the founder of the Temple music and psalmody (47⁸⁻¹⁰). This is all the more remarkable, as Ben Sira was inclined, if anything, to depreciate the efficacy of sacrifices *per se*. Throughout, Ben Sira closely follows the narrative given in the canonical scriptures, and reminiscences of scriptural phraseology are of frequent occurrence. It is clear that he values highly the written word (cf. 48¹⁰ = Mal. 3²³, ²⁴), which he obviously regards as among the most precious possessions of the chosen community of God. It is interesting to note, in this connexion, that the author shows clear indications of acquaintance not only with the Law (Pentateuch) and the Prophets (including Joshua, Judges, Samuel and Kings), but also with Chronicles ($47^{8\text{ff}\cdot}$), Nehemiah (49^{13}), the Psalms (44^5, $47^{8\text{ff}\cdot}$), Proverbs (44^5, 47^{17}), Job (49^9) and perhaps Ḳoheleth (47^{23}). No allusion is made to Daniel, which was not yet extant when the author wrote; and it is uncertain whether Ruth, Lamentations and Canticles were yet regarded as sacred Scripture, as he makes no clear allusion to any of them. The whole forms a carefully articulated composition, falling into strophes, and consisting of 211 distichs.

Chapter 44^{1-15} forms an introductory section to the enumeration of the fathers, setting forth in general terms and under twelve categories the different classes of eminence into which Israel's heroes fall. The reference is to Israel only and does not include the heathen. On the basis of the Hebrew and Greek text, the following title should be prefixed to the chapter: 'Praise of the fathers of old.'

1. *famous men*: the Hebrew, perhaps rightly, reads *men of piety*. If adopted, this reading connotes piety in its broadest sense, the duty rendered to God.

that begat us: perhaps we should read, *in their generation*, that is, in chronological order.

3–7. Note that twelve categories of men are enumerated in these verses.

3. *Such as did bear rule in their kingdoms*: rulers like David and Solomon and warriors like Joshua are meant.

Giving counsel, &c.: prophets like Elisha and Isaiah who combine the functions of prophet and public counsellor are meant.

4. *Leaders of the people by their counsels*: the Hebrew reads *Princes of nations, &c.* Perhaps by 'Princes of nations' such figures as Joseph are meant.

And by their understanding men of learning for the people: the Greek text originally ran: *Scribes of the people in understanding*. It probably misunderstood the Hebrew original, which may be rendered *And leaders in their penetration*. Such trusted leaders as Zerubbabel and Nehemiah may be meant.

Wise were their words: or perhaps *Clever of speech; in their instruction*, i.e. in their scribal instruction. The reference, doubtless, is to the work of the scribes as instructors.

At the end of v. 4 a line has been omitted by the Greek text. This may be rendered *And speakers of wise sayings in their tradition*. *Wise sayings*: i.e. proverbs. The wisdom-teachers are referred to as a class of men who express their wisdom in proverbial form orally.

5. *Such as sought out musical tunes*: or *who sought out music according to rule*. Another suggested rendering is *Perfecters of poetry according to rule*. The reference appears to be to the composition of psalms set to traditional melody. The guilds of Temple-singers would be thought of primarily in this connexion.

And set forth verses in writing: the Hebrew may be rendered *The authors of proverbs in books*, i.e. collections of proverbs under the name of Solomon and others.

6. *Rich men furnished with ability, &c.*: perhaps Job and the Patriarchs are in the writer's mind.

8. *There be of them, that have left a name behind them*: again referred to in vv. 10 ff.

9. *And some there be, which have no memorial*: godless kings, especially those of the northern kingdom, are probably referred to. These are passed over in silence by Ben Sira, as also by the Chronicler.

10. *But these, &c.*: the reference is to the enumeration that follows.

Whose righteous deeds have not been forgotten: perhaps the meaning would be better rendered *And their good fortune shall not come to an end*, i.e. it lives on in the happy and prosperous lives of their descendants.

11. *With their seed, &c.*: cf. Job 21$^{8, 16}$. *their children are within the covenants*: the Hebrew text has *and their inheritance to their children's children*. This line should be supplied to v. 11, and the clause *their children are within the covenants* should be supplied to v. 12a.

Covenant in Ben Sira's phraseology always implies a gracious promise from God. The covenants in the writer's mind included those with Noah and Abraham and possibly those with Phineas, Aaron, and David; cf. 45^{15}.

12. *Their seed, &c.*: substitute for this clause *Their children are within the covenants*, as the first line of v. 12.

13. *Their seed*: Hebrew and Syriac read *Their memory*, rightly. Cf. 39^9.

And their glory: perhaps we should substitute *And their righteousness*.

15 = 39^{10}.

(5) THE BOOK OF WISDOM

Perhaps the most attractive book in the Apocrypha is the Book of Wisdom—one of the latest and most influential products of the Wisdom literature of the Jews. The book falls naturally into three sections: (*a*) chs. 1–6^8; (*b*) 6^9–11^1; (*c*) 11^2–19.

The first section is in form addressed to the rulers of the earth (cf. 1^1, 3^8, 6$^{1-2}$) and draws out a contrast between the destinies of the righteous and of the ungodly who oppress them. The ungodly who are denounced deny immortality, indulge the lusts of the flesh, and scoff at the righteous, who in their turn denounce them (2$^{1-10}$).

A striking feature of this part of the book is the picture given of the impiety and defiance of the ungodly, their gruesome fate after death. The religious teaching also of this section is important. 'The writer enunciates the doctrine of immortality immediately after death, denies that suffering presupposes sin, refuses to admit that early death is necessarily a calamity, or that childlessness is a *mark of divine displeasure.*' [1]

This teaching is largely revolutionary in character.

The second section introduces Wisdom as the speaker (6[9-25]). She confers immortality (6[20-21]); on the other hand, sin brings death, since 'by the envy of the devil death entered into the world' (6[24]). In chs. 7–9[17] Solomon is introduced and delivers a speech, declaring that his life is guided solely by Wisdom and closing with a prayer. The conception of Wisdom in this part of the book is very high. She is described (7[25]) as 'a breath of the power of God, and a clear effluence of the glory of the Almighty', an all-pervading power permeating creation and inspiring not only Solomon but all the great men of old (10[15ff.] and 11[1]).

The third part is different in character. From 11[2] to the end of the book we have an historical survey of Israel's deliverance from Egypt, combined with fervent denunciations of idolatry (see chs. 13–15). After the digression on idolatry the writer once more turns to the Egyptians, and the rest of the book is devoted to contrasting the lot of Egypt and of Israel.

The fundamental principle worked out and illustrated by the writer of this section of the book is the law of measure for measure, cf. 11[16]: 'That they might learn, that by what things a man sinneth, by these he is punished.' The application is pushed so far as to maintain 'that the very thing which proved an instrument of vengeance to the Egyptians became a means of safety to Israel' (cf. 11[5]: 'For by what things their foes were punished, by these they in their need were benefited'). The water in which the Israelitish children were to be drowned was turned to blood for the Egyptians, but flowed from the rock to quench the thirst of the children of Israel in the wilderness (11[4-7]). It seems clear that chs. 11–19 have practically nothing in common with the earlier part of the book. The style of writing, too, is different.

The question of the unity of the book has been much discussed. Many scholars regard it as composite, though some argue for the unity. Eichhorn says, justly, 'The first part is appropriate and

---

[1] Charles, *Apocrypha*, vol. i, p. 518.

concise; the second (or rather last part) inappropriate, diffuse, exaggerated, and bombastic'.[1]

A very attractive hypothesis is that which regards the last part as consisting of the Hellenistic passover Haggada. 'The original Wisdom of Solomon and the Passover Haggada-fragment were probably joined together and then treated as one book' (Kohler). It should be explained that at the home festival which the Jews celebrate for Passover, part of the religious ceremonial consists in the recitation of a long narrative recounting the goodness of God as exhibited in the deliverance of the Israelites from Egypt. In the currently accepted form it is recited in Hebrew and Aramaic. No doubt the Hellenistic Jews had a corresponding form written in Hellenistic Greek, and it is conjectured that a fragment of this has been preserved as stated above in the last part of our present Book of Wisdom. If this is correct we have an extremely interesting survival in these chapters.

The relation of the book to the Old and New Testament is interesting. The first section seems to have in mind Eccles. 7^{15}: 'There is a righteous man that perisheth in his righteousness, and there is a wicked man that prolongeth his life in his evil-doing.' Against this the first section of Wisdom is directed: cf. also the following passages: Wisdom 2^1 and Eccles. 2^{23}; Wisdom 2^2 and Eccles. 3^{19}; Wisdom 2^4 and Eccles. 1^{11}, 2^{16}, 9^5; Wisdom 2^{6-10} and Eccles. 9^{7-9}.

The book probably emanated from Alexandria. Its doctrine of immortality is Alexandrine. It may have been written in Alexandria in the first century B.C., perhaps during its first half. The Jewish scholar, Grätz, finds allusions to the apotheosis of Caligula, A.D. 38–40, but, as Kohler rightly points out, the deification of the Ptolemies goes back to an early period, and he goes on to remark: 'The character of the book as regards the creative Wisdom, Word and Spirit indicates a stage prior to the Philonic system.' It may therefore safely be dated before the time of Philo, i.e. before 40 B.C. The book appears to have been known to St. Paul and the author of the Epistle to the Hebrews. Compare Heb. 1^3, 4^2 with Wisdom $7^{22, 26}$.

NOTES ON SELECTED PASSAGES

(a) WISDOM 1^{1-11}: *True religion and apostasy and their several rewards.*

1. *judges of the earth*: the writer addresses the judges of the earth in the assumed character of King Solomon. Perhaps, however, by

[1] Cf. Eichhorn, *Einleitung in die apokryphischen Schriften des Alten Testaments* (Leipzig, 1795), p. 89.

judges of the earth rulers of the Jewish community in Alexandria are meant, though non-Jewish Egyptian officials may be included. He mainly has in mind apostate Jews who have climbed to positions of dignity and power in the state. Tiberius Alexander, nephew of Philo, was a case in point.

4. Purity of heart and life lead to the knowledge of God. On the other hand, evil sets up a barrier.

5. *a holy spirit of discipline*: the idea of discipline also includes instruction.

will be put to confusion, &c.: the Greek word so rendered is difficult. It may mean scared away.

6. *wisdom is a spirit that loveth man*: it is difficult to fit this line with the context. Grimm explains: 'Wisdom is a spirit that loves mankind, and for that very reason will not leave wickedness unpunished.' But this is not convincing. Perhaps the line is an interpolation based on 7^{22}. It has been suggested that vv. 4, 5 are also interpolated, and if v. 6 is made to follow v. 3 immediately the connexion will be improved.

7. *that which holdeth all things together*: this is a Stoic idea. According to the Stoic dictum the world is permeated by intelligence, as the body by life.

knowledge of every voice: *every human voice* is meant.

8. This all-pervasive power is a guarantee that everything shall be brought to judgement.

11. *refrain your tongue from backbiting*: render rather *blasphemy*; murmuring against God is meant. The word rendered *murmuring* is used in the LXX of the murmuring of the Israelites against God. Cf. Exod. $16^{7, 8, 9}$ (LXX).

(b) WISDOM 9: *Solomon's prayer for wisdom.*

In the following beautiful prayer Solomon prays for the gift of wisdom, pleading his own human weakness and the greatness of his task. It is interesting to compare the prayers that occur in scriptural books. With the following may be compared the fine prayer of Ezra preserved in 2 Esdras $8^{20\text{ff}}$. In 2 Esdras the exordium of the prayer is more elaborate.

1–2. *by thy word; And by thy wisdom*: word and wisdom are here synonymous. The writer probably regards wisdom as God's agent in creation. Later, the Logos, or Word, fulfilled this role.

that he should have dominion, &c.: cf. Ps. 8^6.

3. *rule the world in holiness and righteousness*: the divine purpose in creation was wholly beneficent. It depended upon man's fulfilment of his part.

4. *her that sitteth by thee on thy throne*: wisdom shares God's throne; no higher function could be assigned to any created being.

5. Cf. 2 Esdras 8²⁴ᶠᶠ·

8. *A copy of the holy tabernacle*: cf. Exod. 25⁹, ⁴⁰. Perhaps the writer is thinking of this passage, though the Greek conception of pre-existent ideas or heavenly archetypes may not be excluded. Thus, in later Jewish theology there was a heavenly and an earthly Jerusalem. Cf. Gal. 4²⁵⁻⁶; 2 Esdras 10²³ᶠᶠ·, especially ²⁷.

9. *And was present when thou wast making the world*: wisdom is represented as a spectator at the creation. Cf. Prov. 8³⁰.

11. *guard me in her glory*: the reading is difficult. Perhaps what is meant is the guiding power of wisdom, her glory being the light she sheds over the path of her followers.

14. Unaided human intellectual capacity is entirely inadequate to fathom the divine mind.

15. Greek ideas about the evil of the material may have influenced the writer. He probably did not fully accept these, regarding the body merely as a hindrance to the spirit, not necessarily as in itself inherently evil. Cf. the similar language of St. Paul in 2 Cor. 5¹⁻¹⁰. With the present passage cf. Plato; *Phaedo* 81c.

full of cares: R.V. margin *museth upon many things*.

16. Under earthly conditions men can only with difficulty divine the most obvious things. For the thought cf. 2 Esdras 5⁴⁰.

17. Note the equivalence of wisdom and holy spirit.

(c) WISDOM 18⁵⁻¹⁹: *The evil counsel taken by the Egyptians against Israel results in their punishment.*

XVIII. 5. The main idea of the verse is that for every single child of the Hebrews cast into the Nile a multitude of Egyptians was drowned. Perhaps we should read *myriad* for *multitude*. This is an illustration of the writer's favourite principle of 'measure for measure'.

6. *our fathers*: i.e. the patriarchs. As prophets they knew before-hand what was to befall their descendants. The *Apocalypse of Abraham*, a Jewish work of the second century A.D., works out the idea that Abraham in trance sees the future destinies of his descendants.

8. *By the same means*: i.e. the slaying of the first-born sons. The Israelites were warned by this visitation on the Egyptians that they should protect themselves and their households by smearing the blood on the lintels of their houses.

9. *Offered sacrifice in secret*: i.e. the Passover sacrifice, of which they partook in their own homes.

That they would partake alike in the same good things and the same perils: it is better to translate *that the saints* (i.e. the Israelites) *would partake alike in the same blessings and perils*.

The fathers already leading the sacred songs of praise: read with R.V. margin *already leading the fathers' songs of praise*, i.e. singing the psalms appropriate to the Passover. The writer attributes the later custom to the Israelites at the Exodus.

12. *at a single stroke their nobler offspring*: i.e. the slaying of the first-born.

13. *God's son*: cf. Exod. 4²²; Hos. 11¹.

14–19. Notice the extraordinary vividness of the description. A striking feature is the strong personification of God's word in v. 15. Many scholars hold that the divine Word or Logos is here hypostasized, as in Philo and St. John. Others, however, prefer to regard it as in line with O.T. usage, without any hypostasis. Cf. Hos. 6⁵; Jer. 23²⁹; Ps. 147²⁹. But in any case the personification here is much more intense. It has been suggested that the writer may have had in mind a destroying angel. Cf. 1 Chron. 21¹⁶.

16. *Bearing as a sharp sword*: cf. 1 Chron. 21¹⁶ just cited.

unfeigned: i.e. it was no empty threat.

while it touched the heaven it trode upon the earth: the colossal proportions of the divine Word are thus poetically described. It reminds one of the picture of primeval man, the archetypal man.

17. *apparitions in dreams terribly troubled them*: the better reading is *in terrible dreams troubled them*. These ghostly apparitions added a further note of horror to their situation.

19. Dreams as a means of revealing to those who were condemned the cause of their punishment may be compared with the dream of Nebuchadnezzar in Dan. 2.

ADDITIONAL NOTE I

The affinities of the Wisdom Literature with the literature of the world outside Israel

The subject is well discussed in a little book by the late Hugo Gressmann, *Israels Spruchweisheit im Zusammenhang der Welt-literatur* (Berlin, 1925). The author first sketches the development of the early stages of wisdom in Israel, especially in connexion with Solomon, and in this section of the book there is an interesting discussion of Ps. 19 (first part), which is regarded as a hymn celebrating the activities of the sun-god, which has been worked over by an editor. The second section (pp. 27–32) is devoted to the consideration of the proverbial poetry of Israel in the later period of the monarchy (Hezekiah). Here Gressmann points out that some of the lost early wisdom of Israel can be partly recovered from the Prophets and Psalmists, where material may sometimes be found which illustrates the proverbial poetry. An example is detected in Isa. 10¹⁵ (the axe asserting itself against him who wields it). This illustrates a well-developed type of fable, in which the motif is the rebellion of one or more subordinate parts against the rest. A famous example is St. Paul's (1 Cor. 12¹⁴ff.) use of the idea of the body and the members. The same illustration is employed by Livy, who ascribes it to Menenius Agrippa, but the Apostle certainly derived it from Jewish sources.

ADDITIONAL NOTE II
The LXX and Alexandrine Judaism

Alexandria was the chief centre of the intellectual and religious life of the Jews of the Dispersion. Here they came into close contact with Greek civilization in its most intense form. The Jewish population prospered exceedingly in this wealthy city. Many of them rose to positions of influence and wealth. Greek thought profoundly influenced them, and the results of this influence are seen in many ways. We have noted above how profound this influence was on the formation of the Book of Wisdom, which probably emanated from Alexandria in the earlier part of the first century B.C.

Alexandria has been well described as the 'scene of intense intellectual activity. Attracted by the munificence of the Ptolemies and by the opportunities offered by its great library, many of the most famous Greek philosophers and rhetoricians of the age found their home in the Egyptian capital. Public lectures, open discussions, and voluminous literature were only a few of the many forms in which this intellectual life was expressed. Hence it was in Alexandria that Hebrew and Greek thought met on the highest plane.'[1]

One of the most significant productions of Alexandrine Judaism is the translation of the Hebrew scriptures into Greek. This made an enormous impression on the Jews of the Dispersion, and the origin of the translation has been invested with legend. Thus Josephus cites the tradition that the translation was completed in seventy-two days by seventy-two scholars sent from Jerusalem by Eleazar the High Priest at the request of Ptolemy Philadelphus. The actual fact is that the translation was not the work of Palestinian but Alexandrine Jews, and the dialect of Greek used in it is that of the Egyptian Koiné. It is not the work of a single group but of many different hands working at different times. The quality of the translation is not uniform. The historical fact underlying the tradition seems to be that it was begun in the reign of Ptolemy Philadelphus, who may have encouraged his Jewish subjects in the undertaking (285–247). No doubt the first part of

[1] C. F. Kent, op. cit., p. 260.

the scriptures to be translated was the Law of Moses, i.e. the Pentateuch. Very soon after this was completed the historical writings, Samuel to Kings, may have been added. The remaining books were probably translated between 250 and 150 B.C. At any rate, the grandson of Ben Sira in the Prologue to his Greek translation of his grandfather's book (Ecclesiasticus), writing about

The harbour at Alexandria to-day

132 B.C., implies that he already knew a Greek translation of the Law, the Prophets and the other writings.

The primary object of the translation was to meet the needs of the Greek-speaking Jews, most of whom knew no Hebrew at all; another object may have been to make the Hebrew Bible accessible to the Greek-speaking world generally, and in this way to commend the Hebrew scriptures and to refute pagan calumnies. The best means to do so was to make a Greek version available for the Greek-speaking world. The needs of proselytes may also have been regarded in the production of the translation.

In time the LXX acquired a new importance, and won for itself a position of supreme influence. It became, with the N.T., the

Bible of the Christian Church. In the course of the second and third centuries A.D. a reaction against the LXX arose in Jewish circles. The divergence between its text and that of the official Hebrew O.T. became more and more marked, and a demand arose among the Jews for a more faithful version. Hence arose various revisions of the LXX text (those of Aquila, Symmachus and Theodotion being the most important).

Perhaps the influence of Greek thought on Judaism may be seen most clearly in such a work as the Wisdom of Solomon, which has already been considered briefly above. It is not difficult to detect the apologetic purpose of this remarkable writing. The author evidently desires to commend Israel's faith to the Greek world by showing its substantial agreement with the noblest doctrines of Greek philosophy, and further, to provide the Jews who lived in the Greek-speaking world and who wished to retain the practice of their religion and at the same time to recognize the importance of Greek ideas, with the means of combining these two points of view in their theology and worship. A remarkable feature, as we have already seen, is the tendency to personify the figure of wisdom. This had already taken place under the influence of Greek thought in the book of Proverbs, chs. 8–9, and it is still further developed in the book of Wisdom and later in the works of Philo.

It is possible, however, to press the idea of personification too far, and possibly the author did not wish to regard wisdom as an hypostasis. It was simply an attribute of God shared by man. The theology of the book is remarkable in two ways: (1) It contains the earliest reference in Jewish religion to a personal devil who is identified with the serpent (2^{24}, *By the envy of the devil death entered into the world*). (2) It teaches the doctrine of immortality. Cf. 3^1. Contrast the resurrection doctrine of Dan. 12.

The book also extols the four cardinal virtues of Greek ethics—moderation, good sense, justice and courage.

The book may be regarded as an early synthesis of all that is best in Greek and Hebrew thought.

E. SOME PSALMS OF THE GREEK PERIOD

THE Psalter grew up by a process which involved several collections. It is important at the outset to distinguish between the date when any particular collection of psalms was made and the actual date of composition of the individual Psalms. These may vary considerably.

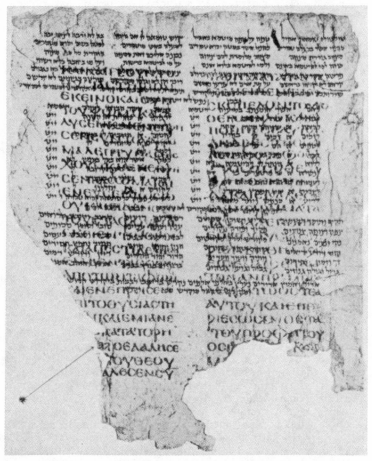

A page from a sixth-century MS. of Aquila's translation of the O.T. from Hebrew into Greek. (The MS. is a palimpsest, a work in Hebrew having been written over the Greek)

The older criticism associated with the name of Professor Cheyne regarded the entire Psalter as the creation of the Jewish Church and as therefore post-exilic. 'The Psalter is post-exilic because of its developed religion. It is the lyric and liturgical reflection of the prophetical teaching which could only arise when that teaching had been absorbed by an entire community. The monotheism that culminates in the doctrine of the Babylonian Isaiah is the assumption or starting-point of the Psalter. The Psalmists depend upon the prophets and succeed them.' The prophets, when they delivered their message, usually at first were isolated individuals. It is out of the question to regard them as the mouthpiece of the Jewish church, and the existence of a number of sacred song-writers such as is presupposed in the Psalter was then impossible. This sharp distinction has, however, been considerably modified by more recent criticism. It is recognized that there are large elements in the Psalter which go back to the pre-exilic period. Their liturgical character as an integral part of the older cultus is emphasized. The work of Mowinckel has been epoch-making in this connexion. It is clear that a large element must be allowed for which consists of old material. But the old material has been profoundly modified and reshaped. In many cases the transformation practically produced a new composition. The process of revision and reshaping must have been drastic. There is no reason to doubt that psalms were sung in liturgical worship before the exile, doubtless in the old-established sanctuaries such as Dan as well as in the Temple at Jerusalem. An interesting indication of such a use occurs in Ps. 89[12] (*The north and the south, thou hast created them: Tabor and Hermon rejoice in thy name*). Here it is obvious that the psalmist is speaking as one who is situated in a country the northern and southern points of which are Hermon and Tabor. This would suit the old sanctuary of Dan, and we may plausibly regard the psalm as based upon a pre-exilic one. An example will illustrate the kind of process that went on. Psalm 19 in its present form consists of two parts, probably originally independent psalms. The first part praises natural light in connexion with the sun (vv. 1–6); the second part is in praise of the Law, the light of revelation (vv. 7–14); this combination, viz. thanksgiving for natural and spiritual light, is a feature of the early Jewish synagogue liturgy.[1] In its oldest form the benediction over light in the synagogue prayer-book may go back as far as the

---

[1] Cf. Singer's Prayer-book, Hebrew and English, pp. 37 ff.

Persian period, and the combination of the two parts of the psalm may have been inspired by the same liturgical *motif*. But the first part of the psalm may in substance be older still. As Gressmann [1] has pointed out, the first six verses may be an old poem or hymn celebrating the activities of the sun-god which has been worked over by a later editor. The worship of the sun was carried on widely; it even found scope in the Temple of Jerusalem in the period before the exile. This illustration illuminates the way in which the oldest material could be reshaped and live on.

That the psalms were brought together in a collection in the post-exilic period may be confidently assumed. The earliest of these collections probably took place in the time of Nehemiah, under the impetus given at that time to the reorganization of the Temple worship. This early collection is mainly identical with the first book of our present Psalter. Further revision and collection of psalms probably took place in the time of Ezra, whose date may be fixed probably some time after 400 B.C. It is not improbable that another collection of psalms was made about 300 B.C., while a final redaction and enlarged collection was made in the Maccabean period. How far new psalm compositions came into existence during the Greek period it is hard to say. We may assume that a good many psalms included in our present Psalter are based on old material which has been revised, while it is practically certain that some at least were actually composed, e.g. Ps. 119.

Whatever may be the date of the *terminus a quo* for the formation of the earliest of the Psalm collections (psalms forming the Davidic collection are contained in Ps. 3–41 and 51–72), the *terminus ad quem* for the formation of the complete collection is determined by the Prologue of the grandson of Ben Sira (132 B.C.). That the collection was substantially complete and regarded as sacred in the Maccabean period may be inferred from the fact that the only direct quotation from the Bible that occurs in 1 Macc. (written *c.* 100 B.C.) is from Ps. 79$^{2-3}$, which is there cited as Holy Scripture (1 Macc. 7$^{16f.}$).

That poems composed in the Maccabean period have been admitted into the Psalter is practically certain. Theodore of Mopsuestia recognized thirteen psalms as such, viz. 44, 47, 55, 60, 62, 69, 74, 79, 80, 83, 108, 109, 144. The most certain of these are 44, 74, 79 and 83. Not improbably the Hallel group (113–118)

---

[1] H. Gressmann: *Israels Spruchweisheit im Zusammenhang der Welt-literatur* (Berlin, 1925).

was formed about the time of the re-dedication of the Temple (in 165 B.C.). They are still recited every one of the eight days of the Feast of Hanukkah (Dedication).

According to Jewish tradition, Ps. 30 must belong to the same period (cf. superscription). But the Maccabean psalms must be regarded as comparatively late insertions into a large, earlier collection. The original meaning of the title 'of David' (or 'Davidic') as applied to certain psalms may have become obscure. It may have denoted a collection of psalms, the beginnings of which were formed early in the pre-exilic period (to be sung by a choir which traced its origin to David?).

At the time of the Maccabean struggle many of the psalms which had long been in the Psalter were revised, to make them express more clearly the feelings of the time. This revision is especially noticeable in Ps. 44, 74 and 79. In the case of Ps. 74 and 79, the revision took the form of an extensive retouching throughout the hymn; in the case of Ps. 44 another strophe was added to the hymn. A detailed study of this psalm will prove an instructive example of how psalms were edited and adapted to later use. Verses 1–8 contain a hymn of victory, breathing in every line the exaltation and confidence of a nation whose armies are triumphing. This is illustrated by the phraseology of v. 5 ff.

Through thee we push down our adversaries;
Through thy name we tread them under that rise up against us ...
thou hast saved us from our adversaries, And hast put them to shame
that hate us.

This reflects feeling at a time when Israel's armies were winning battles. As the community had no such armies in the early post-exilic period it is plausible to suppose that a fragment of a pre-exilic triumphal ode has been utilized here by the later editors.

To this pre-exilic poem which forms the first strophe of the psalm another was added of a rather different character. It begins at v. 9:

But now thou hast cast us off, and brought us to dishonour;
And goest not forth with our hosts.
Thou makest us to turn back from the adversary;
And they which hate us spoil for themselves.

It has been suggested that this is a cry of despair after an unsuccessful rebellion and fits the time (c. 350 B.C.) when Bagoses suppressed the attempt of the Jews to rise against their Persian masters. The second strophe of the psalm (vv. 9–16) is all of this character. It is a notable fact that this strophe is separated from the opening one by the musical term *selah*, the technical meaning of which probably was to indicate that an instrumental interlude was to come in between vv. 8 and 9.

The last strophe, consisting of vv. 17–26, reflects a different mood and a different situation. It presupposes not unsuccessful rebellion but religious persecution—persecution, too, endured by a people conscious of having kept the divine law.

> *All this is come upon us; yet have we not forgotten thee,* /
> *Neither have we dealt falsely in thy covenant . . .*
> *Yea, for thy sake are we killed all the day long;*
> *We are counted as sheep for the slaughter.*

Now, religious persecution of this kind was endured only in the Maccabean period, and we may plausibly suppose that this strophe was added to the psalm then. This is the view of Prof. G. A. Barton,[1] and the conclusion is confirmed by the omission of the term *selah* after v. 16. This musical term had by the Maccabean time become obsolete, and its meaning was forgotten. We cannot trace the process of editing quite so clearly in other psalms, but doubtless there are many other instances of re-editing and adaptation.

It is a fair inference that the growth of the Psalter in a collected form derived its impetus from critical moments in the national history, when the national spirit was deeply stirred, or when some deep impression was made upon the nation. The earliest of the collection is, of course, Book 1, which originally consisted of Ps. 3–41 (Ps. 1 and 2 being prefixed at a later time). Perhaps the title under which it went, namely, Psalms of David, originally meant that these psalms were in a special sense the property of the oldest of the Temple Choirs, which claimed as its patron David. We may, perhaps, assume that it was under the impulse of the national feeling created by the work of Nehemiah that this collection was made. Books 2 and 3 were collected later—we may plausibly suppose in the time of Ezra, and under the impulse given by Ezra's work (some time, probably, between 400 and 380 B.C.). This second collection included Ps. 42–83, to which Ps. 84–9 were afterwards added. Minor collections were embodied, such as the 'psalms of Asaph' and the 'psalms of the sons of Korah'. But perhaps the most striking feature of this collection is the substitu-

---

[1] *The Religion of Israel*, p. 199 ff.

tion of *Elohim* for *Jahveh* as the name of God. Now the name *Elohim* expresses a more transcendental conception of God than *Jahveh*, and was therefore favoured by the priestly school to which Ezra belonged. The deliberate substitution in certain psalms in Books 2 and 3 of the Psalter of the name *Elohim* for *Jahveh* points to the influence of the priestly school. This can be clearly seen in the double recension of certain psalms; cf. e.g. Ps. 53 with Ps. 14, and Ps. 70 with Ps. 40$^{13-17}$.

It is probable, as we have seen, that a third collection grew up in the Greek period, after 300 B.C. There are indications that the Temple worship underwent considerable changes about this time. One important matter was the reorganization that took place in connexion with the division of the priests and Levites into twenty-four courses of service. The exact date at which this occurred is uncertain. It is, however, clear that at the time of the Chronicler (? *c.* 250 B.C.) these courses certainly existed. See Ezra 6^{18}; 1 Chron. 9$^{25-7}$, 23^6, 25^8. As Dr. Keet points out,[1] 'the rearrangement of the system which prevailed in the early post-exilic period was necessary, because the priests and Levites had become so numerous that it was found to be impossible for them all to perform their official functions at the same time. Henceforth, each course was to perform its duty at the Temple for a week, and to complete its week's work on the Sabbath.'

This division of the Levites into twenty-four sections necessarily involved the loss of identity of the old Temple Choirs, which were now fused together. As independent choirs they ceased to exist. 'It now became a matter of chance', says Dr. Keet, 'whether the members of a former choir used their own guild-psalter or not.' A further consequence was the disappearance of the old technical musical terminology which is noticeable in Books 4 and 5 of our present Psalter. Lastly, a great national upheaval took place in the Maccabean period (169 B.C. and following years). We may certainly assume that some psalms were composed under the impression produced by the momentous events of this crisis. It is probable in any case that the third collection of the Psalter was formed during this period. Cheyne has argued that Books 4 and 5 received their present form soon after 142 B.C. This third collection may have been composed originally of Ps. 91–100, 105–7, 111–18, 135–6 and 146–50.

The collection grew. Later there may have been admitted into

[1] *A Liturgical Study of the Psalter*, p. 26 ff.

it separate psalms like Ps. 90, 119 and 137; partly, groups of psalms such as the psalms of degrees (Ps. 120–34), the David psalms (101–4, 108–10, 138–45). Possibly these additions were designed to include in the canonical Psalter all known psalms. The most certain of the Maccabean psalms, as generally recognized, are Ps. 44, 74, 79 and 83. These all occur in Books 2 and 3. To these should be added Ps. 30. Note that the inscription of this psalm fixes it as assigned to the Feast of Dedication or Hanukkah, sometimes called Feast of Lights (cf. John 10[22]). A number of others may also be added; the most certain of these, perhaps, are Ps. 68 and 110. See below notes on select passages. It should be added that, in 1 Macc. 7[17], Ps. 79[2-3] is cited as Holy Scripture (the author of 1 Macc. lived about 100 B.C.).

One useful way that may be taken in approaching the study of the Psalter is to study first of all the clearly defined groups which may in a sense be regarded as a unit, and which may be found in the last part of the Psalter. There is first of all the Hallel. The word Hallel is a technical Hebrew liturgical term, applied to certain psalms and psalm pieces which have as their characteristic key-note the expression Hallelujah, i.e. 'praise ye Jah'. It is specifically applied to one group of psalms, namely Ps. 113–18, which are regarded as a unit in the synagogue liturgy. This group of psalms seems to have been compiled for liturgical purposes at a comparatively late date. It was probably formed in Maccabean times for recitation on the Feast of Hanukkah (Dedication), on the eight days of which it is still chanted in the synagogue.

Psalm 118[4-24] seems to presuppose the Syrian war and recovery of and entrance into the Temple. At the same time the collection embodies other elements. Thus Ps. 118[25-9] seems to be an old song of praise for the Feast of Tabernacles. With this agrees the fact that, according to an old tradition preserved in the Jerusalem Talmud (Sukka, 4[5]), the Hallel was recited on 'eighteen days and one night of the year—the eight days of Tabernacles; the eight of Hanukkah; Pentecost (one day); and the first day of Passover with its (preceding) night'. It is noticeable that Tabernacles and Hanukkah are placed first in this list; and it should be remembered that the latter feast seems originally to have been regarded as a sort of extension or repetition of the former (cf. 2 Macc. 1[9]); Cheyne (*Origin of the Psalter*, p. 33, note n) remarks: 'That the recitation of the Hallel on these occasions [Dedication and Tabernacles] goes back to Simon can hardly be doubted.' A curious indication of its liturgical use may perhaps be seen in the fact that the Midrash on the Psalms counts only *five* psalms in the Hallel, Ps. 115 not being regarded. The LXX and many Hebrew manuscripts treat the latter psalm as part of Ps. 114. The reason assigned in one of the smaller Midrashim is as follows: 'The Torah consists of five-fifths; the Psalter of five-fifths; and the Hallel of five-fifths.'

As regards the elements which compose the group, Ps. 113–14 may be comparatively early, and embodied later in the Hallel; Ps. 117 may be regarded as a liturgical introduction to 118. Features which suggest a Maccabean background may be seen in Ps. 116^{15}, which speaks of the death of the Chasidim. In Ps. 118^{27} the phrase 'he hath given us light' may be an allusion to the Feast of Lights. Note also the threefold division of Israel into Israel, house of Aaron, ye that fear Jahveh (115$^{9\text{-}13}$, 118$^{2\text{-}4}$).

Another Maccabean psalm which will be considered below is Ps. 110, which, as we shall see, contains an acrostic on the name Simon and was probably composed in its present form in honour of Simon Maccabaeus. It seems, therefore, highly probable that the final redaction of the canonical Psalter took place in the Maccabean epoch; and if Ps. 110 was composed in its present form in honour of Simon Maccabaeus, this would bring down the date of the final redaction to at least *c.* 142 B.C. But though the Maccabean redaction was important, and though the impulse given to the national life and national feeling was reflected in the production of new psalm compositions and a revision of the older collections, the importance of the Maccabean contribution must not be unduly magnified. Before the Maccabean period had begun there is explicit evidence that a Psalter in its general structure and content similar to the canonical Psalter was already in existence. For Ben Sira, Ecclus. 47$^{8\text{-}10}$, says, referring to David:

> In every work of his he gave thanks to the Holy One Most High
>   with words of glory;
> With his whole heart he sang praise,
> And loved him that made him.
> Also he set singers before the altar,
> And to make sweet melody by their music
> He gave comeliness to the feasts,
> And set in order the seasons to perfection,
> While they praised his holy name,
> And the sanctuary sounded from early morning.

Another well-defined group is formed by the so-called psalms of degrees, 120–34, which were sung by the pilgrims on their journey to Jerusalem and may more appropriately bear the title Pilgrims' Psalter. Notice also the Hallelujah Psalms, 146–50, which are very similar in character to the Hallel. Both may have been arranged by Simon Maccabaeus.

SELECT PASSAGES FROM THE PSALTER

We may conclude this section by referring in greater detail to a few outstanding psalms; and for this purpose the following may be selected:

Psalms 1–2, 8, 68, 110 and 119. To these may perhaps be added Ps. 45 and 72.

PSALMS 1 and 2.

It is well known that in several manuscripts of Acts 13[33], Ps. 2[7] is referred to as cited in the first psalm. The real explanation of this appears to be that originally Ps. 1 was regarded as the preface to the entire collection and was not reckoned as a separate psalm. On this assumption Ps. 2 becomes the first psalm.

Psalm 1 is an interesting example of a hymn belonging to the Wisdom school. Its key-note is based on the doctrine, so dear to the Wisdom school, that piety is rewarded and impiety punished in this world. It opens with a blessing on the pious (vv. 1–3). First of all he is described according to his conduct—he holds aloof from associating with 'the Scorner'. As Gunkel remarks, Judaism was threatened with constant danger through its close contact with the heathen world, and by Apostate Jews from within; hence the constant emphasis on the separation of the pious.

1. *the scornful*: this is a technical term in the Wisdom literature. It occurs constantly in Proverbs, cf. e.g. Prov. 1[22], 3[34], &c.

2. *His delight is in the law of the LORD, &c.*: cf. Ecclus. 39[1]. '*But he that giveth his mind to the law of the Most High and meditates thereon, will seek out the wisdom of all the Ancients, and be occupied in prophecies.*' Here *the law* is interpreted in its wider sense, to include later developments. Even so, the law of Moses, i.e. the Pentateuch, is primarily thought of. Note the reminiscence of the psalmist's language in Jos. 1[8].

3. Cf. Jer. 17[8], of which this may be an echo.

4–5. The contrasted fate of the wicked. *Like the chaff, &c.*: threshing-floors were placed in high positions where the wind would blow away the chaff. 'The winnower beats out the wheat or barley with a stick and then throws it up in the air; the grain and the crushed straw fall in heaps, but the chaff is blown away' (Cheyne). The winnower, it is implied, is God, who by successive judgements winnows out the corn. Cf. Matt. 3¹² and Jer. 17⁶.

in the judgement: not the judgement of the last day, but the continuous judgement that is brought about by divine action in the present life. Cf. Eccles. 12¹⁴.

6. *knoweth*: i.e. notes with interest, regards. Cf. Ps. 31⁷, 37¹⁸.

the way of the wicked: *way* here is a term describing the outward circumstances of a man's lot (Cheyne): cf. 27¹¹, 37⁵.

perish: perhaps, as Hupfeld suggests, the idea rather is that of going astray, losing one's way; cf. Job 6¹⁸. The caravans go up into the desert and lose their way. Combined with the other sense = perish.

The psalm is obviously a late composition. This is apparent from its tone of reflection and its dependence on Jer. 17⁵ᶠᶠ.. Notice also its preoccupation with the study of the Law and the way in which it describes this in terms of the Wisdom school. The sharp distinction between righteous and wicked which divides Judaism into two camps suggests the strong party divisions of the Maccabean period.

Psalm 2.

This psalm easily divides into four nearly equal strophes. The situation presupposed is that of a rebellion of subject kings against the Jewish king (vv. 1–3): God in heaven laughs their efforts to scorn (vv. 4–6): then the King is introduced, speaking in his own person and quoting a divine decree, establishing his world-wide rule (vv. 7–9): the final strophe warns the subject kings against the folly of setting themselves in opposition to the divine ordinance.

The psalm belongs, as Gunkel points out, to the class of royal psalms, a group which includes not only this psalm but also Ps. 18, 20, 21, 45, 72, 101, 110, 132, 144¹⁻¹¹. All these psalms are distinguished by a common characteristic. They speak of a king. How far these psalms refer to actual reigning Israelitish kings it is difficult to determine. Some of them at least probably refer to the Messianic king, i.e. the ideal king, who was expected to be raised up from the ancient race of David.

Some of these psalms appear to celebrate the accession of the monarch to the throne. This is apparently the case with our present psalm. For Jahveh is represented as saying: 'Thou art my son; *this day* have I begotten thee' (v. 7).

1–3. A widespread commotion of the peoples is referred to. The phrase *the kings of the earth* has a wide reference and cannot be supposed to refer merely to the neighbouring princes. Note that a

AN EASTERN THRESHING-FLOOR

rebellion is described—the nations of the earth are supposed to have been already previously subjected to the Jewish king.

4. *shall laugh*: cf. 37¹³, 59⁹.

5. *Then*: i.e. at the critical moment.

6. *Yet I have set my king upon my holy hill of Zion*: perhaps we should read *But I myself have been appointed ruler as his king upon Zion, his holy hill*. There is some support for this in the LXX. Thus construed, the verse contains the words of the king himself. If the ordinary text is kept the speaker would be Jahveh, who asserts that he has established his king on Zion.

7–9. Here it is clear that the king is himself the speaker.

I will tell of the decree . . . the LORD: most scholars agree that the Lord, i.e. Jahveh, belongs to the first line. A more drastic emendation would make the whole verse run *He spake to me: I gather thee to my bosom* (I have this day begotten thee)—so Gunkel.

This day: probably not the day of the king's birth, but of his enthronement.

10–12. The poet speaks. He advises them to submit. Submission may avert destruction.

10. *Be instructed*: let yourselves be admonished.

11. *Serve Jahveh*: political submission is meant, i.e. submission to Jahveh in the person of his representative. For a similar use of the verb *serve* cf. Ps. 72¹¹; 18⁴⁴. The same verb, however, often connotes service in a religious sense, i.e. worship. This meaning may be present here.

rejoice with trembling: the idea apparently is of joy tempered with awe—a frame of mind which befits Jahveh's subjects. Possibly, however, the text is not in order. With the difficult clause that follows *Kiss the son* it may be reconstructed thus: *And trembling kiss his feet, lest he be angry, &c.*: so Gunkel.

12. *Kiss the son*: kissing was a mark of homage: cf. 1 Sam. 10¹. In a religious sense, 1 Kings 19⁸; Hos. 13² (kiss the calves). The rendering *Kiss the son* is, however, extremely doubtful. The word here and in the Hebrew text (*bar*) is Aramaic, and occurs again in Hebrew in this sense only in Prov. 31². Why should such an unusual word be chosen here? It is noticeable that no ancient version except the Syriac renders *Kiss the son*. Note the variants in R.V. margin. An alternative rendering of the text which may be accepted as possible is *worship purely* (*adorate, pure*), i.e. let your loyalty be unsullied.

ye perish in the way: Cheyne renders *And ye go to ruin*. Hupfeld, *And ye go astray as to the way*. The idea of the treacherous path is implicit here as in 1⁶. The image of the way denotes fate, or destiny.

The most various views have been held regarding the date and occasion of this psalm. Those who try to find some historical background are involved in considerable difficulty. Duhm assumes some reference to a Maccabean prince, e.g. Aristobulus I. Others suggest Alexander Jannaeus. Some even have thought of Solomon's reign. All these attempts to fix an historical background fail, and this suggests that the idealistic element in the psalm is fundamental. The interpretation which regards the king as a purely Messianic figure is attested by the Targum, and in the N.T. (cf. Acts 4²⁸ᶠᶠ·, 13³³; Heb. 1⁵, 5⁵; Rev. 2²⁷, 19¹⁵). It is noticeable that the psalm is already cited in the Psalms of Solomon, 17²³ᶠᶠ. It probably was added to the collection at a late date, but not at the same date as the first psalm. The two are entirely different in character. It seems to be a late reaffirmation of the orthodox Messianic belief in the coming of the son of David, who is pictured poetically as fulfilling in an ideal manner the ancient promise of a world-wide empire, to be conferred by God upon the Israelitish king and confirmed by him again after a rebellion of subject kings.

PSALM 8.

This psalm may be described as a hymn of creation, as summed up in man, the crown and glory of creation. 'The psalm', says Cheyne, 'is virtually a prophecy of the glorification of the race'; cf. 2 Pet. 1⁴. There is an element working in humanity which overcomes all rival forces.

1. *How excellent is thy name in all the earth*: Gunkel divides differently. He renders:

Jahveh, our Lord, how majestic is thy name.
Upon the earth is thy majesty, thy glory on the heavens.

The sentence rendered in R.V. *Who hast set thy glory upon the heavens* is textually very doubtful. For the ascription with which the poem begins cf. Ps. 65².

2. *Out of the mouth of babes and sucklings*: here again the text seems to be corrupt. The received text is difficult to interpret. Cheyne explains *children* and *sucklings* as equivalent to poor unbelievers: cf. Matt. 11²⁵. Praises proceeding from their mouths constitute Israel's stronghold; such poor words as these are powerful enough to still the fiercest enemy. This seems rather strained and hardly suits the tone of the rest of the psalm. Gunkel, following others, renders the third line *Out of the mouth of children thou correctest the overweening, to put the enemy and the avenger to shame.*

the enemy and the avenger: i.e. the revengeful enemy. *Children* in the previous line is a descriptive term of those who are weak and apparently of no account.

3–8 form a little poem of creation.

3. *When I consider, &c.*: the contemplation of the heavens makes the psalmist wonder why God cares so much for man. Notice it is the

starlit sky of which the poet evidently thinks, so much more sug
gestive of vastness and infinitude than the sky by day.

4. *What is man . . . that thou visitest him?* 'Visitest', i.e. with Thy
providence, showest him Thy providential care. The verb *visit* is
used in the Hebrew Bible either in a favourable or in an unfavourable
sense. In the latter case it means 'to punish'.

5–6 describe the nature with which man is endowed and the
sovereignty over the world with which he is invested.

thou hast made him but little lower than god: lit. *Thou makest him to
lack little away from being God.* The allusion here is to the mental and
spiritual endowments of man which raise him above the brute
creation.

crownest him with glory and honour: i.e. as of a king.

6. *Thou madest him to have dominion, &c.*: cf. Gen. $1^{26, 28}$. Cheyne
renders *Thou makest him scarce to be less than God*: cf. Gen. 1^{27}. Gunkel
renders *a god.* Cheyne objects to the rendering *than God* that in the
Psalter God is Jahveh, who is directly addressed in this very clause.
The other rendering *than angels* perhaps limits the term too much.
This rendering, however, has the authority of the LXX.

7. *All sheep and oxen*: lit. sheep and oxen—all of them. Note the
emphasis. *Oxen*, i.e. domestic animals: beasts of the field: wild animals.

The psalm clearly depends on Gen. 1, i.e. the Priestly narrative
of creation, and presumably can have been composed in its present
form only after the publication of the P-sections of the Pentateuch,
i.e. after 400 B.C. It may have taken the place of an earlier composition which perhaps dealt with the creation theme in too
mythological a form, just as Gen. 1 has taken the place of an
earlier and cruder creation story. Note also that the psalm is
parodied in Job $7^{17ff.}$, the Job passage being, presumably, later
than the psalm: cf. also the reminiscence of the same language in
Ps. 144^3.

PSALM 19.

This psalm is clearly composite. It falls into two distinct parts;
vv. 1–6 (= Heb. 2–7) and vv. 7–14 (= Heb. 8–15).

The first part forms another hymn of creation. It celebrates the
creation of natural light, especially as diffused from the sun. The
second part is a hymn of praise for the spiritual light which shines
forth from the Law (Torah). The two parts, though originally
distinct and belonging to different compositions, afford a fine
contrast. For a somewhat similar conjunction compare the two
benedictions which appear in the Jewish Prayer Book (Singer,
pp. 37–40); the first of these in its oldest form was the benediction of

a natural light; the second of them (beginning with the words 'with overbounding love') praises God for Israel's spiritual privileges. It seems natural to suppose that this psalm must have assumed its present form under the influence of the liturgy of the synagogue.

The view just stated does not preclude the possibility—or rather the strong probability—that the first part of the psalm contains some very old mythological material, belonging originally to a hymn celebrating the sun-god. This view has been emphasized both by Gressmann and Gunkel. The old material has been worked over by later editors and transformed.

1. *declare the glory of God*: the divine name here used is *El*, a descriptive name, which is used of God in his wider relations outside Israel. The wonders of the heavens much interested the authors of *Job*; cf. Job 37[18].

firmament: in this sense the word is derived from Gen. 1[22ff]. Its use may imply knowledge on the part of our author of P's narrative of creation, but Gunkel will not allow this.

2. *uttereth speech*: Cheyne renders *is a well-spring of speech*. The Hebrew word means 'to bubble forth'; cf. Ps. 78[2]. There it is especially used of speech spoken under the stress of strong emotion, e.g. oracular speech. 'Every day the heavens renew their testimony to God's glory' (Cheyne). Note that the days are commonly regarded in antiquity as quasi-personal existences; cf. Job 3[1-10].

3. This verse is regarded by Cheyne as a gloss.

4. *Their line*: read *their voice*, i.e. the voice either of the heavens or of day and night. The text reading (*their line*) is usually explained to mean *their dominion*.

In them: can hardly refer to the heavens, which can hardly yield a suitable picture. By a slight alteration the text can be made to read *in the sea*. So Gunkel. So the line runs: *In the sea hath he set a pavilion for the sun*. Gunkel regards this verse as introducing a new strophe. He renders the line *For the sun's disk hath there a pavilion in the sea*. Here the poem takes up ancient mythological material. The sun disappears over the western horizon to his home in the sea, which is here represented in accordance with ancient ideas as a tent, not a house.

5. *Which is as a bridegroom coming out of his chamber*: 'A primitive solar myth has died down into a metaphor' (Cheyne).

bridegroom: here as symbol of youthful vigour. The word for 'sun' in Hebrew is masculine. The term used in Hebrew (*Huppa*) is still employed in connexion with the Jewish marriage ceremony, in which it denotes the canopy which is held over the bride and bridegroom during the marriage ceremony. From Joel 2[16] it may be concluded that the Huppa was originally a part of the nuptial chamber curtained off for the bride.

as a strong man: this is part of the ancient myth. The sun was represented as a warrior; compare also the later representation of Mithra. The Greeks also represented Helios as a fast runner.

6. *His going forth is from the end of the Heaven, &c.*: he traverses the entire heavens from end to end before vanishing below the horizon.[1]

Part 2 (vv. 7–14).

This section of the psalm, contained in vv. 7–14, sets forth the blessings imparted by the Divine law. It may be fitly compared with Pss. 1 and 119. Clearly, as Cheyne says, 'the scriptures are now the great source of spiritual life'. It reflects the later development of Jewish piety and is particularly interesting from this point of view. Notice especially the spirit of joyfulness which the sense of possession of the Divine law imparts to the psalmist. Far from being a burden it is the source of sheer joy. Contrast the way in which St. Paul regards the Law (Rom. 7; Gal. 3), which may perhaps be accounted for by the great development of ordinances, which grew up later out of the observance as a means of safeguarding the divine enactments.

7. *The law of the LORD, &c.*: the law here probably has a larger connotation than the Pentateuch; the latter is still primary—but the Scriptures now include the prophetic canon. To the psalmist it is Torah that is the source of spiritual refreshment.

8. *The precepts of the LORD, &c.*: the psalmist takes a positive delight in observing the precepts of Jahveh. Notice that the sense of joy becomes explicit.

enlightening the eyes: a phrase used also to denote the physical refreshment that comes from satisfying the cravings of hunger; cf. 1 Sam. 14[27].

9. *The fear of the LORD*: an O.T. phrase meaning religion, especially 'the religion regulated by the sacred books'. This religion is 'clean' as contrasted with the immoral accompaniments of heathen religion.

judgements . . . true: judgements mean *ordinances*, *true* means *truthful*, 'because based on the *eternal* laws of morality' (Cheyne).

10. *More to be desired . . . than gold*: this spiritual treasure is more precious than the costliest earthly treasure—a sentiment often reflected in later Jewish piety.

11. *thy servant*: i.e. *thy servant Israel*: cf. Jer. 30[10], or a representative Israelite. Notice the psalmist's feeling that the law by creating the conscience helps to safeguard against transgression. The developed sense of sin is a mark of later Jewish piety.

In keeping of them there is great reward: reward and punishment are

---

[1] See Additional Note V at end.

determined by the observance of the Law. This again is the mark of
later Jewish piety; compare how the theme is worked out in 2 Esdras,
especially ch. 8.

12. *errors*: or 'lapses' due to ignorance or inadvertence; cf. Lev. 4⁵;
Num. 15²². For such 'sins' the law provides a remedy.

13. *presumptuous sins*: for such no remedy is provided in the Law.
They are left to be punished by direct divine action. Cf. Num. 15³⁰.

then shall I be perfect: i.e. living fully within the precepts of the
divine law.

Psalm 19 forms part of a selection of psalms and doxologies
sung in the synagogue service on Sabbaths and festivals (cf.
Singer, p. 20 ff.). Psalm 19 is particularly appropriate. As
Dr. Abrahams in his annotated edition of the Jewish prayer-book
remarks (p. xxxiii): 'We have arrayed before us the glory of God
in the heavens and the glory of the Law on earth. The praise of
God in nature is succeeded by the praise of God as revealed to
man. The Sun warms, the Law enlightens.' An apt commentary
on this is the great saying of Kant that there were only two things
which were a perpetual marvel to him: the starry heavens 'above',
and the moral law 'within' (Montefiore).

PSALM 68.

The problem as to the possible existence of Maccabean psalms
in our present Psalter may conveniently be discussed in connexion
with Pss. 68 and 110. The Maccabean date of Ps. 68 is advocated in
an able article by the late Dr. C. J. Ball in the *Journal of Theological Studies* (xi, p. 415 ff.). In particular he refers v. 22 ('The
Lord said, I will bring again from Bashan'; cf. v. 15) to a definite
historical event in the Maccabean period, namely, the expedition
of Judas Maccabaeus into the land of Gilead, to rescue the Jewish
population, who were threatened with extermination by their
heathen neighbours, cf. 1 Macc. 5⁴⁵ᶠᶠ·. This happened in 164 B.C.
The victory, we are told, was celebrated with solemn pomp in
Jerusalem: 'And they went up to Mount Sion with gladness and
joy and offered whole burnt offerings, because not so much as one
of them was slain.' Dr. Ball suggests that our psalm was the hymn
composed for the festival service on this occasion.

Dr. St. John Thackeray supports the Maccabean date with a
further piece of evidence. He writes:[1] 'The writer of 2 Maccabees
(12³¹ᶠ·), after describing the massacre at Ephron, goes on to say
that the victors "went up to Jerusalem, *the feast of weeks being close*

---

[1] *The Septuagint in Jewish Worship*, p. 58.

at hand." But *after the (feast) called Pentecost* they marched in haste against Gorgias. The celebration of the victory coincided with Pentecost. Dr. Ball, indeed, has a passing reference to that passage, but merely as giving an indication of the season of the year, in illustration of the "bounteous rain" of the Psalmist. It is characteristic of the general neglect of Jewish liturgiology that he omitted to make further use of such strong corroborative evidence. The psalm commemorates a double event, both the victory and the wheat harvest. It is dominated by the two blending thoughts of Jehovah as God of battles and as giver of the land.'

Gunkel, on the other hand, while he relegates the psalm to the post-exilic period, would place it much earlier than the Maccabean—in fact, in the fourth century B.C. He argues that the real enemy of Judaism at that time was Egypt, which between the years of 408 and 343 was independent, asserting its freedom against Persia. To the poet Egypt appears as the oppressive world-power which through its hordes of mercenary troops has brought so much suffering and oppression upon Israel, and the subjugation of whom under Jahveh's yoke will mean deliverance for the chosen people. In Egypt at that time, as we know from the Elephantine papyri, patriotic movements stirred the population to anti-foreign outbursts in which the Jews suffered; so the poet can speak of a new exodus from Egypt. Such a passage as Isaiah 19[19ff.], which gives expression to the hope that Egypt may be converted to Israel's religion, would belong, according to Gunkel, to an earlier period, when the Persian rule was still vigorous, and the feeling of hostility between the Jew and Egypt was not acute.

Gunkel refuses to assign the psalm to any definite historical event. He points to the variety of opinion on the part of those scholars who have attempted to find so definite a background. Thus, Grätz suggests the time of Josiah; others, the end of the Babylonian exile; Ewald, the time of the dedication of the Temple after the exile; Briggs, the later Persian period; Reuss, the wars between the Seleucids and the Ptolemies. At the same time Gunkel fully admits the late date of the composition of the psalm as a whole. It has often been pointed out that it is full of reminiscences of other O.T. passages.

It may be freely conceded that the historical occasion—whatever such occasion be presupposed—will not provide a complete clue to the interpretation of the psalm. Something else must be allowed for, and, more especially, the liturgical factor is all-important. But that the psalm was adapted for use at a particular historical occasion is a plausible hypothesis which has much to recommend it. It is the merit of Dr. St. J. Thackeray's exposition that he combines this with the liturgical factor. In the following exposition Dr. Thackeray's hypothesis is adopted.

1–6. Prayer for deliverance, uttered with such assurance as almost to pass into prophecy.

Let god arise, &c.: cf. the chant to the accompaniment of which the ark went forward in the wilderness, Num. 10³⁵.

2. *As smoke, &c.*: when God arises they shall be scattered like wreaths of smoke.

4. *Cast up a high way*: as for a royal progress; cf. Isaiah 41³.

6. A glance back by the psalmist at the two great returns from Egypt and from Babylon.

a parched land: i.e. a land destitute of spiritual and material blessings. By *prisoners* is meant those who are in exile, and by *the rebellious* is meant those Israelites who lapse into the surrounding heathendom.

7–18. Looking back to the past and to the great deliverances effected by Jahveh, especially from Egypt, the psalmist is strengthened in his firm faith in approaching deliverance. He sketches the journey through the wilderness, the conquest of Canaan, and the occupation of Mount Sion by the great king.

9. *Thou . . . didst send a plentiful rain*: lit. *A rain of free-will offerings thou dost wave.* A rather curious use of the term 'wave' in this context, explained by Dr. Thackeray in connexion with the Feast of Weeks: cf. Deut. 16¹⁰—'Thou shalt keep the feast of weeks . . . with a tribute of a free-will offering of thine hand.' This offering is to be 'waved' by the priest as a 'wave-offering' before Jahveh; cf. Lev. 23²⁰. The ceremony of waving, the movement of the offering towards the altar and back, symbolized its presentation to God and its return by Him to the priest. The psalmist acknowledges the gracious action of the Great High Priest; this freewill offering of the rain alone makes possible that of the worshipper. 'Of thine own have we given thee' (Dr. Thackeray, op. cit., p. 57).

10. *didst prepare for the poor*: cf. Lev. 23²², part of the lection which was read at the feast.

Dr. Thackeray points out that reminiscences of Deut. 33 occur throughout the psalm. These will be noticed later.

11. *The women, &c.*: the heralds of victory are a great host. They proclaim the news of the victory in all parts of the land. The word may be equivalent to *song*; cf. Miriam's song of victory, Exod. 15.

12. *divideth the spoil*: i.e. the spoil that had fallen to her husband: cf. Judges 5³⁰.

13. The difficulty consists in the connexion between the different parts of this verse.

lie among the sheepfolds: this is a phrase denoting taking one's ease in a safe retreat: cf. Gen. 49¹⁴; Judges 5¹⁶. The rest of the verse speaks of the brilliant hues of the dove's wings. What does this mean? They may indicate the rich clothing of some persons in the picture. Some interpreters explain the verse as an address of the women who herald the victory to the men, describing the happy state of Israel after the victory. Then render *When ye lie, &c.*, *then shall Israel be as the wings of a dove, &c.*

Cheyne suggests that we need not demand a close connexion in the sense. 'If line 1 be taken from one old poem, why should not lines 2 and 3 be quoted from another, entirely unconnected with the first?' He renders the whole verse:

Will ye lie among the sheep-folds?
The wings of a dove that is covered with silver, and her feathers with green shimmering gold.

Gunkel deletes line 1 as having got into the text from a possible variant of v. 10. He emends the last line of v. 12, reading *And the treasure house is divided as spoil*, and then proceeds (v. 13), *The wings of a dove covered with silver and her feathers with yellow gold.*

14. Another difficult verse. The explanation of Zalmon is uncertain. There is a small mountain so called near Shechem (Judges 9⁴⁸): the name occurs in the Talmud. The mountain range of the Hauran¹ is called in Ptolemy's geography Asalmanos, and Cheyne suggests that the name in our text may have arisen out of this. He suggests the following text:

[For full is the land of spoil]
When the almighty scatters kings therein
[as the snow when] it snows in Zalmon.

The reference then is to the mass of spoil which litters the district like snow. The text, however, is probably corrupt. Gunkel, following previous suggestions, emends the verse: *Of sapphires sufficient for kings.*

15–23. Jahveh is enthroned on Sion for the deliverance of his people.

15. *A high mountain*: lit. a mountain of domes or rounded tops. Wetstein regards this as 'a picturesque description of the crater formation of this highly volcanic region'. Ball, however, thinks that Hermon with its three rounded summits is intended here.

16. *Why look ye askance*: the grand mountain range of the Hauran might seem to offer a suitable site for Jahveh's sanctuary, but Sion was chosen. Even the peaks of Bashan might well look with envy on Sion.

¹ This volcanic range, about ten miles east of 'Bosorah' and thirty-five miles east of Carnaim (1 Macc. 5²⁶) 'bounded the field of Judas' campaign on the east, as the summits of Hermon on the north' (Ball).

17. Read at the end of the verse: *He hath come to Sinai to the sanctuary.*

18. The poet imagines Jahveh as coming from Sinai with his countless chariots and horses to take part in the triumphal procession of Judas and his warriors up the sacred height of Sion. There he receives his share in the prisoners, to serve as Nethinim in the sanctuary. Among them it would seem are some apostate Jews who had surrendered to the arms of Judas. So Ball, who reads for the third line: *Yea, the renegades almost must dwell with God.*

For the progress of Jahveh from Sinai cf. Deut. 33²; Hab. 3³, ⁸; Judges 5¹.

Thou hast ascended on high: i.e. *Thou art gone up to the height of Sion*; cf. 1 Macc. 5⁵⁴. The Jews described as renegades, i.e. those who lapsed into heathenism, must now, however unwillingly, dwell with God as bond-servants in the Temple.

19. *daily*: i.e. day by day, now as of old.

beareth our burden: or *bears* us, as a shepherd; cf. Ps. 23⁹; Isaiah 40¹¹

20. *a God of deliverances*: Cheyne renders *divine in saving acts.*

issues: Cheyne renders *escapes.* 'Death may be equivalent to Sheol.'

21. A reminiscence of Num. 24¹⁷. Hair was the symbol of strength and pride.

22. This suits the reference to the expedition of Judas Maccabaeus: cf. 1 Macc. 7.

from the depths of the sea: the Hebrew word so translated is used elsewhere, in a figurative sense, of trouble; cf. Ps. 69³, 88⁷. But it hardly affords a suitable parallel to Bashan. Ball suggests the reading *from Zalmon*. He thinks that the scribe was reminded of the deliverance from the Red Sea at the Exodus. For *sea* he reads *my people.* The whole clause now runs: *Jahveh said: From Bashan will I bring back. I will bring back from Zalmon my people.*

24–7. A festal procession is described. Note the mention of Judah, Benjamin and of Galilee. This again fits the Maccabean reference, as these three constitute elements representative of the dominant heads of the Israelitish community in the Maccabean time.

The description is interesting, including as it does references to the presence of singers, musicians and tribal chiefs in festal processions at the thanksgiving service.

24–5. *They have seen thy goings . . . the sanctuary*: Ball renders:

> Stately is thy march, O God—
> The march of my God, my King, into the sanctuary!
> The singers go first, behind are the harpers,
> In the midst are the maidens playing timbrels.

26. Better read: *They bless.* Perhaps the reference is to the singers.

27. The verse describes those who take part in procession.

Benjamin their ruler: this cannot be right. Ball suggests *Led them on*. Zebulon and Naphtali are descriptive terms of Jews from Galilee and the north; cf. 1 Macc. 5¹⁴ and ²³; Judges 5¹⁴⁻¹⁸.

28–31. A prayer for the continuance of divine help. May Jahveh manifest his power in fresh victories.

commanded thy strength: Cheyne renders, slightly emending the text, *Command, O God, thy strength*. 'Command' has the sense 'give a commission to'. God's strength is personified.

Strengthen, O God, &c.: Cheyne renders: *Show thyself strong, O God, Thou who [before] hast wrought for us*.

29. Ball reads: *unto thy temple at Jerusalem to thee let kings bring the gift*. Cf. 1 Macc. 10³⁹; 2 Macc. 13²³.

30. 'The most obviously corrupt verse in the Psalms' (Ball). The *wild beast of the reeds* symbolizes the warlike empire of the Nile valley. *The multitude of the bulls*: i.e. of fierce kings.

kill the calves of the peoples: the text appears to be corrupt. Ball proposes to read, *consume the tribes from Pathros, greedy for pelf*.

scatter the nations that delight in battles: 'From Pathros' was proposed by Nestle = Upper Egypt.

trampling under foot: For the Hebrew text so translated the emendation *from Pathros* is easy. Cheyne renders the line *that rolls itself in mire for gain of money*. As already pointed out, the wild beast mentioned symbolizes Egypt. For the bulls we may compare the Apis bull. The long-continued strife between Syria and Egypt for the possession of Palestine would justify such a sentiment as is here expressed. Possibly, however, as Ball suggests, the whole verse is an insertion; its omission improves the logical connexion.

31. The prediction of the second Isaiah shall be fulfilled. Egypt and Ethiopia shall lavish their treasures on God: cf. Isaiah 43³, 45¹⁴.

Ethiopia shall haste to stretch out her hands unto God: Cheyne regards the phrase as referring not so much to prayer as to the offering of gifts: cf. Isaiah 18⁷.

32–3. The fine doxology addressed to all nations.

To him that rideth upon the heaven of heavens, &c.: cf. Deut. 10¹⁴. 1 Kings 8²⁷. By *the heaven of heavens* is meant 'the highest heaven'.

34. The first line is rendered by Cheyne: *Ascribe ye unto God strength which shelters Israel*. So nearly the Targum.

35. *terrible*: cf. Ps. 47³.

giveth strength and power, &c.: cf. Ps. 29¹¹.

[Dr. St. John Thackeray points out that reminiscences of Deut. 33 occur throughout the psalm, but in the closing invitation to worship these are blended with phrases derived from Ps. 29 (the older Pentecost psalm). Note especially v. 33, the first part of which is a reminiscence of Deut. 33²⁶, while the second line is derived from Ps. 29⁴. Verse 35 of our psalm = Ps. 29 end. Dr.

Thackeray goes on to remark: 'It was fitting that the older Pentecost psalm should supply the model for the finale of its rival which was coming to supplant it in the festival ritual'.]

PSALM 110.

Cheyne describes this psalm as 'divine oracles and lyric anticipations addressed to the king'. He goes on to remark: 'To me it appears like an imitation of Ps. 2.' Gunkel remarks that the King of Israel appears to have been accustomed, like the Babylonian and Egyptian kings, to be the recipient of oracles and prophecies. Can the psalm be referred to any definite historical occasion? Some scholars maintain that it can, and assign it to 141 B.C., when Simon Maccabaeus was accepted as prince and governor by the people of Israel and appointed to be High Priest, though he was not in the direct line of the High Priestly family (cf. 1 Macc. 14[35]). It is to be noted that Simon owed the dignity of High Priest and tetrarch to the election of his own people, not, like his predecessor, Jonathan, to the favour of a foreign monarch. This view is supported by the interesting fact that the oracle beginning with the word 'Sit thou' forms an acrostic on the name Simon.

1. *The LORD saith unto my lord*: the word translated *saith* is a technical term for an oracle. Cheyne renders *Jahveh's oracle touching my lord*.

Sit thou at my right hand: or, as Cheyne renders, *be enthroned at my right hand*. Mount Sion is the symbolical representation of the mountain of God. Jahveh upon his throne summons Israel's king to share it with him; cf. Ps. 2[5]. The king of Israel is thus Jahveh's deputy and rules by divine appointment. Here the reference would be, according to the Maccabean interpretation, to Simon.

2. *the rod of thy strength*: *Thine overpowering sceptre* (Cheyne). *Rule thou*: again the words of Jahveh.

3. *in the day of thy power*: i.e. the public proclamation of Simon as governor. The verse describes the enthusiastic adherence of crowds of Israelites to the royal banner; *in the beauty of holiness*: more exactly, 'in holy attire', i.e. in the High-priestly vestments.[1]

from the womb of the morning: the muster is in the early morning, and the youthful army, full of vigour and freshness, is figured by the dew (cf. Hos. 14[5]; Isaiah 26[19]).

4. *for ever*: i.e. for life.

Melchizedek is referred to because he embodied in his own person the united offices of king and priest; cf. Gen. 14[18]. Melchizedek appro-

---

[1] Cheyne, by a slight emendation in the text, reads: '*upon* the holy mountains', i.e. of Jerusalem, whence the army marches forth.

priately typifies a new order of High Priest, apart from the line of Zadok. This is especially appropriate to the assumption of the High Priesthood by the Maccabean prince, who, although he belonged to a priestly family, was not of the line of Zadok. The name Melchizedek also happily suggests the chief attributes of the Messianic king, righteousness and prosperity.

After the order: a better rendering, *after the manner*.

the lord: i.e. Jahveh.

Shall strike through: or, *shatter*. The same verb is repeated in v. 6: cf. Ps. 68²².

6. *He shall judge among the nations*: this is one of the functions of the Messiah.

7. Cf. Jud. 7⁵; 2 Sam. 23¹⁵.

Gunkel does not accept the Maccabean date of the psalm. He points out that the priestly function was sometimes exercised by pre-exilic kings (cf. 2 Sam. 6¹⁸; 1 Kings 8¹⁴, ⁵⁰). But the mention of Melchizedek is difficult to reconcile with a pre-exilic date, and it admirably suits the new order of High Priesthood which came in with the Maccabeans, and more particularly with Simon.

F. THE RISE OF APOCALYPTIC AND THE BOOK OF DANIEL

PROBABLY the oldest complete apocalyptic book is Daniel, which was probably put into its present shape between the years 167 and 165 B.C. The book of Daniel, like the book of Revelation, has forced its way into the Canon, though both books stand only just within the canonical border-line. But outside the Canon both of the Old Testament and of the New a whole series of apocalyptic books exists. The most important of these which have affinities with the Old Testament are associated with the name of Enoch.

1. (i) *The Ethiopic Enoch*, a compilation of materials drawn from Enochic books of various dates. As printed in Charles's edition the oldest parts are contained probably in chs. 1–36 and 72–108, which may be dated about 100 B.C. and later; the similitudes contained in chs. 37–71 are the latest and most important element and may be dated not long before the Christian era. The Ethiopic translation, it may be added, is based upon a Greek version, a large section of which has been recovered; and this, again, ultimately upon a conjectured Semitic (Hebrew or Aramaic) original, which is lost. Then (ii) there is the Slavonic book of the *Secrets of Enoch*, which has survived in a version of a lost Greek

original, and may be plausibly dated some time within the first century of our era (before 70 A.D.).

2. *The Assumption of Moses* (Latin = Greek = Hebrew), 4 B.C.–A.D. 10.

3. *The Apocalypse of Ezra* (= 2 Esdras 3–14), A.D. 90–120.

4. *The Syriac Apocalypse of Baruch*: about the same date.

5. *The Testaments of the XII Patriarchs*: in its present form, first century A.D., but groundwork is earlier.

6. *The Apocalypse of Abraham*: c. A.D. 100 or a little later. To these may be added the Jewish parts of the *Ascension of Isaiah* and the *Book of Jubilees*, which, however, is not an apocalyptic book as a whole, though it contains apocalyptic elements. The same remark applies to the Psalms of Solomon (first century B.C.). Of Hellenistic writings proper the oldest part of the Sibylline Oracles may be mentioned as largely influenced by Apocalyptic.

There was thus quite an extensive literature of Jewish apocalyptic, which was largely borrowed or adopted by Christians and owes its survival (in Christian translations) to the fact that it was popular and widely read in Christian circles.

Before we come to deal more particularly with the book of Daniel, a word may be said about the general characteristics of apocalyptic thought as represented by its literature.

Perhaps the most striking characteristic of these books is their *supernatural colouring*. The two poles of apocalyptic thought are not so much *present* and *future* on the plane of earthly development, as *above* and *below*. Earth is but a shadow of heaven; the issues are really determined in the realm above. The future age is conceived as a sudden irruption of celestial forces from the other world. It is for this blinding but glorious catastrophe that the apocalyptist longs and yearns with painful eagerness. The other-worldly spirit thus reaches, in these books, its most sublimated expression.

This supernatural colouring is also reflected in the form of the apocalyptic books. They are full of strange and cryptic symbolism (e.g. the animal symbolism of Daniel and parts of Enoch); they employ the vision and the dream as regular vehicles for revelation; there is also a rich angelology and demonology. Doubtless the employment of cryptograms and mystic signs (such as the number 666, and the 'beast' in the Apocalypse of St. John and the 'little horn' in Daniel as symbols of Nero and Antiochus respectively) was dictated partly by prudence. Nevertheless the particular symbols chosen reflect the mysterious character so much loved by these writers. But the mystery is no mere literary mystification. The apocalyptists were conscious that divine secrets must contain in them something incomprehensible by merely finite intelligence, and this feeling sometimes comes to fine expression, as in 4 Ezra 4 (= 2 Esdras 4).

This feeling for the mystery that so largely surrounds things divine will account for a feature of the apocalyptic literature which must strike every student who examines it at all—its mixed character of half revelation, half concealment.

Another peculiarity is its pseudonymous character. This feature has been a source of real difficulty to those who recognize that these books are by no means destitute of religious value. In the case of the book of Daniel, which has secured for itself a place within the Canon of Holy Scripture, and which has played so important a part in later religious history, and especially has profoundly influenced the whole religious outlook of the N.T., this difficulty has been acutely felt. The book of Daniel purports to be a record of certain experiences, including a series of visions which are represented to have been given to a pious Jew named Daniel, who lived in Babylon during the Exile, and whose life and work are set forth as a means of encouraging those who had to face religious persecution at the hands of Antiochus Epiphanes.

THE BOOK OF DANIEL

INTRODUCTION

SOME most complicated questions of criticism and interpretation arise in connexion with this book. These are fully discussed in the two most recent and important commentaries which have appeared, Montgomery's (I.C.C. 1927) and Dr. R. H. Charles's (Oxford University Press, 1928). It will only be possible here to indicate these questions and briefly to call attention to certain salient points.

One remarkable feature of the book is its use of two languages, Hebrew and Aramaic—the latter being a form of Palestinian Aramaic—the opening chapters (i–ii, 4a) and the closing chapters (viii–xii) being written in Hebrew, the intervening ones (ii, 4b to vii) being in Aramaic. What is the explanation of this curious phenomenon? Various theories have been proposed. Dr. Charles accepts the view that the whole work was originally written in Aramaic, but that the opening chapters and the closing ones were translated into Hebrew—the sacred language—to allow of the book being incorporated into the Jewish Canon. The difficulty about this view is to account for the fact that only parts of the book are so translated. Why not the whole? It is more plausible to suppose that the book was put together by a member of the party of 'the pious', Chasidim, who himself was responsible for the Hebrew parts which he freely composed, while he incorporated the Aramaic parts from another source or sources. This view would regard the Aramaic parts as essentially older than the Hebrew parts; and in fact many scholars have been impressed with the comparatively older character of the Aramaic employed in these sections. A strong case may be made out for the view that the Aramaic parts, at any rate chapters ii, 4b to vi, belong in their original form to the third century B.C. If there has been some slight revision and modernization of the language of these chapters this may plausibly be ascribed to the activity of copyists.[1]

Another point to be noticed is the remarkable chronology of events which is implied in the framework of the book itself. Chapter 1 opens with a statement which is historically inaccurate. It states that in the third year of Jehoiakim (reigned 608–597), i.e. in the year 605, Nebuchadnezzar came up against Jerusalem and besieged it, with the result that Jehoiakim was obliged to submit. Part of the vessels of the sanctuary were carried to Babylonia, and apparently some Jewish captives also, among whom were included Daniel and his companions. Now, no capture of Jerusalem during Jehoiakim's reign by Nebuchadnezzar is recorded in the book of Kings; and such a siege is very improbable before the date of the battle of Carchemish (604 B.C.), when Pharaoh Necho was overthrown by the Babylonians. Till that event the whole of Judah with its King was subordinate to Egypt. The first deportation of Jewish exiles to Babylonia took place in 597 after the end of Jehoiakim's reign, and after that monarch's death.

But much more important than this is the chronology of the Babylonian, Median, and Persian monarchs which is represented in the book. According to this representation Daniel flourished in the reign of Nebuchadnezzar (died 561 B.C.) and of his immediate son and successor, Belshazzar, who was succeeded by Darius the Mede—the sole ruler of the Median Empire—and Darius was followed by Cyrus. Now Belshazzar was neither the immediate successor nor son of Nebuchadnezzar. He was, in fact, the son of the last Babylonian King Nabunaid, though he may have been

---

[1] See further Additional Note VI at end of volume.

associated with his father on the throne.[1] The Empire of Nabunaid was conquered and annexed by Cyrus, who became King of Babylon in 539. The true succession, as fixed by contemporary evidence, is as follows: Nebuchadnezzar, 604–561; Evil-Merodach (Amel-Mardûk) his son, 561–559; Neriglissar, 559–555; Labashi-Mardûk (555—9 months) was succeeded by a usurper, Nabunaid (555–538), the last King of Babylon. Then follows the Persian period, beginning with Cyrus, 538–529; Cambyses, 529–521; Darius I (Hystaspis), 521–485; Xerxes I, 485–464; Artaxerxes I, 464–424; Darius II (Nothus), 424–404; Artaxerxes II (Mnemon), 404–358; Artaxerxes III (Ochus), 358–338; Darius III (Codomannus), 336–331; Battle of Issus: End of Persian Period, Greek period begins.

Darius 'the Mede', or Darius Hystaspis, according to the unhistorical view which appears to have prevailed during the Greek period among Jewish writers, was the sole ruler of a mythical 'Median' Empire which *preceded* the Empire of Cyrus. This completely deranges the true historical order of events. Let me quote what Professor Torrey says on this subject.[2] 'Neither the author (or authors) of Daniel (he remarks) nor any of the other Jewish writers show any interest in this Median power or its history. The duration of its rule over Babylonia was believed to have been very brief, to have included, in fact, the reign of only one king. We read in Dan. 5^{30}, 6^1, that upon the death of the last Babylonian King, Belshazzar, his kingdom was taken by Darius "the Mede", and we are told with equal distinctness that this Darius was immediately succeeded by Cyrus, the first king of the Persians. . . . The author of Daniel would have begun his list of Persian kings thus: Cyrus, Xerxes, Artaxerxes I Longimanus, Darius II Nothus, &c.' Dr. Torrey believes that the Chronicler's history of Israel represents precisely the same view of the royal succession, and, accordingly, of a brief Median rule, preceding the Persian. According to Dr. Torrey the 'Darius' referred to by the Chronicler in *Ezra* is Darius II (Nothus). He remarks: 'The Chronicler makes no mention of Darius Hystaspis "the Mede"' before Cyrus for the same reason that he fails further to include Artaxerxes III (Ochus), namely, because these kings, as he supposed, had nothing to do with the history of the Jews. . . . According to his view, Zerubbabel and his companions finished the Temple under Darius II (Nothus), and the Artaxerxes who befriended Ezra and afterwards

---

[1] See Boutflower, *In and Around the Book of Daniel*, p. 118 f.
[2] *Ezra Studies*, p. 38.

Nehemiah was Artaxerxes II (Mnemon). Dr. Martin Thilo,[1] in a small monograph of forty-three pages, discusses the puzzling phenomena of the chronology of the book of Daniel. He begins with the third year of Jehoiakim (Dan. 1[1]), which is the date given for Nebuchadnezzar's coming to besiege Jerusalem. How is this date to be explained? The author points out that if the regnal years of the Jewish kings, as these are given in the books of Kings, are added up from the building of Solomon's temple to the last king, the sum of 430 results, and if to this is added fifty years to cover the period 586–537 inclusive, the number 480 results, as the interval from the first building of the Temple to the second, this number corresponding exactly to that of the interval from the exodus from Egypt to the building of Solomon's temple (1 Kings 6[1]). It is suggested that the author of Daniel reckoned back as follows. Counting 50 years from 537 to 586, he added 11 to 11 (22) years to cover the reigns of Jehoiakim and Zedekiah, and so reached the number 72 ; 71 would be the second year, and 70 would be the third year of Jehoiakim. This would account for the 70 years of Jer. 25[11f.] and 29[10], taken as an exact and not as a round number.

The next chronological datum discussed is the question of the 62 weeks referred to in ch. 9[26] ('And after the threescore and two weeks shall the anointed one be cut off, and shall have nothing'). Here the reference, as is generally agreed, is to the murder of Onias the Third about the year 170 B.C. The clause rendered in the R.V. 'And he shall have nothing' should run 'And he shall have no one' (sc. to succeed him), i.e. he shall have no legitimate successor. Reckoning from 605 B.C. to 173 B.C. inclusive, the result is 61 weeks plus 5 (605–173 is 432 ; 432 ÷ 7 is 61 plus 5). The author seems to have reckoned as follows: 605–537 is 70 ; 536–173 inclusive is 364 ; thus the whole is 364 plus 70, 434, that is, exactly 62 weeks.[2] This is the bare result. It is ingeniously worked out and all the relevant factors are discussed. Regarding the last week of years the author is equally ingenious. He first of all divides it into 7 × 365 days = 2,555 days, and brings this into relation with the puzzling and apparently inconsistent reckoning of the time when the daily offering in the Temple ceased (variously reckoned as consisting of 1,150, 1,290, and 1,335 days). How the author deals with this puzzle the reader must consult his book to discover. Other points

---

[1] *Die Chronologie des Danielbuches* (Bonn: A. Schmidt), 1926.
[2] The 'weeks' referred to above are periods of seven years each.

are discussed, including the first year of Darius the Mede, the third year of Cyrus (Dan. 10[1]), and also the problem of the composition of the book is referred to. This last discussion is very interesting. Dr. Thilo regards the author as a member of the learned scribal class, and thinks that he was using Aramaic sources, especially for the Apocalyptic parts. Here he is acting as a redactor. When he plays the part of author in the proper sense of the word he writes in Hebrew, and in the Hebrew parts he occasionally freely reproduces his sources. In chs. 2–7 the author (i.e. the author of chs. 8–12) has interpolated certain sections.

THE DATE OF THE BOOK AND CHARACTER OF THE STORIES

Can the exact date of the composition and putting forth of the book of Daniel be fixed? Within certain limits, yes. It seems clear that it was written by a member of the party of the 'pious' (Chasidim) after the desecration of the Temple, but before the death of Antiochus, and before he had started on his eastern campaign. The writer, too, was apparently unaware of the important part played by Judas and presumably wrote before the Chasidim joined the forces of the latter.

We may safely, then, assume the commonly accepted date for the composition and publication of our book and proceed to illustrate its religious and doctrinal importance when viewed in the light of its historical origin and its influence on later religious thought.

It has already been pointed out that the stories in the first part (chs. 1–6) which may be derived partly from tradition are not to be pressed as if they were put forth as sober historical narrations, but are to be regarded rather as in the nature of Midrash, stories narrated with an edifying purpose. The late Dr. C. J. Ball, referring to these stories, admirably describes their true purport and significance. After pointing out that the conception of a deliverance from a fiery furnace was traditional among the Jews, in all probability from very ancient times, he goes on to remark: 'And we have to bear in mind a fact familiar enough to students of Talmudic and Midrashic literature, though apparently unknown to many expositors of scripture, whose minds conspicuously lack that *orientation* which is an indispensable preliminary to a right understanding of the treasures of Eastern thought, I mean the inveterate tendency of Jewish teachers to convey their doctrine, not in the form of abstract discourse, but in a mode appealing directly to the imagination, and seeking to arouse the interest and sympathy of the man rather than the philosopher. The Rabbi embodies his lesson in a story, whether parable, or allegory, or seeming historical narrative, and the last thing he or his disciples would think of is to ask whether the selected persons, events, and circumstances, which so vividly suggest the doctrine, are in themselves real or fictitious. The doctrine is everything; the mode of presentation has no independent value. To make the story the first consideration, and the doctrine it was intended to convey an afterthought, as we with our dry Western literalness are predisposed to, is to reverse the Jewish order of thinking, and to do unconscious injustice to the authors of many edifying narratives of antiquity.'—*Speaker's Comment. on Apocrypha* (ii. 307).

If we look at these stories from this point of view we can see at once how aptly they fit the situation in 167 or 166 B.C. during the time of the great tribulation. The first story expresses the lesson of loyalty to the Jewish law regarding food, against the command of a foreign king. A similar demand was made by Antiochus when, according to 1 Macc. (1⁴⁷), he ordered the Jews to 'sacrifice swine's flesh and unclean beasts' (cf. also 2 Macc. 6⁵, ⁸). The third story tells of an image set up by the monarch which he required all to bow down to and worship. In a similar way Antiochus made it obligatory on the part of the Jews to take part in the Greek cult, and especially to worship the image of 'Zeus Olympius', i.e. the 'Abomination of desolation' in which, as often pointed out, could be detected the features and likeness of Antiochus himself, which was set up on the altar of burnt offering in the desecrated Temple. In the next narrative Nebuchadnezzar is humbled because of his pride and implicit denial of God. The moral of the story is that no mortal king can with impunity deny that his kingship is derived from God, and his tenure of it is dependent upon his recognition of this fact. In the story Nebuchadnezzar's pride is humbled to the dust, and before his sovereignty is restored to him he is made to confess his folly and acknowledge his dependence upon the divine power. The application to Antiochus, with his arrogant claims to divinity amounting to blasphemous usurpation, is obvious. The story of Belshazzar's feast (ch. 5) depicts a scene of proud and sacrilegious revelry, followed suddenly by retribution. Readers at the time when the book was first published would recall the stories current of the riotous feasting and excess at Daphne near Antioch in celebration of Antiochus's victories.

The decree of Darius in ch. 6 forbidding any one to ask a petition
of God or man, save the king only, would suggest the arrogant
egotism of Antiochus in likening himself to divinity and proclaiming himself 'God manifest', these claims outrivalling all
others. It is thus clear that these stories are adapted to the circumstances of the time, and their application would have been
easy and inevitable. 'Some disguise', says Prof. Porter, 'was of
course necessary if a book were to assail the ruling power. Here
the disguise is that of the story, in the later chapters it is that of
vision, and throughout the assumption of exilic date veils the
treasonable teaching of the book.'

THE VISIONS

The stories, then, are to be valued not as fact, but for the teaching they were meant to enforce. Their use of tradition does not
signify that they are historical in character. 'We must', says
Prof. Porter, 'suppress our modern historical sense in order to
appreciate the freedom with which history was adapted and story
invented, and history and story blended, for practical religious
purposes.' Of the visions that form the second part of the book
(chs. 7–12) the first contained in ch. 7 is of very great importance.
The vision proper is contained in vv. 1–14; the rest of the chapter
is mainly concerned with its interpretation. It has often been
pointed out that there is a lack of adjustment between the material
of the vision and the interpretation. Some points in the one are
ignored in the other, and in one or two particulars points are added
in the interpretation to which there is nothing corresponding in
the vision (e.g. that the fourth beast had 'nails of brass', that
the little horn became greater than the other, and that it made
war with the saints and prevailed against them). None of
these features come out in the original vision. It may be inferred
from these phenomena that there are elements in the original
vision which belong to a fixed tradition. To this fixed tradition
belong the winds and the stormy sea and the emergence of
the beasts that stand for the godless kingdoms. We have, in
fact, in this material another form of the old myth of the dragon
of the watery chaos. The sea is the anarchic element in the
material world, and from it emerge the evil forces which have to
be overcome before order and light can prevail. The apocalyptist
is working upon material provided for him by ancient tradition.
He is not freely inventing, but he shapes the material and adapts

it to his special purposes. It is to be noticed that his interest is focused upon the fourth beast, and more particularly upon the little horn. This detail is exaggerated out of all proportion in the picture as a whole, because it is the supremely important thing to the writer.

Another very important feature in this vision is the mysterious figure of one 'like unto a Son of Man'. The old view that this term designates the Messiah can hardly be sustained; for the personal Messiah plays no part in the scheme of redemption—the overthrow of the tyrant Antiochus; and the establishment of the rule of the Saints is effected by God Himself directly. Nevertheless, the Danielic 'one like unto a Son of Man' has played a great role in the development of Messianic doctrine. The kinship between this mysterious figure and the heavenly 'Son of Man' of the similitudes of 1 Enoch is clear enough, and probably also extends to the *Man* of 4 Ezra 13. The author of Daniel used the phrase 'one like unto a Son of Man' in contrast with the beasts who represent the world empires, as a symbol for the people of Israel. But it does not follow that the figure 'like a man' (or son of man) has no individual or personal significance. On the contrary, it seems probable that the term is a descriptive one for an angelic being—presumably Michael in the thought of the writer of Daniel—who acts as Israel's representative and counterpart. The figure is thus both a symbol and a person. This view of the facts will explain the development of the term in the similitudes and 4 Ezra. The author of Daniel may have been influenced, in using the term 'Son of Man', by the figure of the Cosmic Man, who in apocalyptic tradition was gradually invested with Messianic attributes. Originally, in apocalyptic tradition, this *Man* or *Son of Man* was conceived as a heavenly being or angel, and was invested with attributes proper only to Jahveh Himself.

The idea of a heavenly being who thus comes to view as a feature in old apocalyptic tradition is the source of the conception of the heavenly Messiah—the Son of Man—of the similitudes of the book of Enoch. We have already seen that the heavenly being 'like unto a Son of Man' of Dan. 7 was probably identified by the author of Daniel with Israel's angel prince Michael; this angelic being was later, it would seem, invested with Messianic attributes, and so became the pre-existent heavenly Messiah of the book of Enoch, who is to judge both men and angels. His standing designation in the similitudes is 'this (or that) Son of Man', seldom 'The Son of Man'. In other passages in the same section of the book he is called 'the Righteous One', 'the Elect One', 'the Elect One of righteousness and of faith', and God's 'Anointed' (i.e. the Christ).

This view of the significance of the figure of one 'like unto a son of man' has this in its favour: (1) it explains the development of the term in a Messianic sense—indeed, apart from this view, it is difficult to see how the development of the heavenly Son of Man idea can be explained; (2) the writer of Daniel holds the belief very strongly in guardian or representative angels. Michael, the angel-prince, is Israel's representative in the heavenly sphere, and his victory over the angels of other nations in heaven, and his receiving the kingdom, would mean precisely Israel's victory over enemies on earth and attainment of world-rulership. Clearly Michael plays an all-important part in determining Israel's fortunes, according to the view of the author of Daniel. He, with Gabriel, fights against Israel's enemies, the angels of Persia and Greece, and his appearance as Israel's champion at the height of its distress will mean the coming of salvation and glory (cf. Dan. 12[1]). It is to be noticed that in Rev. 12[7] Michael is pictured as the destroyer of the dragon. The question has therefore been raised whether, either in our writer's own view, or in the older tradition of which he made use, the one like a man was not himself the destroyer of the water-beast. If so, then 7[11-12] would describe this victory, and in v. 13 the conqueror would be seen rising up from his conflict with the sea-monster, borne on a cloud to the presence of God, where he receives as a reward for his victory rulership over the world. But however this may be, it is at least probable that the writer of Daniel conceived 'one like unto a son of man' to be an angel, a view which was apparently shared by the writer of Rev. 14[14].

The second vision of the ram and the he-goat is simply an historical sketch, thinly disguised, of the rise of the Hellenic Empire, under Alexander the Great, his conquest of Persia, and the development of his empire through separate kingdoms. It culminates in a description of the proceedings of the 'little horn', i.e. Antiochus Epiphanes.

The one difficult point that emerges in this vision is the period assigned to the Temple's desecration. It is said in v. 14 that the daily sacrifice shall be omitted for 2,300 evenings and mornings, i.e. for 1,150 days. How is this number to be explained? It does not correspond to the $3\frac{1}{2}$ years of 7[25] and 12[7] ('time, times and a half a time'). In 12[11-12] the numbers are given as 1,290 and 1,335 days respectively. It has been suggested that the difference of numbers implies difference of authorship. Probably one or other has been added after the original composition of the book. If the number 2,300 evenings was added after the actual re-dedication it is probably exact. In this case the interval will be about 3 years and 2 months. The $3\frac{1}{2}$ years may be regarded as symbolical and not exact.

The third vision, if vision it may be called, contained in ch. 9, is mainly concerned with the interpretation of the duration of the exile and the date of the rebuilding of the Temple. Daniel in his study of the scriptures is perplexed as to the meaning of Jeremiah's prediction (Jer. 25[11ff.] and 29[10]) that the exile should last 70 years. Daniel utters a prayer of confession and supplication for forgiveness of the sins of his people ; and then receives a revelation from the angel Gabriel that the 70 years of Jeremiah was to be interpreted to mean 70 weeks of years. The original prediction had been a source of perplexity—hundreds of years had passed since the destruction of Jerusalem in 586, and now about the year 167 the Jewish community was still under the foreign yoke, and suffering more than ever before at the hands of a heathen tyrant. How the 70 weeks are to be explained is still a matter of uncertainty. A solution widely accepted by modern scholars may here be detailed. According to this, the first 7 weeks (= 49 years) embraces the period 587–538, i.e. from the destruction of Jerusalem to the edict of Cyrus; the 362 weeks that follow embrace the period 538–171 B.C. (171 = year when the legitimate High Priesthood had ceased); the last week (= 7 years) = 171–164 B.C. On this construction the middle period of 62 weeks ought to embrace 434 years, whereas, according to the true chronology, the interval is one of 367 only. The probable explanation of this discrepancy is to be found in the inexact knowledge possessed by the author of Daniel of the time-limits of this period. He did not possess the necessary *data* for reaching an exact chronology.

One can see at once the appositeness of this disclosure to the crisis of the hour when the book appeared. Here was a real difficulty to pious souls who were steeling themselves against the bitter persecution then raging against the profession of their religion. Had not God, through His prophet, assured Israel that their sufferings should be ended after 70 years of exile ? The 70 years had long since passed, and Judaism was fighting for its life. To such souls the reinterpretation of the 70 years as 70 weeks of years, the term of which had almost expired, must have brought real relief. They could now nerve themselves for one final effort of endurance, convinced that the storm would soon spend itself—and their faith was soon brilliantly justified.

The last vision (chs. 10–12) consists simply in the sight of the angel Gabriel and the hearing of his words. There is no vision of God or of symbolic figures representing historical nations, persons or events. Gabriel does indeed disclose some significant happenings in the heavenly sphere with which the fortunes of Israel are intimately associated; but the language employed is not symbolical but literal, and without disguise. Yet it is to be noticed that the visionary character of the experience is strongly emphasized. The disclosure made by the angel is preceded by a long period of preparation on the part of the seer, consisting of fasting and prayer; and the effect of the disclosure on Daniel himself is elaborately described. The artificial and pseudepigraphic character of this composition it seems impossible to question or deny. It is thus described by Prof. Porter: 'It professes to be a story of far future events, told to the seer during the reign of Cyrus by Gabriel, and the fact that the story has remained so long unknown is due to the hiding and sealing of the book, by order of the revealing angel, until the end came near (cf. 10^{14}, $12^{4, 5-13}$) . . . .'

The late date of the writing is unmistakably revealed by the fact that there are probably errors, certainly striking omissions and abbreviations, in the early part of the history, and that the writer's knowledge and interest increase as the reign of Antiochus IV is approached, and culminate in that reign. At a certain easily recognizable point, however, namely at 11^{40}, the agreement of the angel's disclosures with known history ceases, and we have an account of a third and triumphant invasion of Egypt by Antiochus and his death in Palestine on his return, which is not in accordance with the facts. At that point, evidently, the form of prediction passes over into prediction proper, and that, of course, is the point at which the writer himself stands.

One or two points of considerable theological interest come out in this vision. In the first place (1) the idea is elaborately worked out that behind the scenes of earthly conflict there are spiritual forces at work, in the form of angels, whose conflicts determine the fortunes of the corresponding earthly scene. The angelic champions of Israel, Gabriel, and Michael contend on behalf of Israel first with the angel of Persia and then with the angel of Greece. (2) Another conception of considerable theological importance is the portrait of Antiochus as the embodiment and consummation of evil. There is something demoniacal and superhuman in the picture thus given, and Antiochus becomes the prototype of Antichrist. It is the obverse of his arrogant and blasphemous claim to deification. The figure of Antichrist assumes different embodiments, in later eschatological tradition, e.g. he was identified later with Nero; but apart altogether from these identifications the Antichrist idea became a permanent element in Christian eschatology.

But the most striking advance in theological ideas, and one that marks a real difference of outlook between the older prophecy and apocalyptic, is the emphasis placed in this vision on the idea of the *resurrection of the dead*. It appears there in a much more definite form than elsewhere, and is enunciated with much greater assurance and conviction. It, of course, became a dogma of orthodox Judaism; but its firm establishment in the Jewish religious consciousness is due to the apocalyptists. The belief first emerges into clear expression in the apocalyptic literature. In the apocalyptic section Isa. 24–27, which almost certainly is older than the book of Daniel, the belief is expressed that death will be abolished in the Messianic Age, and that the righteous dead will be raised to share in the coming glory of the nation: *He hath annihilated death for ever* (Isa. 25⁸). While any resurrection for the wicked is categorically denied in Isa. 26¹⁴, it is affirmed, on the other hand, that the righteous shall live again:

Thy dead shall live; awake and shout for joy, Ye that dwell in the dust!
For a dew of lights is thy dew (O Jahveh) and Earth shall bring forth
shades. (Isa. 26¹⁹)

In Daniel the belief assumes a fixed and permanent form as part of the Apocalyptic hope, and here both righteous and wicked are expected to share in the resurrection to receive the reward of their deeds (Dan. 12², ¹²). The writer uses the term 'many', not 'all'; and apparently he has in mind only the very righteous, and the very wicked, and not the large intermediate class. In fact the author of Daniel seems to have in view especially the martyrs who had suffered death on account of their faith; and it is worth noting that the association of martyrdom with the resurrection persisted, and reappears in the N.T. Apocalypse (Rev. 20⁴ᶠᶠ·; cf. 2 Macc.). For some time uncertainty prevailed as to whether the resurrection should be confined to the righteous only, or should embrace righteous and sinners alike. According to Josephus (*Ant.* XVIII. 14) the former view was that of the Pharisees, as it certainly was of the author of 2 Macc. (6^{26}, $7^{9, \ 14, \ 26}$, $12^{23f.}$, 14^{46}). It is also repre-sented in the Gospels; cf. Luke 14^{14} and 20^{36}, where the righteous are described as 'sons of the resurrection'. Both theories are combined in the Johannine Apocalypse, where the martyrs are raised first, at the beginning of the millennium, to reign with Christ 'a thousand years'; then at the final consummation, after the thousand years have ended, all the dead are raised to be judged.

The book of Daniel brings the reader into the very heart and soul of Judaism when it was faced with the most tremendous crisis of its history. Produced in the midst of this crisis, when the Terror was at its height, it performed a signal service to true religion by its passionate advocacy of resistance to the heathen persecutor, and its fearless assurance of speedy relief. The great tribulation that fell upon Judaism marked a crisis indeed. We have to remember that the idea of a persecution of a religion, so familiar to later generations, was at this time something entirely new. The later martyrs could face with courage what was to them at worst only a transitory moment of pain. But, as Mr. Edwyn Bevan has pointed out, 'the Jewish martyrs were the pioneers on this road; to them this affliction was an appalling surprise; death, remember, had not been to their thinking the gate into life, but a darkness which God in the case of His faithful servants held back till they had enjoyed their full measure of days. And now?—How did the old easy comfortable doctrine of the happy end of the righteous sound to those carried to the tormentors? . . . What did it mean that God had delivered up His people to the enemy? The daily sacrifice on the altar at Jerusalem, the pledge and the means of communication between the Lord and Israel, had ceased; it was an open breaking-off of relations. To the faithful it must have seemed that the ground was gone from under their feet, and that before their eyes was only a void of darkness'.

It was at this moment of gloom and perplexity that the message contained in the book of Daniel was given. It came to wounded and bewildered hearts as a voice from Heaven—a trumpet-call to resist even unto death, the dark horizon being illumined with the promise of divine deliverance, even from death. 'And they that be wise shall shine as the brightness of the firmament; and they that turn many to righteousness as the stars for ever and ever.'

'It was a great moment in the history of religion'—it has been said—'when these words obtained a place in the consciousness of Israel. Through the grim conflict with torture and death the elect people was being led to the new vision: the Spirit which had guided and taught them in the past did not fail them now; the thought of their teachers still reacted under His inspiration to the need of the day. The martyr could now go down to the gulf of darkness with a transcendent prospect upon the farther side.'

The book of Daniel is one of the classical documents of religion. It marks a new type of literature created by the faith and expectation that inspire martyrdom.

There are moments of agony in the experience of humanity when the human spirit achieves a great advance by rising to the height of a supreme conviction which henceforth remains unshakable and permanent. Such a moment is revealed within the life of Judaism by the book of Daniel. The faith of the Jewish martyrs, revealed and inspired by the book itself, passed through the Terror to the inevitable Triumph. Henceforth Judaism is a stronger and more vital organism, endowed with the new powers of expansion, and above all with a proud self-consciousness which nothing can daunt. For the first time in the history of Religion the blood of the Martyrs has become the seed of the Church.

G. THE ETHIOPIC BOOK OF ENOCH
(1 ENOCH)

THE book of Daniel exercised a profound influence on other apocalyptic writings and contributed to their development. The most important of these is the so-called Ethiopic Book of Enoch or 1 Enoch—a composite work consisting of sections selected from a wider Enochic literature. It is styled the Ethiopic Book because it happens to have been preserved in an Ethiopic translation. The original language was Aramaic. It was apparently translated from Aramaic into Greek, and a considerable fragment of this Greek translation, embracing chs. 1–32 plus ch. 89, sections 42–9, has survived. The book is obviously, in its present form, a compilation, containing excerpts or specimens of a larger Enoch literature which once flourished in independent form.

The book falls into a number of loosely connected sections which form independent writings. The first part embraces chs. 1–36, which subdivide into the following sections: A, chs. 1–5, introduction; B, chs. 6–16, Enoch's preaching to the fallen angels

(chs. 6–11 form a legendary introduction to the preaching);
C, chs. 17–36, the travels of Enoch (two recensions contained here,
namely, chs. 17–19 and 20–36).

The second main division of the book is the similitudes or
parables, about which it will be necessary to say something in
detail presently. This is followed by chs. 72–82, which may be
entitled the Book of Astronomy. Here, Enoch describes the
luminaries of heaven and their various functions, giving their
names and places of origin, as the Archangel Uriel had informed
him. It is a sort of crude attempt at a statement about the science
of astronomy. At the end Enoch commends his books and their
wisdom to his son, and strongly asserts the truth of his reckoning
the year at 364 days.

The next main division is the Dream Visions, chs. 83–90, containing two visions, namely 83–84, and 85–90. In these two dream-
visions the whole course of human history is surveyed. An interesting feature of this part of the book is the picture of the 70 shepherds
to whom was entrusted the guidance of the affairs of the world.
They rule in four groups of 12, 23, 23, and 12. The first group
carries the rule up to the exile. The second group apparently
carries the story down to the end of the Persian period. The third
group, beginning with Alexander, extends to some time in the
Greek period. The fourth group is introduced by the birth of some
Jews who began to open their eyes and cry to their fellow-countrymen, ch. 90[6]. This apparently marks the breaking in of an en-
lightened sect or party to which the writer belongs. According to
Schürer this party is the Maccabeans. According to Charles the party
of the Chasidim. A notable martyr is referred to in ch. 90[8], and then
a leader is described, v. 9 and following, who has been identified as
Judas or John Hyrcanus, or possibly some later person. If the
party referred to is that of the Pharisees, the allusion may be to
their gaining power in the Sanhedrin. At the end of the second
vision God abolishes the old Jerusalem and introduces a new and
greater Jerusalem in its place, in which he himself dwells. A
Messianic community inhabits this city. Enoch and Elijah are
brought from Paradise to join it. Ultimately the Messiah is born
and becomes the head of the community, ch. 90[37-8].

There follows the Apocalypse of the Ten Weeks (contained in ch.
93 plus ch. 91[12-17]). This apocalypse covers the history of the world,
which is described in a series of weeks. The first seven weeks cover
the history down to the writer's present. The eighth and following
weeks refer to the future. Week eight is the period of the sword,

when the present woes will be reversed, and the righteous will slay the wicked. At the close of this week the Messianic Age will appear and the new Jerusalem will be built.

The ninth week is devoted to missionary preaching, which will be followed by the conversion of the world. The tenth week ends in the Final Judgement, which is confined to the angels. A new heaven appears, and an unbroken righteousness reigns. Another important section is contained in the Book of Admonitions and Consolations (ch. $91^{1\text{-}11}$ + 92 + 94–104) (chs. 106–8 appear to be later additions). This section of the book is not purely apocalyptic in form. It contains a series of warnings and consolations, and reflects the hope and faith of the righteous. It appears to be a Pharisaic production directed against the Sadducean party, at a time when the latter were in supreme power. The date of the book may belong to the reign of Alexander Jannaeus, when the Pharisaic party was much oppressed. Alexander reigned from 103–76 and was succeeded by his widow, Alexandra, in whose reign, 76–67 B.C., the fortunes of the Pharisees took a turn for the better. Thus, the date of the writings will fall between 100–76 B.C. The persecutors depicted in the book are Jewish rulers. It may be described as a book of Pharisaic martyrs.

Perhaps the most important section of the Ethiopic Book of Enoch is chs. 37–71, containing the similitudes. This remarkable section depicts the pre-existent heavenly Messiah, who is to judge both men and angels. It is strikingly different in tone and in character from the rest of the Ethiopic book. The enemies it refers to as the enemies of God and His people are foreign monarchs, not Jewish rulers. This section is largely dependent on the book of Daniel, especially Dan. 7. Perhaps the most probable date for its composition would be some time in the reign of Herod. The phrase which occurs in the book, 'The mighty kings and high ones of the earth', would then be interpreted to mean Augustus and Herod. It must be admitted that the references to the writer's situation and background are very vague. But such vagueness and reserve may have been a precaution on the writer's part, which we can well understand of one living under the despotism of Herod. This writing has suffered interpolation, a number of Noah-passages having been inserted (ch. $39^{1,\ 22}$; cf. ch. $54^{7\text{-}55}$; chs. 60, 65–69^{25} inclusive). Chapter 71 forms an addition of a peculiar kind, identifying the heavenly Son of Man with Enoch. Thus it is clear that the book is purely Jewish, since the interpolations are Jewish. The whole section containing chapters 37–71 sharply divides portions of the book which belong together, namely chs. 1–36 and chs. 72–105.

The author of the Book of Jubilees appears to have been acquainted with our book in some of its parts. The Ethiopic Book of Enoch obviously contains the work not of one person but of a circle of pious people. A convenient designation of the book is Charles's symbol, Enoch I. As we shall see, there is also an Enoch II and III.

The whole of this Enoch literature is of special importance because it reflects in its bizarre and peculiar features the hopes and fears of the pious in the Maccabean times, and bears eloquent witness to the tendency in those circles towards the transcendental type of piety. In its content it is not purely apocalyptic, but contains traces of an attempt to evolve a godly type of wisdom, embracing by the side of pure prophecy a sacred geography, astronomy, and heavenly lore and ostensible revelations concerning terrestrial and celestial secrets.

H. I AND II MACCABEES

THE first book of Maccabees is an important historical source for the Maccabean Age, written by a Jew who was strictly orthodox and a patriot. He was evidently a native of Palestine, with the life and localities of which he shows an intimate acquaintance. The tone of the book suggests that he belonged to the Conservative party among the Jews, represented by the Sadducees. He was a loyal adherent of the Law, and he shows a marked interest in and sympathy for the Jewish High Priesthood; and it is significant that not the slightest allusion is made to a belief in a future life.

The articulation of the book is clear. It falls naturally into the following divisions: ch. 1^{1-9}, a brief introduction concerned with the conquests of Alexander and the division of his kingdom; ch. 1^{10-64}, the causes of the Maccabean revolt; ch. 2^{1-70}, the opening of the struggle, headed by Mattathias; chs. $3^{1}–9^{22}$, an account of the events that took place while Judas was head of the insurgents, including the purification of the Temple and the re-dedication of the altar. Religious liberty is attained; ch. $9^{23}–12^{53}$, Jonathan in command. The Hasmonean High Priesthood is established; chs. $13^{1}–16^{24}$, the leadership of Simon and the happiness of the country under his rule and its enjoyment of political independence. The book closes with a brief allusion to the rule of John Hyrcanus.

The composition of the book is probably to be assigned to a date somewhere between 100 and 70 B.C. Possibly, however, parts of the book go back to an earlier date. It was written in Hebrew, as Jerome expressly states. The Hebrew original seems to have been superseded at a comparatively early date by the Greek version. The book is of first-rate importance as an historical source and also as a religious document.

Very different both in tone and character is the second book of Maccabees. The aim of the book is dominated by an apologetic rather than by a purely historical purpose. It shows how the Temple has been rescued again and again from the direst peril, and how the foes who threatened it have come to a bad end. It has been suggested that the book may perhaps to some extent have been dictated by hostility against the Jewish temple of Leontopolis in Egypt. It presupposes the existence of the feast of Purim for the Diaspora (it is called the day of Mordecai, ch. 15[36]). It is acquainted with the legend of Aristobulus, the teacher of King Ptolemy (ch. 1[10]), and according to Bousset it must therefore have been produced in the Roman epoch.

On the other hand the third book of Maccabees is dependent on the second, and Philo already knows the book. Bousset would fix the date after A.D. 40 and well before A.D. 70.

The second book is not used by Josephus, but appears to be referred to by the author of the Epistle to the Hebrews 11[35]. Composed originally in Greek, it must have been written by a Jew of the Diaspora, who represents the Pharisaic standpoint.

I. THE BOOK OF ESTHER

IN its present form this writing is a very late production linguistically; and the Feast of Purim, which it is obviously the purpose of the book to recommend, appears not to have been introduced into Palestine till a late date—the earliest historical mention of it occurs in 2 Maccabees—and it may well have been brought in, as has been suggested, in the Maccabean period, c. 130 B.C., when anti-foreign feeling was strong. But where did it come from? As Sellin remarks: 'The book must be based on some kind of historical foundation, for there must have been some reason for the introduction of this new, originally non-Jewish festival, and this is, no doubt, to be looked for in some occasion of persecution and deliverance of the Babylonian-Persian Jews in the Persian period.'

It has been suggested that the Jews were influenced by the Babylonian New Year or Puchru Festival, which may serve to explain certain mythological features.

'According to the results arrived at above,' says Sellin, 'the purpose of the book is to recount how the Jews in Babylon came to give a new interpretation to this dual feast, and to take part in it, and, moreover, as a purely secular festival. In view of this secular character of the feast, the Divine name is entirely avoided in the book, although the author was obviously a believing Jew (cf. ch. 4¹⁴, 8¹⁷). We cannot, therefore, be surprised that the feast was only introduced in Palestine some decades after the Maccabean rising (it is not yet mentioned in I Macc. 7⁴⁹), and that there was strong opposition to the inclusion of the book in the Canon (cf. Megilla i. 7 in the Palestine Talmud).'

J. THE PSALMS OF SOLOMON

AT the close of the Maccabean period there arose a collection of psalms, known as the Psalms of Solomon. An admirable edition exists in English, edited by the late Dr. Ryle and Dr. James, under the title *Psalms of the Pharisees*. The existence of this collection clearly shows that at the time when it was put together the canonical Psalter was closed. The death of Pompey is clearly referred to in the second of these psalms (48 B.C.). The psalms were originally written in Hebrew and have been preserved in a Greek translation and also in a Syriac translation. They reflect the piety of the Pharisees and the disillusionment that had set in regarding the Maccabean dynasty. The seventeenth of these psalms is specially important, as reflecting the Messianic hope as held in Pharisaic circles. Part of this striking psalm may be cited here. It contains a beautiful description of the Messianic king, which in its ideal aspirations is not surpassed in the loftiest passages of the Synagogue Liturgy:

A righteous King and taught of God is he that reigneth over them;
And there shall be no iniquity in his days in their midst,
For all shall be holy and their King is the Lord's Messiah.
For he shall not put his trust in horse and rider and bow,
Nor shall he multiply unto himself gold and silver for war,
Nor by ships shall he gather confidence for the day of battle.
The Lord himself is his King, and the hope of him that is strong in
*   the hope of God.*

And he shall have mercy upon all the nations that come before him in fear,

For he shall strike the earth with the word of his mouth even for evermore, He shall bless the people of the Lord with wisdom and gladness.

He himself also is pure from sin, so that he may rule a mighty people, and rebuke princes and overthrow sinners by the might of his word.

And he shall not faint all his days, because he leaneth upon his God; for God shall cause him to be mighty through the spirit of holiness, and wise through the counsel of understanding with might and righteousness.

And the blessing of the Lord is with him in might, and his hope in the Lord shall not faint.

And who can stand up against him? He is mighty in his works and strong in the fear of God.

Tending the flock of the Lord with faith and righteousness; and he shall suffer none among them to faint in their pasture.

ADDITIONAL NOTE III

Alexander the Great in Jewish Legend

Alexander appears in Jewish history as having made a visit to Jerusalem which is recorded by Josephus in *Ant.* XI. viii. 4–6. According to this account the conqueror went to Jerusalem after the capture of Gaza (332 B.C.) and was met by the High Priest Jaddua and a company of priests and a multitude of citizens. When Alexander saw the High Priest he reverenced God and saluted Jaddua, much to the surprise of his generals. Alexander explained that he had seen the High Priest in a dream clothed in the very same habit when he was at Dios in Macedonia and that he had given him a message promising him dominion over the Persians. According to the story, Alexander then entered the Temple and offered sacrifice to God under the High Priest's directions. Then follows a curious passage about the book of Daniel: 'And when the book of Daniel was showed him, wherein Daniel declared that one of the Greeks should destroy the empire of the Persians (cf. Dan. 7^6, $8^{3-8,\ 20-2}$ and 11^{3-4}) he supposed that himself was the person intended.' The conqueror was so highly pleased that he granted the Jews signal favours, which he extended also to the Jews of Babylonia and Media.

In the Talmud and Midrash the accounts given of Alexander are purely legendary. As an example the following may be quoted from Yoma 69*a* (= *Megillath Taanith* III):

'When the Samaritans had obtained permission from Alexander to destroy the Temple in Jerusalem, the high priest Simon the Just, arrayed in his pontifical garments and followed by a number of distinguished Jews, went out to meet the conqueror and joined him at Antipatris, on the northern frontier. At sight of Simon, Alexander fell prostrate at his feet, and explained to his astonished companions that the image of the Jewish high priest was always with him in battle, fighting for him and leading him to victory. Simon took the opportunity to justify the attitude of his countrymen, declaring that, far from being rebels, they offered prayers in the Temple for the welfare of the King and his dominions. So impressed was Alexander that he delivered up all the Samaritans in his train into the hands of the Jews, who tied them to the tails of horses and dragged them to the mountain of Gerizim: then the Jews plowed the mountain [demolished the Samaritan Temple].'

It is evident that this is a distorted version of an event with which Alexander had nothing whatever to do, namely, the destruction of the Samaritan Temple on Mount Gerizim by John Hyrcanus I (108 B.C.). For other fantastic legends about Alexander, see the *Jewish Encyclopedia*, i. 342 f.

ADDITIONAL NOTE IV
Greek and Latin Names among the Jews

The tendency was pronounced to adopt Greek names among the Jews in the Greek period. Sometimes the Greek name bore a certain resemblance to the Hebrew name. Thus Joshua was Grecized into Jason. Dr. J. Jacobs, writing in the *Jewish Encyclopedia*,[1] says: 'In the Hellenistic period Greek names became quite usual among the Jews, especially those of Alexander, Jason, and Antigonus. Even the name of a god like Apollo occurs (Acts 18[24]). Other names are Apollonius, Hyrcanus, Lysimachus, Demetrius, Dosa, Nicanor, Pappus, Patroclus, Philo, Sosa, Symmachus, Tryphon, Zeno. The same occurs among women, as Alexandra and Priscilla. Roman names also occur, as Antonius, Apella, Drusus, Justinus, Justus, Marcus, Rufus, Tiberius, and Titus. It was during this period that the practice arose of giving a son the name of his grandfather, as was done in the high-priestly family the members of which were named alternately Onias and Simon

[1] *Jewish Encyclopedia*, s.v. 'Names', vol. ix, p. 154.

THE HIGH PRIEST. An illustration from Walton's Polyglot Bible

from 332 to 165 B.C. Similarly, a little later, in the family of the Hillelites, the names Gamaliel and Judah succeed each other with only an occasional occurrence of Simon and Hillel. Towards the end of the period, owing to the intermixture of foreign languages, the use of double names for the same person began to be adopted, as in the instances of Simon Peter, John Mark, Thomas Didymus, Herod Agrippa, and Salome Alexandra.'

The later Rabbis also in numerous cases bore Greek names.

ADDITIONAL NOTE V
Sun Worship in the Temple

That the Sun Worship which went on in the Temple towards the end of the pre-Exilic period, and is referred to by Ezek. 8[16] ('And he brought me into the inner Court of the Lord's house, and behold, at the door of the temple of the Lord, between the porch and the altar, were about five and twenty men, with their backs towards the temple of the Lord, and their faces towards the East; and they worshipped the sun towards the East'), made a deep impression upon the Jews is clear from the interesting fact, mentioned in the Mishnah (*Sukkah* v. 4), that among the ceremonies of the Feast of Tabernacles was one in which two Priests, standing on the steps which led down to the Court of the Women, proceeded to the gate *that goes out to the East*. Then they turned to the West and said:

'Our fathers who were in this place, turned their backs to the temple and their faces to the East, and they prostrated themselves to the Sun towards the East; but we lift our eyes to God.' R. Jehudah says: *'They used to repeat: "We belong to God, and lift our eyes to God".'*

Another interesting fact is to be found in the survival of a chamber in the later Herodian Temple which in its name PAR-VAH probably bears witness to the Sun Worship formerly practised within its precincts. As Gressmann has pointed out (in the *Zeitschrift f. d. alttest. Wissenschaft*, 1924, p. 323), the original form of the name seems to be preserved in the word PARBAR of 1 Chron. 26[19], and this name may be explained from the Sumerian BARBAR (BABBAR)—'shining'; thus Ê-BAR-BAR —'the shining house', was the name given to the Sun Temple at Sippar, Larsa, Lagasch, and Babylon, and appears to have been the name given to the Chapel of the Sun in the Temple of Jeru-salem.

ADDITIONAL NOTE VI

The Languages of Palestine in the Greek Period

The Book of Daniel affords an interesting example of the use among the Jews of more than one language. In this case the languages in question are Hebrew and Aramaic. A third language with which many Jews were acquainted in the Greek period was, of course, Greek.

The gradual extension of the Aramaic language among the Jews affords an interesting problem. When precisely it had become so dominant among them as to supplant to a large extent the use of their own proper language, Hebrew, cannot exactly be determined.

In any case it had won a commanding position by the second century B.C.

The use of Aramaic as a kind of *lingua franca* throughout the region of Mesopotamia during the period of the Assyrian and Babylonian Empires is well known and well attested. Under the Persian monarchs it was used as the official tongue in the same region. The author of the books of Chronicles, who compiled the books we know as Ezra and Nehemiah, used Aramaic documents in the compilation of his work (cf. Ezra $4^{8\text{-}22}$, $5^{1\text{-}6}$, $7^{12\text{-}26}$).

'In point of fact', says the writer of the article 'Aramaic Language among the Jews' (*J.E.* ii, p. 69), 'at the time of the second Temple both languages were in common use in Palestine; the Hebrew in the academies and in the circles of the learned, the Aramaic among the lower classes in the intercourse of daily life. But the Aramaic continued to spread and became the customary popular idiom, not, however, to the complete exclusion of the Hebrew. Nevertheless, while Hebrew survived in the schools and among the learned—being rooted, as it were, in the national mind—it was continuously exposed to the influence of Aramaic. Under this influence a new form of Hebrew was developed which has been preserved in the Tanaitic literature (i.e. the Mishnah and parallel literature), embodying the traditions of the last two or three centuries before the Common Era. So that even in those fields where Hebrew continued the dominant tongue it was closely pressed by Aramaic.'

The subject is well discussed by Mr. Segal in the introductory chapter of his *Grammar of Mishnaic Hebrew* (O.U.P., 1927).

Another interesting point which deserves notice is the fact that in the Tosefta Tractate *Yadayim* the question is discussed whether those parts of Scripture which are written in the Aramaic language 'defile the hands', i.e. whether the Aramaic passages can be considered canonical. This bears witness to the feeling that Aramaic was hardly worthy to be the medium of inspired Scripture, and might be adduced as an argument in favour of the view held by some scholars that the opening and closing chapters of the book of Daniel were originally extant in Aramaic and were afterwards translated into Hebrew, in order to make the work more acceptable as a canonical writing. This view is plausible but not entirely convincing.

The place occupied by Greek in Palestine during the two centuries which preceded the birth of Christ and the century which followed is more difficult to determine. That it was an important element is clear from the fact that a very large number of Greek words have penetrated into Rabbinical Hebrew. It is probable, indeed, that Greek was the second language to many Jews in this period. The question is admirably discussed by Gerhard Kittel in his important book, *Die Probleme des palästinischen Spätjudentums und das Urchristentum*, Stuttgart, 1926. Kittel makes it clear that Greek played an important part as a second language throughout Palestine during this period. Jesus himself may well have known Greek. The Fourth Gospel was evidently written by a Jew, and if, as is probable, it was written in Greek, it was the Greek of an Aramaic-speaking Jew, in fact, it may be inferred that down to A.D. 70, and even later, an educated Jew of Palestine would know a certain amount of Greek. The disastrous cleavage between the Jews and the Greek-speaking world came later after the termination of the revolt of Bar-Kokba and its ruthless suppression in A.D. 135.

See further the article 'Greek Language, and the Jews', in *J.E.* vi, p. 85 ff.

APPENDIX

A SHORT BIBLIOGRAPHY

For the history of the period the most recent and important work is the *Cambridge Ancient History*, vol. vi, 'Macedon 401–301 B.C.', 1927; vol. vii 'The Hellenistic Monarchies and the Rise of Rome', 1928. Reference should also be made to volume viii, 'Rome and the Mediterranean'.

Of the older works, Schürer, E., *A History of the Jewish People in the Time of Jesus Christ*, 6 vols., Edinburgh, 1890–1 (English

translation from the German), is still useful. The later German
edition in 3 vols. is dated Leipzig, 1901–9. W. D. Morrison's *The
Jews under Roman Rule*, London, 1891, may also be mentioned as
well as the works of Dr. Edwyn Bevan (*The House of Seleucus*,
2 vols., 1900, 1901, and *Jerusalem under the High Priests*, 1904).

For the individual books of the Bible dealt with in this volume
reference may be made to the various introductions to the literature of the Old Testament, especially Driver, S. R., *Introduction
to the Literature of the Old Testament*, 9th edition, Edinburgh, 1913;
Cornill, C., *Introduction to the Canonical Books of the Old Testament*,
London, 1907; Sellin, E., *Introduction to the Old Testament*,
London, 1923. The latter volume is enriched with a valuable
bibliography, by the late Professor Arthur S. Peake, to which
reference may here be made for fuller details.

Of smaller works, Gray, *A Critical Introduction to the Old Testament*, London, and Box, G. H., *A Short Introduction to the Literature of the Old Testament*, 4th edition, London, 1930, may perhaps
be mentioned here.

For the literature dealing with the particular books reference
may be made to Dr. Peake's bibliography as cited above. The
more important items are referred to in the course of the preceding
commentary.

The standard authority for the Apocrypha and Pseudepigrapha
of the Old Testament is the Oxford corpus edited by Dr. R. H.
Charles, 2 vols., 1913. This elaborate work by a number of
scholars includes English translations of the various books, with
full introductions and commentaries. In smaller form there is the
series edited by W. O. E. Oesterley and G. H. Box, *Translations
of Early Documents*, published by the S.P.C.K., 1917 and following
years. The books are dealt with separately in this series, each
being provided with an introduction. Oesterley, W. O. E., *The
Books of the Apocrypha, their Origin, Teaching, and Contents*,
London, 1914, will also be found useful.

INDEX

NAMES AND SUBJECTS

Index

THE OLD TESTAMENT

CHRONOLOGICALLY ARRANGED

by EVELYN W. HIPPISLEY, S.Th.

*Licensed Teacher in Theology, Tutor to Women Theological
Students, King's College, London.*

N.B.—The dates of the Kings of Israel and Judah are taken from
the article 'Chronology of the Old Testament' in the *Encyclopaedia Biblica*; and the articles in Peake's commentary and in
Hastings' *Dictionary of the Bible* on the separate books have
been consulted. Other books which have been used are the
International Critical Commentary, the *Westminster Commentaries*, the *Expositors' Bible*, the *Century Bible*, Dr. Driver's
Introduction to the Literature of the Old Testament, Dr. Oesterley's
Books of the Apocrypha, and Dr. Charles' *Apocrypha and Pseudepigrapha*.

Principal Foreign Power = the principal foreign power with which
Israel was in contact at the time.

Inscriptions = inscriptions, chiefly on Babylonian and Assyrian
monuments which refer to events in the history of Israel. These
are mostly translated in the Appendix to Dr. Foakes-Jackson's
Biblical History of the Hebrews. The Code of Hammurabi,
Selections from the Tell el-Amarna letters, and the Babylonian
Flood Stories are published by S.P.C.K. (1s., 4d., and 6d. each).

The Book of Genesis, divided into sources by Dr. T. H. Robinson.
is published by the National Adult School Union (1s.).

Book.	Contents.	Origin.

The Hexateuch	Genesis to Joshua—contains four strands of narrative :
	    (i) Jahvistic, Judaean in origin, *circ.* 850 B.C. ;
	    (ii) Elohistic, Ephraimitic in origin, *circ.* 750 B.C., both written from a prophetic standpoint ;
	    (JE combined *circ.* 650 B.C.).
	    (iii) D Deuteronomic revision, 7th century B.C. ;
	    (JED combined early in Exile).
	    (iv) P Priestly author and editor, 5th century B.C. ;
	    (JEDP combined and re-edited before 3rd century B.C.).	

N.B.—*No analysis of sources is given, but large portions belonging to the Priestly writer are indicated, as it is important to recognize the later standpoint.*

Genesis	i–xi. Prehistoric Narratives. xii–xlix. Stories of the Patriarchs.	JEP.
Exodus	The Exodus and Wanderings.	JEP (xxv–xxxi, xxxv–xl P).
Numbers	The Story of Wanderings.	JEDP (i–x. 28, xvii–xix, xxvi–xxxi, xxxiii–xxxvi P).
Joshua	The Conquest of Canaan.	JEDP (xv–xix P).
Judges	The Conquest of Canaan and Settlement of Tribes.	Compiled from old material (perhaps JE) by a Deuteronomic editor, 6th century B.C.
1 and 2 Samuel	History of Establishment of Monarchy, and Early Kings.	Two strands of narrative of 9th and 8th centuries B.C. woven together by a Deuteronomic editor, 6th century B.C.
1 and 2 Kings	History of Kings of Israel and Judah from Solomon to Fall of Jerusalem.	Compiled from Court and Temple records and biographies of prophets by a Deuteronomic editor, and re-edited during the Exile.

Important Events.	Date B. C.	Principal Foreign Power.	Inscriptions.
		First Babylonian Empire, 2050–732 B.C.	
Ḥammurabi's Code of Laws, based on an older Sumerian Code.	circ. 1950		Code of Ḥammurabi.
			Tell el - Amarna Letters (1450–1370).
			Stele of Raamses (Rameses) II (1300–1234) found at Beth-shan, showing that Semites had built city of Raamses.
	circ. 1230	Egypt.	Stele of Merneptah (1234–1225 B.C.).
Crossing of Jordan.	circ. 1196		
Philistines settling in Canaan, circ. 1200 B.C.			
SAUL	1025		
DAVID	1000		
SOLOMON	970		
Division of Kingdom.	933		
Kings of Judah. *Kings of Israel.*			
REHOBOAM JEROBOAM	933		
ABIJAM	916		
ASA	914		
NADAB	912		
BAASHA	911		

Book.	Contents.	Origin.
Amos	Warning to Israel by a Judaean.	Prophecies delivered in the reign of Jeroboam II (2 Kings xiv. 23-9), 760-746 B.C.
Hosea	Warning to Israel by an Israelite.	Prophecies delivered in reign of Jeroboam II, and later (2 Kings xiv. 23-xv), 746-734 B.C.
Micah	Denunciations of Israel and Judah by a Man of the People.	Chapters i-iii—prophecies delivered in reigns of Jotham. Ahaz, and Hezekiah (2 Kings xv. 32. xvi, xviii-xx)—739-693 B.C. Chapters iv-vi anonymous prophecies, added later.
Isaiah i-xxxix	The Statesman - Prophet's Warnings to Jerusalem.	Prophecies delivered in reigns of Uzziah, Jotham, Ahaz, and Hezekiah (2 Kings xix. 20, xx), 739-701 B.C. (omit xiii-xiv. 23, xxi, xxiv-xxvii, xxxiv, xxxv, and possibly other passages which are post-exilic).

Important Events.	Date B.C.	Principal Foreign Power.	Inscriptions.
Kings of Judah.　*Kings of Israel.*			
ELAH	888		
ZIMRI	887		
OMRI	887		
AHAB	876		
JEHOSHAPHAT	873	Assyria	
Battle of Ḳarḳar	853	(Shalmaneser	Moabite Stone.
AHAZIAH	853	III. 859).	Ḳarḳar Inscription.
JORAM	853		
Completion of Jahvistic narrative.	850		
JEHORAM	849		
AHAZIAH	842		
ATHALIAH　　JEHU	841		
Jehu pays tribute to Shalmaneser.	841		Black Obelisk of
JOASH	835		Shalmaneser.
JEHOAHAZ	814		
JOASH	797		
*AMAZIAH	795		
AZARIAH or UZZIAH	789		
JEROBOAM II.	782		
JOTHAM (regent)			
Compilation of Elohistic narrative	750		Tiglath-Pileser III
ZECHARIAH	743		reduces Hamath.
SHALLUM	743		
MENAHEM	743		
JOTHAM	739		
Menahem pays tribute to Tiglath-Pileser III.	738		Tribute of Menahem.
PEKAHIAH	736		
AHAZ　　PEKAH	735		
Ahaz pays tribute to Tiglath-Pileser III.	734		
HOSHEA	730		Hoshea placed on throne by Tiglath-Pileser III.

* The Biblical Chronology here obviously needs reconstruction. The dates given here are those of Marti in *Encyd. Biblica* ; cf. Steuernagel, *Einleitung*, and Box, *Isaiah*.

Book.	Contents.	Origin.
Jeremiah	Warnings and Pleadings to Jerusalem.	Prophecies uttered in reigns of Josiah, Jehoiakim, Jehoiachin, and Zedekiah (2 Kings xxii–xxv). Earlier prophecies written down by Baruch ; later prophecies, especially xlvi–li, added by a compiler during or after the Exile — 626–500 B.C.
Zephaniah	Doom of Wicked Nations.	Prophecy uttered *circ.* 626 B.C., when the Scythians were threatening Jerusalem, and edited in post-exilic times.
Deuteronomy	The Law-Book (with additions) found in the Temple, on which Josiah based his reform.	A revision of the earlier laws, compiled *circ.* 640 B.C.
Nahum	Doom of Nineveh	Chapters ii and iii written *circ.* 612 B.C. ; chapter i a post-exilic acrostic poem.
Habakkuk	Moral Problem raised by God's use of Chaldaeans.	Chapters i and ii written *circ* 600–550 B.C., when Chaldaea, i.e. New Babylon, was becoming powerful ; chapter iii a lyric ode of post-exilic date.
Ezekiel i–xxxii	Prophecies of Doom, and Denunciations of Jerusalem and foreign nations.	Written in Babylon before the Fall of Jerusalem by an exile banished in 596 B.C.
Ezekiel xxxiii–xxxix	Picture of the Restitution of Israel.	Written in Babylon after the Fall of Jerusalem—584–572 B C.

Important Events.	Date B. C.	Principal Foreign Power.	Inscriptions.
Kings of Judah. Kings of Israel. Fall of Samaria *End of Kingdom of Israel*	721		Capture of Samaria by Sargon II.
*Hezekiah Invasion of Sennacherib Manasseh Amon Josiah	{ 720? { 715? 700 692 638 637		Siloam Inscription. Invasion of Sennacherib.
	625	New Babylonian Empire founded by Nabopolassar.	
Finding of Law-Book (2 Kings xxii) Reform of Josiah Fall of Nineveh Battle of Megiddo Jehoahaz Jehoiakim Battle of Carchemish Jehoiachin First deportation to Babylon Zedekiah	621 621 612 608 608 607 605 597 596 596	Nebuchadrezzar King of Babylon 604–561.	
Fall of Jerusalem *Exile.*	586		

* See Dr. Robinson's note, p. 232. If the view is accepted that Hezekiah was associated with Ahaz for a time, this would dispose of part of the discrepancy.

Book.	Contents.	Origin.
Ezekiel xl–xlviii	A Vision of the Ideal Theocracy.	Written after 572 B.C.
Lamentations	A Book of Dirges.	These poems, arranged as acrostics (except ch. v), are of exilic date.
Isaiah xl–lv	The Promise of Return.	Prophecies delivered by an unknown author at the close of the Exile, probably between 549 and 538 B.C. The Servant-Songs are possibly later.
Obadiah	Doom of Edom.	Verses 1–14 belong to an exilic prophecy; the rest is probably post-exilic.
Leviticus xvii–xxvi	The Law of Holiness.	Old Laws of Priestly character grouped together towards the close of the Exile.
Haggai *Zechariah* i–viii	Call to rebuild the Temple.	{ Prophecies delivered 520 B.C. (Ezra v, vi). Prophecies delivered 520, 518 B.C.
Isaiah lvi–lxvi	The Restored Community: its Faults and its Blessings.	Prophecies delivered by an unknown author in Palestine *circ.* 450 B.C.
Malachi	Rebuke of the Moral and Religious Condition of the Jews.	Probably delivered *circ.* 450 B.C.
Ruth	A Pastoral Idyll.	Probably used as a Tract for the Times about Foreign Marriages in Nehemiah's day.
Job	A Wisdom-Book, treating of the Problem of the Innocent Sufferer.	Probably based on an older story by a post-exilic author.
Leviticus	The Priestly Code of Laws.	Compiled during the Exile, and possibly published by Ezra.
Joel	The Day of the Lord.	The date is probably early in the fourth century B.C.

Important Events.	Date B.C.	Principal Foreign Power.	Inscriptions.
Cyrus overthrows the Medes.	549	Persian Empire.	
Capture of Babylon by Cyrus.	538		
Edict of Cyrus.	538		
The Return.			
Return of Zerubbabel and Joshua (Ezra i, ii).	537		
Building of Temple.	520–516		
Dedication of Second Temple (Ezra vi. 16).	516		
		Artaxerxes I.	
Return of Nehemiah (Neh. ii).	445		
Nehemiah's second visit (Neh. xiii. 7).	433		
		Artaxerxes II.	
Ezra's Return.	? 397		
		Artaxerxes III (Ochus).	
Jaddua, High Priest (Neh. xii. 11).	351		
Samaritan Schism.	335		

Book.	Contents.	Origin.
Zechariah ix–xiv	An Apocalyptic Vision.	The work of a post-exilic prophet or prophets, *circ.* 320 B.C. or later.
Jonah	An Evangelical Allegory.	Written *circ.* 300 B.C., and probably based on an old tradition.
1 and 2 Chronicles	History re-edited from an ecclesiastical standpoint.	Compiled, with additions, from previously existing sources by a Temple Levite, *circ.* 300–250 B.C.
Ezra } *Nehemiah* }	Narrative of the Return and Rebuilding of the Temple.	Compiled by the Chronicler, *circ.* 300 B.C., from City and Temple records, Aramaic documents, and memoirs.
Proverbs	One of the Wisdom-Books of the Hebrews, containing Moral Maxims.	Several collections of Proverbs of various dates combined by an editor, *circ.* 250 B.C.
Song of Songs	A Marriage Drama, showing the triumph of faithful love.	Probably written in Jerusalem during the Greek period.
Esther	A Didactic Romance.	Written, perhaps on an historical basis. *circ.* third century B.C., to defend the keeping of the Feast of Purim.
Ecclesiastes	A Wisdom-Book, containing the Meditations of an Unsatisfied Man.	Written *circ.* 200 B.C.
Psalms	The Hymns Ancient and Modern of the Second Temple.	Five books of gradual growth, containing 'Praise-Songs' dating probably from the time of David to the second century B.C.
Daniel	An Apocalypse of Encouragement.	Probably founded on an older story, and written *circ.* 168 B.C. to encourage the Maccabaean party.

Important Events.	Date B.C.	Principal Foreign Power.	Inscriptions.
Alexander the Great becomes ruler of the world.	331	Macedonian Empire.	
Conquest of Palestine by Alexander.	331		
Death of Alexander and division of his Empire.	323		
		Ptolemaic and Seleucid Empires.	
Palestine under the Ptolemies of Egypt.	311		
Antiochus III conquers Palestine.	198		
Persecution of Jews by Antiochus IV (Epiphanes).	169		
Maccabaean Revolt against Antiochus Epiphanes.	167		

A list, chronological as far as possible, is appended of the principal
in the Alexandrian Canon (the Septuagint), but not in the
were never included in either Canon, but are important as greatly

Book.		Contents.	Origin.
APOCRYPHA.	APOCALYPTIC.		
Ecclesiasticus (Wisdom of Jesus, son of Sirach.)		A Wisdom-Book, containing counsels for daily life.	Written in Hebrew, probably *circ.* 180 B.C., and translated into Greek by the author's grandson, *circ.* 130 B.C.
Tobit		An Idyll of Home-Life.	Written probably in Aramaic, *circ.* 190–175 B.C.
	Book of Enoch	A series of Apocalyptic Visions.	Written in Palestine by several Hebrew authors belonging to the party of the Ḥasidim, between 170 and 64 B.C.
Prayer of Azariah			An addition to the Greek text of Daniel, probably written in Hebrew, *circ.* 170 B.C.
Song of the Three Children.		The Thanksgiving of the Three for Deliverance (*Benedicite*).	Dating from the Maccabaean triumph, *circ.* 165 B.C.
1 Esdras		History of the Jews from the reign of Josiah to the Proclamation of the Law (639-? 400 B C.).	Written probably at Alexandria between 170 and 100 B.C.
Rest of Esther		Contains additional details as to Esther, probably imaginary.	A Greek interpolation in the Hebrew text, *circ.* 150 to 100 B.C
Judith		A story of the Deliverance of Israel from Assyria by a Jewess.	Written *circ.* 150 B.C. and edited *circ.* 60 B.C.
Baruch		A work in four divisions, containing prayers of Exiles and messages to Exiles	Written by three authors, probably between 2nd century B.C. and 2nd century A.D.
	Testaments of the XII Patriarchs.	The Dying Commands of Jacob's Twelve Sons.	Written, probably in Hebrew, by Ḥasidim, *circ.* 130-10 B C. (contains later Christian interpolations).
3 Maccabees		History from the reign of Seleucus IV to the death of Nicator (176–161 B.C.). (Parallel with part of 1 Maccabees, but not so trustworthy.)	Probably abridged *circ.* 40 A.D. from a larger work by an Alexandrian Jew, written *circ.* 120 B.C.

Apocryphal and Apocalyptic Books. The *Apocrypha* were included Palestinian Canon (Massoretic Text). The *Apocalyptic* writings influencing New Testament thought and phraseology.

Important Events.	Date B. C.	Principal Foreign Power.	Inscriptions.
		Seleucid Empire.	
Maccabaean Revolt.	167		
Re-dedication of Temple.	165		
Death of Judas Maccabaeus.	160		
Jonathan, High-Priest.	160		
Simon, High-Priest, and Ethnarch	142		
Independence of the Jews.	142		
John Hyrcanus.	135		
Rise of Pharisees and Sadducees.			
JOHN HYRCANUS, King of Judaea (Hasmonean Dynasty).	107		

Book.		Contents.	Origin.
APOCRYPHA.	APOCALYTIC.		
1 Maccabees		History of the Jews from the accession of Antiochus Epiphanes to the death of Simon (175–135 B.C.).	Compiled from existing sources in Hebrew by a devout Jew, between 1co and 90 B.C.
Story of Susanna		A Story in praise of the wisdom of Daniel.	Probably written to support new laws as to witnesses, *circ.* 100 B.C An addition to the Greek text of Daniel.
Story of Bel and the Dragon			Perhaps written originally in Aramaic ; an addition to the Greek text of Daniel, *circ.* 100 B.C.
Wisdom of Solomon		A Wisdom-Book inculcating the beauty of Divine Wisdom.	Written by an orthodox Alexandrian Jew, *circ.* 100-50 B.C.
Prayer of Manasses.		A Jewish Penitential Psalm.	Perhaps written in Greek —date uncertain.
	Psalms of Solomon or *Psalms of the Pharisees.*	Eighteen Psalms, containing important Messianic teaching.	Written in Hebrew by a Pharisee, 70-40 B.C., probably for use in synagogues.
	Book of Jubilees	The narrative of Genesis, rewritten from a later standpoint.	Written in Hebrew by a Palestinian Jew, *circ.* 40-10 B.C. or later.
	Secrets of Enoch	An Account of the Creation.	Written in Greek by an orthodox Alexandrian Jew between 30 B.C. and 50 A.D.
2 Esdras		An Apocalypse, containing Visions of Ezra at Babylon.	A Jewish work, probably belonging to 1st century A.D., with later Christian interpolatiohs.

Important Events.	Date B. C.	Principal Foreign Power.	Inscriptions.
ARISTOBULUS I.	105		
ALEXANDER JANNAEUS.	104		
ALEXANDRA.	78		
HYRCANUS II and ARISTOBULUS II dispute the throne.	69		
Rise of the House of Antipater.		Roman Empire.	
Pompey enters Syria and conquers Jerusalem.	65		
Judaea divided into five districts.	57		
Antipater becomes Procurator of Judaea.	47		
HEROD, King of Judaea.	37		
Herod marries Mariamne, the last of the Hasmoneans.	35		
Herod's Temple begun.	20		
Death of Herod.	4		

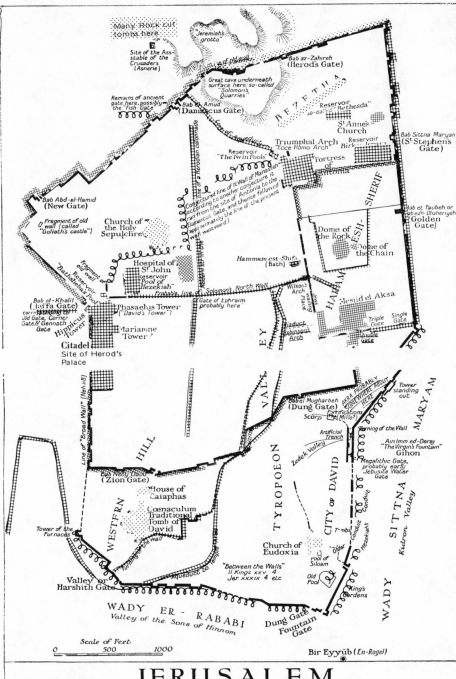

JERUSALEM

Many Rock cut tombs here

Jeremiah's grotto

Site of the Ass-stable of the Crusaders (Asnerie)

Old wall

Bab az-Zahireh (Herod's Gate)

Great cave underneath surface here, so-called "Solomon's Quarries"

Remains of ancient gate here, possibly the "Fish Gate"

Bab el Amud (Damascus Gate)

Reservoir so-called "Bethesda"

St Annes Church

Reservoir "The Twin Pools"

Triumphal Arch "Ecce Homo Arch"

Reservoir Birk

Bab Sittna Maryan (St Stephen's Gate)

Fortress of Antonia

Conjectured line of N.Wall of Manasseh according to another conjecture it ran from the site of Antonia to the Damascus Gate, and thence followed approximately the line of the present wall westward

Bab Abd-el-Hamid (New Gate)

Fragment of old wall (called "Goliath's castle")

Church of the Holy Sepulchre

HARAM ESH-SHERIF

Dome of the Rock

Dome of the Chain

Bab et Taubeh or Bab edh-Dhaheriyeh Golden Gate)

Fragment of old wall

Reservoir Bathsheba's Pool

Hospital of St John

Hammam est-Shifa (Bath)

Pool of Hezekiah

Gate of Ephraim probably here

Probable line of Solomon's North Wall

Wilson's Arch Wailing Place

Mesjid el Aksa

Bab el-Khalil (Jaffa Gate) corresponding to Old Gate, Corner Gate, & Gennath Gate

Phasaelus Tower ("David's Tower")

Marianne Tower?

Hippicus Tower

Viaduct Robinson's Arch

Triple Gate

Single Gate

Double Gate

Citadel Site of Herod's Palace

Line of "Broad Wall" (Nehem 8)

Bab el Mugharbeh (Dung Gate)

Scarp

Fortifications (Millo?)

AKRA PROBABLY SOMEWHERE ABOUT HERE

Tower standing out

TYROPOEON VALLEY

Artificial Trench

Turning of the Wall

Ain Imm ed-Daraj "The Virgin's Fountain" Gihon

Zedek Valley

Megalithic Gate, probably early Jebusite Water Gate

WESTERN HILL

House of Caiaphas

Bab Neby Daud (Zion Gate)

Coenaculum Traditional Tomb of David

CITY OF DAVID

Conduit

SITTNA MARYAM Kidron Valley

WADY

Tower of the Furnaces

Turning of the wall

Aqueduct to

Church of Eudoxia

"Between the Walls" II Kings xxv 4 Jer. xxxix 4 etc

Pool of Siloam

Old Pool

Older

Hezekiah's Conduit

Tombs

King's Gardens

Valley or Harshith Gate

WADY ER - RABABI
Valley of the Sons of Hinnom

Dung Gate
Fountain Gate

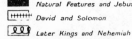

Scale of Feet
0   500   1000

Bir Eyyūb (En-Rogel)

JERUSALEM

Natural Features and Jebusites

David and Solomon

Later Kings and Nehemiah

Herodian

Early Christianity to Arab Conquest

Arab and Crusader

W.T.Wright